Reading Pleasures

THE NEW BLACK STUDIES SERIES

Edited by Darlene Clark Hine
and Dwight A. McBride

*A list of books in the series appears
at the end of this book.*

Reading Pleasures

Everyday Black Living in Early America

TARA A. BYNUM

UNIVERSITY OF ILLINOIS PRESS
Urbana, Chicago, and Springfield

Publication was supported by a grant from
the Howard D. and Marjorie L. Brooks Fund
for Progressive Thought.

The cataloging-in-publication data is available
on the Library of Congress website.

LCCN 2022025000
ISBN 978-0-252-04473-1 (cloth : alk.)
ISBN 978-0-252-08683-0 (paper : alk.)
ISBN 978-0-252-05378-8 (ebook)

For my mother, Ethel V. Locks
12 January 1952–26 January 2021

and my sister, Tia Anise Bynum
23 January 1985–18 November 2021

Contents

Acknowledgments

To say I've always wanted to write a book isn't entirely true. But, I did want to write this one. I learned quickly that this book is real and in your hands because of the inspiring help, support, and advocacy of so many people. Too many, in fact, have begged, prayed, demanded that I write (and publish) what follows. Too many have, also, lifted me—in prayer, in song, in laughter, in community—when I struggled to put pen to paper. This book is my thank-you to all of those who compelled, prayed, funded, and encouraged it into being (with a nod as well to those who are not named in this list):

Dwight A. McBride, Darlene Clark Hine, Dawn Durante, Dominique Moore, Ellie Hinton, Kelly J. Baker, Deborah Oliver, the University of Illinois Press, and the production and marketing staff;

The staff—in particular, the archivists, librarians, curators, grant makers—of the Rhode Island Historical Society, American Antiquarian Society, John Carter Brown Library, Library Company of Philadelphia, Newport Historical Society, National Endowment for the Humanities, Omohundro Institute of Early American History and Culture, and the Rare Book School;

Deirdre Cooper Owens, Jasmine Smith, Erica Armstrong Dunbar, Jim Green, Krystal Appiah, the Library Company of Philadelphia's Program in African American History, and the Mellon Foundation;

Hodson Trust–John Carter Brown 2018–2019 Fellowship, Neil Safier, Kimberly Nusco, Bertie Mandelblatt, Adam Goodheart, Patrick Nugent, Airlee Ringgold Johnson, Hodson Trust, Washington College and the C. V. Starr Center for the Study of the American Experience, and the John Carter Brown Library;

Departments of English and African American Studies, and Avery Research Center at College of Charleston;

Paul Erickson, Ashley Cataldo, Elizabeth Pope, the American Antiquarian Society, and the National Endowment of the Humanities;

Keith Stokes and the Rhode Island Black Heritage Society, Bertram Lippicott III, Ingrid Peters, and Newport Historical Society;

Dominique Hill, Tammy Owens, Karina Fernandez, Jackie Jeffery, Yaniris Fernandez, and Hampshire College's National Endowment for the Humanities' Challenge Grant;

Autumn Womack, Cheryl Wall and Rutgers University's Department of English Postdoctoral Fellowship in African American Literature;

Towson University's Department of English (and, in particular the PTRM committee of 2014–2015);

Daniel Richter, Amy Baxter-Bellamy, and the McNeil Center for Early American Studies and its Wednesday Brown Bag and its Friday Seminar crews;

Michael Moon, Jonathan Goldberg, Hollis Robbins, and Johns Hopkins University's Departments of English and History;

Katherine Chiles, Derrick Spires, Matthew Brown, Phil Round, Alyssa Smith, and University of Iowa's Obermann Center for Advanced Studies, University of Iowa Department of English, University of Iowa's Program in African American Studies, University of Iowa's Diversity through Distinction Fund;

My students at Towson University, Rutgers University, College of Charleston, Hampshire College, and University of Iowa;

Cassander Smith, Brigitte Fielder, Joe Rezek, Kabria Baumgartner, Molly Warsh, Nicole Breault; Ebony Okafor, Jameta Barlow; Karen Schafer; Elyshia Aseltine; Elyssa Tardif; Bryan Conn, Jason Hoppe, Christiane and Tim, Jordan Alexander Stein; Heather Smith; Barrye Brown, Mari Crabtree, Shannon Eaves and the M/T/W/Th/F writing group; Earl Johnson Jr., Gary Davenport, Matthew Pettway; Donika Kelly, Melissa Febos, Louisa Hall, William Menefield, Shalisa Gladney, Ashley Howard; Jessica White, Tsajai Gonzalez, Ebony Burnside, Linda Mbeki; Khadijah Mitchell and Gerard Jameson; Shani Mott, Nathan Connolly; the Means family; the Beauttah family; the Locks and House families; the Bynum family; Nyasha Grayman-Simpson, Fatimah Aure, Maya Burgos, Kristen Hodge-Clark, Keina Hodge, Dominica J. Henderson, Aja D. Jackson, Valene Whittaker, Lauren P. Wills, Carol Croxton, Rianna Matthews-Brown, Sabrina Johnson Turner; Stephanie Ray, Antoinette Perry-Banks; Stacee Dorsey, Carla Allen, Lisa Locks; and my father, James O. Bynum.

Reading Pleasures

The Matter of Black Living

Black Interiorities
(with a Nod to Poet Elizabeth Alexander)

This is not a book about suffering. It's not about protest or resistance, slavery or freedom. It is a book about the many ways that Black people feel when white people—as an idea or a voyeuristic gaze—aren't looking. It is a book that looks for those good feelings that are neither governed nor legislated: joy, excitement, or enthusiasm. What this book argues is that we—as scholars, students, or as a general public—don't talk enough about what feels good to Black people when there is no white gaze. It's assumed that to be Black is to be set out by this white gaze; to be Black means to be outside, outdoors, and to be made public and accessible to an oppressive, white sensibility.[1] Outside—of government, of personhood, of community—the "Black body" must resist and fight to get in. It seems to be Black is imagined as a collective and unsettled experience that must suffer a constant surveillance under an intrusive white gaze. There is no way in, no way inward.

But I've learned where there is an outside there must be an inside, and there are so many other ways to read the experiences of everyday living. Surely, as writer Toni Morrison describes, the inside "is formed by the inwardness of the outside, the interiority of the 'othered,' the personal that is always embedded in the public." This inside, at times, must be what Morrison explains further as "a social space that is psychically and physically safe."[2] Even as I take heed of literary scholar Farah Jasmine Griffin's admonition to recognize interiority as a necessary antecedent to public and resistive acts, I use interiority because it is neither public nor is it totally hidden, and it's true that everyone has an inside.[3] It is necessarily personal. It's in what's personal that interiority can and does show itself in the various ways that a person can and does reveal what and who matters.

Interiority is, as literary scholar Kevin Quashie explains, the "source of human action": it is where imagination can do its creative work and where feelings feel freely.[4] It has depth, and its uses are manifold. There is an interior to Black subjectivity that remembers what it means to be without the burdens or limits of white supremacy. Poet Elizabeth Alexander speaks of this interiority as the "inner space" wherein lies those "selves that go far, far beyond the limited expectations and definitions of what Black is, isn't or should be."[5] It is the site of the "somewhere" that the self can go and just be in love, in joy, or quite simply, amidst possibility. It is there where "White people never got to us," Toni Morrison writes, "in that private place where we lived and where we exercised skill and power, be it over biscuit dough or quilts, railroads or levees, architecture or baskets."[6] It is there, where language and representation reconcile, "beyond the power of the state to regulate," where feelings feel or speak for what cannot be said.[7]

Feelings gather meaning where no one else can see. Feelings acknowledge what matters to the person who feels them. In this private place, away from a real or imagined white gaze, there is the quiet of creativity. It's in the processes of creation—baking, writing, friendship, or loving—that reveals the truth of this interiority; it's the truth of knowing fully what it means to be human and to make meaning out of one's very human living. Inside, interiority's quiet can do its work as "a metaphor for the full range of one's inner life—one's desires, ambitions, hungers, vulnerabilities, fears."[8] What this interiority, in its quietude, gets at is, as writer Ralph Ellison explains it, "something subjective, willful, and complexly and compellingly human."[9]

And it's there inside where living, from time to time (albeit not always) feels *good*.[10] Joy lives there, and it has stories to tell. Where a person can feel inside his or her body, to own it, to delight in and experience its affective power, feelings realize thoughts and judgments that determine what is reasonable, right, or pleasing.[11] And feeling good doesn't always privilege or necessitate a meaningful collective identity or even racial politics. It's dangerously individual and, at times, a collective practice. I suspect those who can access this inside space—where feelings happen and one's humanity is never questioned—know what it means to "feel right" or to feel "an appropriate response" not only "to the scenes of suffering and redemption that the reader has witnessed" but also to everyday living and to the experience of feeling on behalf of someone else.[12] Where there are good feelings or right feelings, there is also the reality of an inside.

This book neither offers nor does it presuppose a singular narrative of feeling, interiority, or pleasure. It does gather various and compelling stories about the ways in which four early American writers, poet Phillis Wheatley, ministers John Marrant and James Albert Ukawsaw Gronniosaw, and pamphleteer David Walker feel good and write about it despite living while enslaved or nominally free. I read these four writers because each feels good often enough to write about even though their pleasures may look differently.

Wheatley delights in writing letters to a friend about the sale of her books or the ever-present spectacle of war. Gronniosaw and Marrant, in their respective narratives, memorialize their love for their Christian God because this god loves each of them. Walker appeals to his brethren because he knows that if they get angry enough to claim their victory, they will eventually enjoy the pleasures of a citizenry in a new American nation where slavery no longer exists. I have learned that it's not always easy to imagine good feelings in the lives of Black persons. There's a suspicion that if the enslaved are somehow happy or delighted that then they may have deserved their enslavement or worse yet, enjoyed it. However, for Wheatley, Gronniosaw, Marrant, and Walker, good feelings do happen, and they write about those feelings. It is true that where there are good feelings, there is also the reality of an inside—an interiority where a messy and joy-filled humanity is lived. Each of them talks about this inside and those resulting pleasures anticipate a pending or inevitable satisfaction and a hoping for what is not yet seen.

It is funny that Wheatley, Gronniosaw, Marrant, and Walker don't seem to need what we want from them presently—to prove their humanity, to resist publicly all of the time, or to feel burdened by the white gaze. Joy is inevitable for them; their faith promises joy. They are Christian and, more specifically, Protestant. Despite any expectations that single-mindedly privilege and observe their suffering, they read their lived experience in order to speak of that which communicates feeling good: maybe a kiss, a conversation, an appeal or a prayer to God with a community of believers who feels with them. And, what they write or publish tends to the very meaning of their complex, fleeting, and uncertain lives. Their work requires me to turn inward and toward a simple fact—Wheatley, Gronniosaw, Marrant, and Walker understand what pleases and feels good and what makes their lives matter.

As I look for their interiority, I'm asked to go inside too, into the work, the text, and into the very possibility that there is an inside to find. And this "turn inward requires contemplation, requires a quieting of the mind, requires stillness" and a belief that this turn serves a preparatory function.[13] I read this interiority as an invitation into a different story of selfhood, literacy, and community that pursues a kind of genealogy and ways of readings that privilege matters of feeling. I read for this interiority because it helps determine just what matters more. It demands the kinds of close reading that accept, as fact, interiority as a site of subjectivity and the making of meaning. It privileges those feelings that lead the reader to community, friendship, and a sense of providential mission. The lesson of interiority and this pursuit of good feeling is that reading pleasures are possible if only we take seriously a simple premise—Black lives do, in fact, matter.

What Is Feeling Good; or, "They Took Pleasure"

When I speak of feeling good in the writings of Wheatley, Gronniosaw, Marrant, and Walker, I'm describing what looks like those quotidian and simple pleasures that make life easier.[14] Maybe it's a gift, a friendly conversation, a political victory, or religious faith. It's any manner of loving and enjoyment. I don't mean to use pleasure—or good feelings—as a simple euphemism for sex or sexuality. Pleasure can name those experiences, but it is not exclusively sexual nor limited to bodily exercises. I mean to evoke what James Baldwin calls "sensual" or a way of being that promises to "respect and rejoice in the force of life, of life itself, and to be *present* in all that one does, from the effort of loving to the breaking of bread."[15]

Pleasures speak to that which is mundane, various, and so compellingly human. Pleasures are, at times, made by desire. Desire is a decidedly human longing. It longs for what poet Kevin Young explains as "a heroic act of reinvention" that can't help but to hope for some form of its own satisfaction.[16] As desiring seeks its remaking, satisfaction, and even its anticipation, it compels the experience of pleasure. For this reason, pleasure needs a dissatisfaction or discomfort to urge the desiring that will ultimately seek it. Dissatisfaction or discomfort inspire a desire to appease, satisfy, or comfort.

What Baldwin calls sensual and what I put forth as pleasure or feeling good is an ontological pursuit. It's an ongoing way of being that insists on one's presence at the site of any discomfort, dissatisfaction, a disrespect, or quite simply, a "diss," even as it also insists on desiring and ultimately, the very possibility of a deep, deep joy. Pleasure bears proof of the taking care or the tending to an inward self, an interiority and a larger community because, as cultural geographer Katherine McKittrick argues, it's a "collaborative praxes."[17] It depends upon an individual and bodily experience of desiring, satisfaction, and ultimately feeling good, even as it must collaborate to experience fully what kinds of good feelings are possible. What is certain is that pleasure is expected and worthy of our curiosity. In fact, there is no way to truly read individual suffering without also asking questions about pleasure. There is no way for these Black lives to matter if we don't consider how these lives matter to themselves and to those who love them.

Not only does each write about their pleasure, I study Wheatley, Marrant, Gronniosaw, and Walker because their writings are in print. They are popular. They are easily accessible and well-cataloged. Their works are a part of a long-standing scholarly conversation. Each of them is a kind of "first" in a so-called African American literary tradition: the first to publish a book of poetry or a wildly sought-after conversion or captivity narrative, or the first to self-publish a pamphlet that may inspire slave revolts and a series of legal prohibitions against literacy. As a "first" in this literary tradition, each allows the tradition to tell its origin story in a way that never promises or guarantees pleasure or interiority (because the tradition wouldn't ever guess that each of these writers has an inside, let alone joy). Rather, it promises and celebrates a reading practice that memorializes a racialized identity as it suffers its way into being.

This literary tradition must, as my students once told me, "keep it real." When I asked what this phrase means, students chimed in to offer descriptors that tried to move "keep it real" from abstraction to "real." To "keep it real" meant to express, to live, to hold on to what is real—remnants of bygone days preserved in manners of speech, styles of dress, and history books. To be "real" and to keep it was cool. Its history was hot, southern, plantation slavery. Its present was urban, impoverished, and folk; it was always inarticulate and uneducated speech and, to use their word, "ghetto." Most importantly, it resisted and opposed unnamed technologies of power (read: white privilege). And its stories made for a tradition that could never expect pleasure. Pleasure was far too risky and threatened the sorts of politics-making that profit from a collective suffering.[18] But, comedian Dave Chappelle's famed skit, "When Keeping It Real Goes Wrong" (2004) is right. "Keeping it real" can and does go wrong.

Even as the title pages of their texts identify their enslaved status or as a "Negro," "colored," or "Black" person, the letters of Phillis Wheatley, the narratives of Marrant and Gronniosaw, and David Walker's appeal refuse a simplistic reading or the expectations of a literary tradition. What they resist are those insistent, single-minded readings that obsess over their racialized subjectivity, objectivity, or agency. Marrant makes no direct mention of his racial identity. For Gronniosaw, "Africa" is a paradoxical site of his sinful torment and his mythic, Eden-like childhood. Walker and Wheatley question race-making while, at the same, offering to readers a new way of thinking about selfhood and community. It seems, if we read closely enough, racial identity is not their "ultimate concern."[19] God is. What they have in common is a Christian faith that matters to them and sometimes, seems to matter more than our need for specific racialized categories. Because they can't anticipate our twenty-first-century concerns, I read closely for and take seriously their sincerity and their faith. I believe them when they profess their Christian faith because I suspect that for Wheatley, Marrant, Gronniosaw and Walker, it is, in fact, a meaningful way to live.

Despite their many differences of time, gender, and geography, they share a concern for and a belief in a Christian faith that pleases them even as it also demands the cultivation of a proper inner life. Faith is as much an inward expression as it is an outward fellowship. In this way, they are believers whose faith brings them together intertextually—by way of friendship or collaboration, masonry, Protestantism, the popular itinerant minister the Reverend George Whitefield, or publishing—in mobile, Atlantic, Protestant communities.

Theirs is a faith in a Protestant God (and most often Methodist) who can provide when necessary and is certain of their worth despite what sociopolitical conditions might suggest. "Your observations," Phillis Wheatley writes in a 30 October 1773 letter to her friend, Obour Tanner, "on our dependence on the Deity, & your hopes that my wants will be supply'd from his fulness which is in Christ Jesus, is truely worthy of your self."[20] Because she is certain that Christ will satisfy her wants, Wheatley confesses her dependence on her Savior, at times, because of her bodily or emotional weakness. John Marrant and James Albert Ukawsaw Gronniosaw narrate their stories of salvation; God saves each man repeatedly from starvation, bodily harm, or certain death. Every story they tell testifies to the providence of God, and their titles hint at the "remarkable particulars" and "wonderful dealings" of their dutiful Savior. David Walker prays that his readers might feel godly truth, "and may God Almighty, who is the Father of our Lord Jesus Christ, open your hearts to understand and belief the truth."[21] For Walker, the truth is in God's Word—that slavery is not God's will. Faith governs their lives, and God is greater than man. Their faith demands that they cultivate an inner life as well as right ways of living.

Theirs is a readerly faith. The Christian reader must feel inwardly his or her way to knowing God and the self. This kind of reading, then, names an everyday practice of discernment and a sensory experience that correlates often (albeit not always) with a spiritual faith and a particularly, Christian faith. It calls the reader inward; readers experience what's read as bodily, interior, and private. It mimics the enthusiastic means by which the faithful receive godly word and insight.

When reading happens in this way, it happens in the body. The heart feels. Eyes see or the "ear takes on the function of reading," Hortense Spillers explains.[22] Listeners are readers too. And yet, the ear is only part of how this reading happens. Spillers observes an aurality that remembers, in part, a decidedly Christian manner of reading. This manner of reading requires only a belief in a Christian God whose manner of salvation opens the heart of the believer to the Word of God. Reading the Word demands an affective engagement not only with the book but also with the meaning of words as they are heard or seen.[23]

While the ear hears words, the eyes must do the work of seeing properly. Reading, in this affective way, happens inside the self, deep down at the heart of what matters, at the site of the self whose feelings determine what constitutes meaning. This affective literacy resists publicity yet pursues community, and for good reason. This literacy demands a trust of the self that takes the reader into the site where an individual humanity reveals its affective sensibility.

What results from this experience of the Word awakens believers to an enthusiastic fellowship with God that opens the eyes to sight and the ears to hearing; the believer can see and hear what the unconverted cannot.[24] The wholehearted believer can testify to God's ability to save, to create a new man out of a former sinner, and to make a reader out of those, by the grace of God, deemed capable and worthy. Those who can "read" God's Word into their hearts fulfill—Marrant explains—"the evidence of their interest is 'Christ in them.' Coll. i. 27. and he [Christ] fills not only their heads with this doctrine, but their hearts and affections with his spirit, they derive virtue from Christ, to cure their spiritual diseases, to purify their hearts, and to bring forth fruits unto God. Deeply sensible, that without Christ, they can do nothing."[25] The believer cannot help but to feel rightly, with "their hearts and affections with [Christ's] spirit." Suddenly, the believer emerges as a new man with eyes and ears that can read into hearts and feel where others cannot. But there are those readers who take up the practice of reading as a moralistic and faithful quality of the self. These are the good readers. These are the readers who practice the requisite faithful reading in order to get into what's inside the Word, words, or text—into the value of belief, into the truth of feeling, and into the ability to feel beyond the individual self.

Theirs is an imaginative faith. It "is the substance of things hoped for, the evidence of things not seen."[26] Their faith is necessarily active, unwavering, and engaged. It demands prayer and engagement in a way that privileges a deep longing. But, it's in the longing that faith emerges, and its hoping serves its purpose. There is a pleasure in the anticipatory processes of faith and in its profound trust of a forthcoming evidence. In spite of what each cannot see—freedom, the abolition of slavery, books not yet printed or sometimes, love, and family—Walker, Wheatley, Marrant, and Gronniosaw take up this faith and live in its certain pleasures. Their faith is certain that God will and does make their living right. Their faith serves them well. It offers them a language with which to create fellowship, friendship, and publishing opportunities even as it teaches that good feeling happens inside those who are deemed worthy readers, those whose faith affords them access to this inward site. How the writers name this site varies—sometimes it's even referred to as "heart" (or the Holy Spirit's point of entry as in the case of Marrant and Gronniosaw). But, what they speak of is an interiority, where language meets representation, where God meets the faithful—in words or in the Word or where feeling good happens. Their language, curiosity or any "joy unspeakable," at the site of this interiority, can and does direct my reading.[27] I've learned as I read each letter, narrative, or appeal we shouldn't take for granted that even small pleasures make life more enjoyable to live.

When I read as if their lives matter, I don't have to wonder anymore about how their lives anticipate a twenty-first-century demand for resistance, survival, or abjection. Reading as if and because their Black lives matter lends me the "critical generosity" that is willing to imagine that Wheatley, Marrant, Gronniosaw, and Walker matter to themselves and to those who love and know them.[28] Their living bears witness to the kinds of materiality that not only accepts a collective or individual humanity as fact but also the pleasures that admit to what matters to their lives. Theirs is a pleasure, like many, that begins with the desire for something—a letter, a friend, a god, or love. Their living is didactic. It serves those Christian readers who they expect to learn from their lives. Imagine how much fun David Walker has setting the type for his appeal;[29] even as he must speak his anger, he must also strategize its formation in print—every italic, pointed finger, footnote, and capital letter. I suspect that Wheatley enjoys reading her letters from her sister-friend, Obour Tanner. Not only does she enjoy reading, she must delight too in the very beauty of her penmanship, her signature in particular and its emphasis on the "P" in Phillis and the "W" in Wheatley.[30] John Marrant and James Albert Ukawsaw Gronniosaw celebrate their faith and take readers to the sites of their conversion in order to declare themselves worthy of salvation.

Reading #BlackLivesMatter

Right now, I can't help but to consider #BlackLivesMatter as an invitation to its particular kind of reading practice. I've come to this conclusion by way of a misreading or a misunderstanding. I didn't read Twitter's response to the murders of many Black women and men as an appeal for a particular sort of reading—at first. I heard its protest, its urgency, as a kind of quiet declaration, without exclamation points or capitalized letters. No pointed fingers or grammatical adornments in the way of David Walker's appeals. Just a hashtag and three words: Black, lives, matter. I had missed its desiring or its appeal to and for meaning. I missed it because I only heard its anger. I read resistance and a refusal to accept the brutality and terrorism of white supremacy and nothing else. I forgot that even anger, protest, and grief want for or desire something until I heard students announce its truth as a declaration, demand, and an insecurity—Black lives matter—and claim its rage, its grief, and its future trip into the messy possibilities of its desires and pleasures. Students, in our various class discussions, invoked the hashtag in a manner that has since reminded me that anger must desire after what it cannot have (for a time). Anger is only necessary when a desire is denied, inaccessible, or unsatisfying. Anger is frustrated by its lack or, quite simply, by someone's proverbial "no." Even as a negation or an absence induces it, anger engenders recognition at the expense of what it really desires. But anger doesn't just seek publicity for its own sake with no end in mind. It doesn't just shout or yell without purpose or without a greater desire for something or someone. Anger, despite its noise or silence, desires, asks, and longs for what it can't have. It's anger (or angry) for this reason.

What I missed in its anger and call for resistance or refusal is the very possibility and pursuit of its pleasures. Even when it's angry, #BlackLivesMatter is yearning and asking. I have learned that behind the urgency and its pursuit of recognition, #BlackLivesMatter baits us—without the help of traditional forms of grammar or punctuation—to ask those questions that it never will, at least not out loud. It refuses the burdens of its questions because #BlackLivesMatter needs its reader to pursue what it won't ever ask:

Who are these Black lives?
To and for whom do Black lives matter?
Why is this perceptible question or idea worth stating?
What does it mean to matter?

Where Black lives matter, there is not just the shared experience of rage and grief. There's an enthusiasm that "refuses the dominant order: the feeling of exultation, emerging as a form of knowledge that is a necessarily collaborative praxes, cites and sites of Black joy and love."[31] The mere refusal of the "dominant order" might elicit those sites (and cites) of joy that McKittrick imagines. Protest isn't just resistance or a pronouncement of a collective suffering, but it can also be a source of enjoyment, passion, and community building. Where Black lives matter, there is also the possibility of the delightful and pleasurable experience of collective action, living, and loving too. The possibility of pleasure or delight neither trivializes suffering nor is it less real than trauma. I am returned to the obvious; there is, in fact, pleasure where Black lives matter. It's there where play and enjoyment can happen, and it does.[32] Pleasure creates those ways of knowing and feeling that realize the true work of the hashtag—namely, to fashion and care for affective ways of being together. There is joy in its witness, its storytelling, and its truth-seeking. It's a pleasure to know that Black lives do matter and have always mattered.

What #BlackLivesMatter teaches—in its brevity—is a way to read the experiences and significance of Black lives with a nod, of course, to what matters and to whom it matters. For this reason, it seems to me that the hashtag functions as a reading primer. As a reading primer, its historiography of experience, of the ways in which feeling and materiality mark Black living, also lends me an interpretative way of reading that privileges its truth—Black lives do matter—and hints at (even if it can't say it) those ways of shared and intimate knowing that are demonstrative and private. It assumes and expects familiarity and, of course, anticipates the pleasures that its desiring seeks. It resists the burdens of time and suffering because where Black lives matter, suffering isn't always a thing about which to worry, and neither is time. Black lives matter when and where they do. Its way of reading seems to reproduce Barbara Christian's experience of reading: "How and what do we (the many we's) read and how and what *should* we read? Of course, one could say and it must be said, even stressed, that to read is not only to validate the self but also to participate in 'the other's' view of the world, the writer's view."[33] What we learn to read, in fact, is not only someone else's worldview. We learn to read and write the other's view as our view, and together, we share and swap those stories we don't want to say, those stories that are better shared or left unsaid. Because our stories are archived and gathered as part of this collective observation, #BlackLivesMatter, we are not alone. We are asked, rather, to feel and to look for those stories wherever they are found, lost, or unspoken.

#BlackLivesMatter primes its readers to make and read meaning as part of collective, affective experiences. The reader learns how to make meaning out of what's felt and shared; maybe, it's something akin to an intimacy, a shared pleasure, or a mutual grieving. Because the reader who accepts its offering to feel together might understand that those words "for example, do not convey meaning, but *potential* for meaning. That potential, that opportunity for choice, becomes *meaningful* only when it is performed and accessed in a certain context."[34] The reader attends to the hashtag's potential meanings when she or he can read its feeling and declare to and for whom it belongs. It belongs to these "shared stories, communal activities, and collaborative possibilities wherein 'one *must participate* in knowing.'"[35] This sharing speaks what literary critic Kevin Quashie calls a "rhetorical intimacy." Quashie explains that this intimacy needs no specified addressee. Despite its lack of a specific conversant, the hashtag reproduces rhetorical intimacy with every mention. Its language "suggests a manner of engagement that is consonant with" its technology.[36] It seeks after the familiarity of experience.

Even as it seeks, #BlackLivesMatter lends familiarity to those who can cite experiences, names, or publicity that engender its meaning. It creates language that has "potential" for some other kind of feeling or action.[37] And the potential is not only in its creativity or its ability to make Black living legible. There is a potential, too, in an understanding of Black living as a worthy and pleasurable matter.

#BlackLivesMatter is useful as a modality of reading because its disruptive and generative. It offers me a way to read, albeit with a bit of anachronism, Wheatley, Gronniosaw, John Marrant, and Walker with a "critical generosity" and a belief in their real, multidimensional materiality.[38] Reading in this way and in pursuit of what and who matters allows me to play with or take seriously the idea that their Black lives—whether as indices of racial identity, cultural category, or as a mark upon the skin—have always mattered to them and those who love them. I use "play"—with a nod to Treva B. Lindsey and Frances Smith Foster—to suggest participation and enjoyment as I think critically about this writing.

When Lindsey characterizes her critical practice as a "playground," she remembers to me the various ways in which critical reading is just as fun as the creation of the text. That's the "trick," Foster might say. "We should not merely study the recordings of humankind," writes Foster, "We must use our tricks (feats or skills), we must perform our tricks (duty or work), we must cultivate our tricks (personal habits) so that . . . we help humanity endure and prevail."[39] With the trickiness of play in mind, this manner of reading expects me to disrupt the expectation that life for Walker, Wheatley, Gronniosaw, and Marrant is too challenging to enjoy or to experience fully simply because the American political system says so. It unsettles the kinds of voyeurism that can only read resistance or an antecedent suffering onto this early writing. It rejects the ways of seeing that can only read Black living as a collective way of being mediated through a collective experience of suffering. Protest is not the only way to experience living, and its forms of resistance aren't the only way to inspire a resistive scholarly practice.

#BlackLivesMatter's reading practice also beckons us to remember those ways of reading that need neither books nor book learning. Book learning and the pursuit of traditional forms of literacy aren't the only kinds of reading. When books fail or when there is no book to read, I have learned that what is left are those "compellingly human" ways of reading.[40] I mean to use reading to name an interpretative sensibility that requires instead an experiential or affective literacy and a greater willingness to make sense of living. This manner of reading has had many names: "geopolitical literacy," "visual literacy," or a sort of affective common sense.[41] It might just feel right or like an inexplicable knowing. It's a reading practice that isn't limited to books and takes in the full materiality of any perceived text. And text is defined broadly as experiential or that which requires an interpretation. Experience functions as legible text that must be read closely.

Phillip Troutman calls it a "geopolitical literacy" or the application, acquisition, and dissemination of "geographic and geopolitical knowledge and information" in a way that makes meaning and affects a collective consciousness. Troutman explains further that "it represented words in motion, news and information categorized and passed on surreptitiously" and it also "represented a mode of gathering and transfer of knowledge." This literacy requires ways of knowing and a skillful discernment in order to "'read' the social and political landscape."[42]

Toni Morrison figures it as a "visual literacy" that relies on "the colors, the shapes, the sounds, the smells, all the other senses and it makes for . . . a third dimension, an artist's true dimension, how to read your world as well as how to read texts."[43] Even though Morrison's use of "visual" is a bit of a misnomer, her reading of this kind of literacy admits to the many ways in which reading happens. For Morrison, reading can register affectively upon the body and ultimately determine how the reader feels in his or her world.

Reading closely can yield an understanding of reading as a creative process, as a way to interrogate or consider those affective experiences that suggest Black people feel good, at least, sometimes. Kevin Young thinks of this sort of reading as an *"aliteracy"* that he understands to be "the ability to read situations and power structures more than books." As a kind of affective or feelings-centered reading, Young's "aliteracy" insists on particular ways of knowing and understanding how these feelings are felt or represented. Young explains, "*aliteracy* approaches more what we say when we say 'she read him,' as in figgered him for a fool." Feelings and the bodies in which they live are read as legible and, certainly, not everyone can read them. Nevertheless, as Young says, "from what is left unsaid, even unsayable, we get insight."[44]

Reading, then, demands a listening in, a sounding out, an attention to the in-between and what's left unsaid yet speaks as a gesture, an interruption, or a misplaced word. The reader has a responsibility—to the text and to the author—to lean into what he or she feels. It is a profoundly creative and interpretative act of belief that requires readers to trust, to interpret or discern, what they feel as yet another way of knowing. When reading is an imaginative and at times, faithful matter, it acts as "a process of faith and belief—a faith that leads to wholeness for an individual and for a community."[45] At times, this reading practice yields the pleasures of an anticipatory faith; the reader delights in the affective experience of knowing an individual and collective wholeness that suggests a godly intervention.

Living Pleasures

I am reading Phillis Wheatley's letters again. Her various, extant letters—from 1770 to 1779—aren't often cited even though many are easy to find in the back of the Penguin edition of her *Complete Writings*. But, I like the way she speaks. Her paragraphs are often short, but her concerns and language meander. She can and does move from mundanity of travel and illness to the certainty of God's love in the midst of a political contest that will, inevitably, turn into a war. I like the way her prayers let me know who she matters to and what matters to her. Her correspondence begs me to wonder if a hashtag can look backward in time. Wheatley doesn't need a hashtag, and time won't let her have one anyway. She doesn't need to conclude her letter with #BlackLivesMatter because she seems to know its truth. It's me that must learn how much Wheatley's Black living must have mattered to herself and to someone else. I have to read her letters closely enough to hear just how her living mattered to herself and to someone else.

Take for example the sale of Wheatley's book, *Poems on Various Subjects, Religious and Moral*, first published in London and "printed for" A. Bell. In 1773, Wheatley's letters frequently make reference to her published work because it's then that her book is first in print. "'I have rec'd the money,' the famed poet writes, 'you sent for the 5 books & 2/6 [2 shillings, six pence] more for another, which I now Send & wish safe to hand.'"[46] The books are sent to Wheatley's friend, Obour Tanner, who has sold and collected the monies for the sale of the books. By this 6 May 1774 letter, I have met Tanner already, and I know who she is and to expect her. She first appears, in Wheatley's extant correspondence, as "Arbour Tanner in Newport [Rhode Island]" two years before, in a 19 May 1772 letter. Wheatley greets her as "Dear Sister" in nearly every letter. It seems that Tanner is for Wheatley a sister—a sister-in-Christ, a sister-in-love, and in friendship too. They worship God and pray together; and, for right now, it seems they sell books together as well. Wheatley has already asked Tanner to get subscribers to purchase her book, "as it is for my benefit."[47] Her request works. Tanner is selling Wheatley's books in and around Newport with the help of her pastor and Wheatley family friend, the Reverend Samuel Hopkins. How Tanner coordinates the sale of Wheatley's books is not quite clear. Wheatley doesn't specify to whom Tanner sells (and Tanner's letters are not yet extant). Hopkins's pastorate is a church home to mutual acquaintances (or at least, familiar names to)—Cato Coggeshall, John Quamine, and Bristol Yamma—of Wheatley and Tanner.

What is certain is that Tanner helps Wheatley make money. And the money, with Tanner's help, finds its way from Newport to Wheatley in Boston. Wheatley counts her money, inventories her books, and prepares—"I have recd by some of the last ships 300 more of my Poems"—to send off a further shipment.[48] Wheatley doesn't get enough credit for selling her wares and collecting what's owed her, and there's even less talk of the many ways she may have enjoyed her money or even her success as a published poet.

In her Protestant way, Wheatley certainly praises God for his continued observance of her health and welfare. Though she never quite says how much she enjoys her fame or its privileges, her lists of books sold and accounts received gets me to question Wheatley's pleasures yet again. Mentions of her books make it into the letters. I suspect that, if they are worthy of note, they matter to Wheatley. What seems evident to Wheatley—that her life and its concerns and its pleasures are meaningful—must prompt me to consider what else I might understand about her if and when I accept her everyday living and its materiality as fact. Wheatley's mention of her book sales, as part of the larger conversations of her letters, invites me to wonder what is uncovered in the archive or library if we search for the materiality of Black life and its pleasures. What forms of creativity and curiosity or pleasure might a text reveal? Wheatley's letters are not hard to find, and neither are those pleasures that seem to delight her. She believes deeply in a Christian God who provides for her. She has friends and addressees with whom she corresponds often. What she writes down in those extant letters hint at what she enjoys, what concerns her and who she is.

While her fame is uncommon, Wheatley's faith, friendships, and acquaintances are not. Each letter confesses to the inside stuff, the quiet that makes her a good writer and a better friend, a seller of her books, and a Christian woman. She has an inward, private life—rife with complexity—

within which she lives out those feelings, desires, and pleasures that evince her interiority. Not only do her letters reveal what's inside her; each puts her in a conversation with someone else. It's their traveling conversations—ferreted by named persons across New England's geographies and an ocean too—wherein Wheatley claims a bit about who she is and with whom she is. She weaves these names in and out of her correspondence. There's Obour Tanner, the Countess of Huntingdon, George Whitefield, John Peters, John Quamine, Mr. Zingo Stevens, and others who locate her within a geography of those people, places, and ideas that may matter to her. I suspect—if the library or archive ever permit it—these names might have something to say about how much she matters to them.

With every mention of a name, Wheatley instantiates—what Katherine Clay Bassard calls—a "writing community." Bassard uses this term "as a theoretical rubric through which to attend the 'unfolding'" of this early writing. Bassard imagines her use of writing community "as a corrective to the term 'tradition'."[49] While tradition can name various sorts of "devotion" and "invention," its mention in scholarship privileges a linear chronology that is often fixed and limited by its origin story and its commitment to temporality.[50] Because Wheatley is the first—young woman, enslaved—to publish a book of poems in colonial America, she authors a literary tradition. As a kind of beginning Wheatley's is a story of a heroic genius. What Wheatley authors satisfies a collective "amazement at her achievement," writes Kevin Young, "as if we too sit on her jury of skeptical, prominent, dubious, white gentlemen"—because, without her poetry, there is no Frederick Douglass or Toni Morrison.[51] There's no story or tradition without her *Poems* or without her frontispiece.

If her only story is that she is "first," then it's a story that is far too limiting and too isolating. Wheatley's writings, in fact, refuse the singularity of the *Poems* frontispiece or any expectation that she has a singular story to tell. For Bassard, Wheatley is not simply a "first" to publish a book of poetry or to begin a literary tradition. Wheatley is not part of either a "series of unrelated beginnings" or "separate and isolated publishing 'events'."[52] But Wheatley and her *Poems* are part of many, interconnected stories. "We must remember that even Wheatley," explains Young, "though that all-too-rare figure of 'public poet,' enjoyed a private community of Black voices and words, including Jupiter Hammon and her beloved friend Obour Tanner."[53] And, there must be more even if their works aren't present or if the relationships are unclear. Maybe Wheatley does hang out with Tanner's acquaintances from First Congregational Church, Sarah Searing, or Phylis Lyndon. Wheatley writes her way into community that invokes—as Hortense Spillers explains—what is "both a groping and a given."[54] What are shared are those gestures of acceptance and feeling that admit to a community-building friendship and intimacy.[55] This community, with its exchange of letters, ideas, and shared feelings gropes toward a discursivity and those conversations that expect its potentiality or what's yet to be. It imagines itself as part of its present, a collective and shared future.

What's given is the expectation and certainty that community functions as a sort of sociality and commonality. This sociality "invoke[s] the sense of a boundary or border (community) that remains actively and dynamically in the process of its own renegotiation (writing)."[56] Wheatley participates in its common language that constantly revises and renegotiates its terms of relation. What results is a kind of unfolding community that would, in Wheatley's words, "revive in better times," and alter "forever the 'master narrative' of American authorship."[57]

When Bassard uses "writing community," she names an emergent print culture that literary scholar Joseph Rezek refers to as "the print Atlantic." Bassard's writing communities yield print cultures that, as Rezek argues, connect "the English-speaking publics of the Atlantic into a single, though internally various, culture."[58] The print Atlantic extends Bassard's term to its real or imagined output, namely printed texts that might serve their authors "as a medium for the enactment of a self-determining, collective political presence" or as a way "to speak so and for themselves about matters they considered worthy of written words."[59] It is mobilized around its Protestantism and its commitment to publishing. Together, these terms—writing community and a resulting print Atlantic—work to "stress the importance of a media-specific approach to writing" and its relational pursuits.[60]

Rezek observes "a politics of materiality" as part of this printed Atlantic and, in doing so, examines the meaning that books gather as aesthetic and commercial objects. What matters to Rezek is the manner in which writing turns into print and creates meaning in a bound and circulative form. Not only does the very act of writing create legibility or a kind of "interpretative community," but so does printing or publication.[61] Surely, the printed stuff—books of poetry, narratives, and pamphlets—matters because it leaves a text to read or discern. It engages with systems and processes of printmaking, paper production, ink, circulation, and selfhood. Frances Smith Foster repeatedly observes that the printed materiality of these early writers "worked to communicate physical and metaphysical realities and to develop their moral, spiritual, intellectual, and artistic selves."[62] The printed text performs those realities and evidences the many ways that these writers experience and influence the world as part of what Joanna Brooks calls a "positive collective incorporation."[63]

Even as this politics of materiality encourages questions of publics, consumption, and book history, I can't forget that there is also a pleasure in this materiality. There is a pleasure in the experience of the materiality of the text, in its writing and reading and in the communities, which make this materiality possible. There's pleasure in the touch of the book or the choice of its binding and the practice of reading, in all of its various forms. Pleasure is part of the book's circulation.

The writing community might only gather together, at least in some contexts, because the book is worthy of reading or discussion. It's for these reasons that, while Wheatley may not serve me best as a "first," she does guide me. She contributes to this print culture as well as generates the pleasures of consumption that her readers enjoy. Their enjoyment, at times, looks like a passing mention of her verse or a play on her words, maybe even the kinds of wordplay that suggest a shared interest. There's a resulting interplay or what scholars often refer to as an intertextuality that suggests authors read across texts and borrow ideas, tropes, and concerns. "This form of revision," literary historian Henry Louis Gates Jr. proposes, "grounds each individual work in a larger context and creates formal lines of continuity between the texts that together constitute the shared text of Blackness."[64] It's not just a shared racialized identity. This interplay or intertextuality suggests an intimacy between texts, authors, and readers across identity categories; this continuity demands a sharing that asks for a turning inward and a recognition of self in the language of another. There's a common language that makes this interplay of ideas, tropes, and meaning possible. I mean to use interplay to also get at the pleasures to which play speaks; the book may be important to exchange of ideas, and so is the playfulness of the exchange and the very idea of revision as curiosity and delight.

Writing Pleasures

Phillis Wheatley's mentions—of place and persons—lead me to consider her as part of this larger interplay and its greater early American textual archive of letters, narratives, journals, and sermons. When I read Wheatley as a participant and not as singular, then her writing community emerges, as does her interests in reading and writing for what matters or is pleasing to her. For this reason, I read too the writing of those who may also have heard of Wheatley or those names that Wheatley mentions: in particular, John

Marrant, James Albert Ukawsaw Gronniosaw, and David Walker. Wheatley's travels to meet Selina Hastings, the Countess of Huntingdon—though she never does get to see her—persuade me to read the writings of Gronniosaw and Marrant. The countess funds this early writing community, and its subsequent publications answer particular calls to worship and pray. What Gronniosaw, Marrant, and Wheatley write creates the textual interplay that allows them to cultivate the interiority and make possible a greater experience of individual (and, at times, collective) pleasure. Wheatley, Gronniosaw, and Marrant use the financial support of the countess to realize—by way of their writing and publication—what might serve their shared faith. Wheatley and Gronniosaw dedicate their books to the countess. Both will have their writings published in Newport, Rhode Island, and by way of the countess, they may have learned about each other.[65] Wheatley, in a 17 July 1773 letter to the countess, may have referred to Gronniosaw as "an African so worthy to be honor'd by your Ladiship's approbation & Friendship as him whom you call your Brother," according to Wheatley biographer, Vincent Carretta.[66] I can't say for sure that Wheatley is referencing Gronniosaw or that Gronniosaw ever makes it to Boston. I don't know if he ever meets Wheatley in person, but he too understands the utility of his faith and the support of the countess and George Whitefield.

Not only does Wheatley make use of the countess's support, she, Marrant, and Gronniosaw benefit as well from Reverend George Whitefield, the countess's chaplain. Whitefield's influence is well-noted. Wheatley writes an elegy for him. Whitefield strikes a young Marrant to the ground with his words in Marrant's *A Narrative of the Lord's Wonderful Dealings with John Marrant, A Black* (1785). Gronniosaw, in *A Narrative of the Most Remarkable Particulars in the Life of a James Albert Ukawsaw Gronniosaw, an African Prince* (1774), longs for the day when the good minister might greet him as a brother-in-Christ.

Gronniosaw's story follows him from Baurnou in West Africa into enslavement and the favor of God's saving grace. He speaks his narrative, as an elderly man, to an amanuensis in England and, in so doing, his story is printed into a transatlantic "writing community." Editions of Gronniosaw's *Narrative* are published in England and Newport, where Obour Tanner lives and where she worships at the church of the Reverend Samuel Hopkins. A year after Wheatley's death and a decade or so after the 1774 Newport edition of Gronniosaw's narrative, John Marrant publishes his ordination sermon as a narrative with the editorial help of W. Aldridge.

Marrant tells a redemptive story of his wayward youth in Charleston, South Carolina. His story takes him from colonial and wartime South

Carolina to Britain where he, like Gronniosaw, earns the patronage of the Countess of Huntingdon. He learns God's Word and trains as a minister. His efforts take him away from Britain to Nova Scotia and Boston. In Boston—five years after Wheatley dies—Marrant is welcomed by Prince Hall, founder of the African Freemasons, and even though Marrant's stay is brief, he befriends a community that fellowships with the Free African Union Society of Newport and other mutual aid groups along the East Coast. This community includes Obour Tanner, Cato Coggeshall, Zingo Stevens, John Quamine, and Bristol Yamma—all of whom Wheatley names in her correspondence.[67]

None of them can know pamphleteer and Boston-area merchant David Walker. Each passes away long before Walker ever writes his appeal with a preamble and four articles to the "coloured citizens of the world." Walker is nonetheless tied to these early writers. Phillis Wheatley's popularity is part of Boston's local lore. And, David Walker and John Marrant are Freemasons. Walker must have read or heard Marrant's 1789 Sermon to his fellow mason, and he surely shares Marrant's commitment to Christian faith and racial uplift.

While Marrant may have aspired to leave the United States as part of an early repatriation plan to settle Sierra Leone, Walker appeals for an American citizenry. Walker criticizes the hypocrisy of the American pro-slavery sensibilities and its founding declarations of equality and freedom. He argues, too, against colonization programs. Because he understands that this country belongs to his brethren, he appeals for a citizenry that can live freely and with an honest Christian faith. What Walker shares with Marrant, Gronniosaw, and Wheatley is knowledge of how much life and the lives of others matter.

Each author knows how much he or she matters and where to put what matters too. The chapters of this book consider the intersections of this materiality, pleasure, and interiority in order to wonder: When we assume that the living matters of Wheatley, Gronniosaw, Marrant, and Walker, what else can we learn, hear, or read? What happens when we accept their faith and pleasure as meaningful? What if we accept and believe in their pleasures as we read their writings?

* * *

Chapter 1 reads the extant, intermittent correspondence of Wheatley and Obour Tanner. Wheatley's letters to Tanner—from 1772 to 1779—evidence the deep-down pleasure that comes from the satisfaction of her desire to, as Audre Lorde says it, "shar[e] deeply any pursuit with another person," to listen and to be heard, to love and be loved.[68] For Wheatley, these letters share a deep and abiding faith in a Christian God whose ability to love, create, and author her life inspires this epistolary space of mutual language and exchange. Wheatley's epistles are a series of private correspondence that reveal an intimacy that happens at a site of their exchange. When both women receive each other's letters and presumably read them or have them read, each access—what Lorde calls—an "erotic" power upon which their friendship grows. Wheatley and Tanner participate in a network of correspondence that allows them to ferry their letters across a great distance. If Wheatley teaches us how reading—in this private kind of exchange—makes friendship, then James Albert Ukawsaw Gronniosaw, in his *Narrative* (1774), teaches us how to use publicity and accounts of conversion to call for new ways of understanding Christianity, personhood, and of course, reading pleasures.

Chapter 2 counters the scholarly assumption that Gronniosaw's narrative is an account of an emergent African American racial consciousness or an example in a burgeoning slave narrative genre that begins with Briton Hammon. Gronniosaw's story situates him in a transcultural discourse of religious conversion. He chronicles his transformation from sinner to believer as he recalls his encounters with God's providence: in West Africa, the wilderness, and the Middle Passage as well as a slave in America and a freeman in England. Gronniosaw aims to teach his readers what it means to desire after God and to be saved by God. Gronniosaw writes himself into the conversion narrative tradition of John Bunyan and the biblical Paul. What his narrative offers is his life story as an African man with the help of biblical stories (of Paul and Jesus) that help him tell a prophetic narrative version of his life. Gronniosaw uses his story to predict and convey his worthiness as a Christian. In this way, this African man professes his faith in Jesus Christ.[69] He, much like John Marrant, deems himself worthy to tell his story because he is a true believer and because Christ is his hero and Savior. This chapter points to a new way of reading Gronniosaw. It argues for a reading of his narrative as a proof of his worth as a child of God and his intimacy with God. His story prepares the way for those who seek after what is unspeakable and unknowable before a spiritual conversion.

Chapter 3 observes an intertextual conversation that happens between John Marrant's "talking book" scene and that of James Albert Ukawsaw Gronniosaw *Narrative* (ca. 1772). Marrant and Gronniosaw put forth two differing perspectives on reading, though there is one end—namely, to practice Christian faith in the right way. Gronniosaw and Marrant have ideas about how the right kind of Christian behaves. A good Christian experiences the pleasures of reading God's Word rightly. John Marrant's multi-genre narrative dramatizes the intersections of faith and identity that inform his self-making. Marrant makes a Christian self, not a specifically racialized one. His religious vocabulary registers a profound belief in something other than his physical, racialized, and earthly body—that is, God. He speaks by way of his biblical revisionism.

Take for example Revelation 5. Marrant rewrites this revelation as the story of a Native American "princess" who cannot read, an unrequited kiss, and a series of misses: a misunderstanding, a mis-seeing, or a mis-hearing. And this scene, in its various iterations, isn't necessarily a true story. It's not supposed to be literal. Rather, it's a story to get readers to think about desire and its limitations. When desire doesn't strive toward God, it is disruptive and ill informed. It's carnal and misguided. It assumes, for example, that books talk (literally) when, in fact, they don't. The book, its silence, and the reader are designed to create a feeling that lends its presence to the narrative. The story wants us to feel a desire for God and to act upon it. This story invites the reader to learn its meaning, to feel it, and to experience inwardly its words as a revision of God's Word because if Marrant's reader can feel it rightly, deep down inside, he or she can learn just what it means to know God and who God is. It engenders an optimistic desire that anticipates its satisfaction. The princess misunderstands what Marrant knows. Marrant is the ultimate believer and, as a result, can enjoy the pleasure that comes from knowing the power of the godly word. By way of the princess's story, he realizes his call to ministry.

In the years following the publication of Marrant's narrative, when John Marrant joined up with Prince Hall and his Freemasons, I'm sure he had no idea that one day David Walker would join their ranks. What I am certain of though is that Walker's *Appeal* (all three editions) participates in a genealogy of fraternalism and brotherhood that one finds in Marrant, Prince Hall, and elsewhere. David Walker uses the tenets of Freemasonry and Christian faith to build an argument for the profound transformation of Black people's sensibility and collective identity in the United States.

Chapter 4 recognizes how David Walker appeals not only for political action but also for a new national sensibility. This new nation may not be as egalitarian or integrated as scholars sometimes hope, but it will certainly afford Walker's brethren the opportunity to feel freely and delightfully as whole citizens. It is the pursuit of this new way of joyful feeling that Walker anticipates will have his imagined brethren feeling good. Walker's notable anger is not an end unto itself. It's only a beginning. When his brethren get angry at their enslavement, they can experience the good feeling that comes from making the world anew.

Pleasuring Readers

Reading Pleasures unsettles and disrupts the unspoken expectation that, for Black people, life, as Ralph Ellison summarizes, is lived as "an abstract embodiment of a living hell." Living is, in fact, a daily practice, a getting up and a lying down. Living is a conditioning, an exercise that can only make sense, at times, because there is something or someone in whom to take pleasure or with whom to feel good.[70] What's inside of our living is chaotic and affective. It isn't always easy to find or access, especially without photographs or hashtags. It is legible to those who are literate enough to read its pleasures. It's interiority—the depths of one's very human understanding of self—that gives pleasure its power. Because interiority and its resulting pleasures are imaginative, it possesses a materiality that refuses the limits of agency and resists certainty.

Interiority asks us to rid ourselves of the fear of what's unknown and what resists counting. It has something to say if we are willing to listen into what it has left and what it will leave. Reading for pleasures is a necessary way to seek to understand just what makes living easier and worthy of sharing. Reading for pleasures posits a way of reading that privileges mundanity, where authors tell jokes and stories of feeling good—because even Phillis Wheatley tells jokes. David Walker promises happiness. And, John Marrant tells the story of his younger self, hoping to prank an audience of churchgoers, in order to celebrate how his faith changed him. James Albert Ukawsaw Gronniosaw wants to share the good news of his faith. We can laugh with them if we just read closely enough to observe the limits of suffering and the very real possibility of a profound pleasure.

CHAPTER 1

Phillis Wheatley's Pleasures

The frontispiece of Phillis Wheatley's *Poems on Various Subjects, Religious and Moral* (1773) compels us to stare at her body, fixed as it is in form and time. The engraving—one of the first of its kind to share the likeness of a young, African woman and her poetry—greets readers with this seated, young woman. She wears a bonnet and holds a quill pen in her hand. In the border that surrounds her, there is her name, Phillis Wheatley, and a nod to her political status as "a servant to John Wheatley of Boston."[1] She sits alone in what is assumed to be an empty room, except for her chair and the desk that holds a sheet of paper, an inkwell, and an unnamed book. Her gaze is pensive and elsewhere. The frontispiece seems to direct us to what is still most noteworthy and, at times, compelling about how we read what may matter to her—namely, who she is and to whom she belongs. It publicizes Wheatley's body to her readers, at the behest of her patron, Selina Hastings, the Countess of Huntingdon. Her body is there to be read as a "genius" and a curiosity to those who doubt the intellectual acumen of this African girl. And, it's her body that readers, presently, know how best to see and to read.

While the frontispiece asks readers to look at Wheatley's body, her poems and her various writings call us to what's inside this body. The engraving doesn't memorialize much of Wheatley's story. Rather, in the pages that follow the frontispiece, the poems bring readers inside her imaginative musings. Her poems take readers into her interiority, into what literary scholars Christopher Castiglia and Julia Stern define as those "feelings, fantasy, desire, and affect (which we define as the emotional weather system that is expressive of one's imagined emotional states)."[2] When Castiglia and Stern imagine the interiority of early American persons, they speak of it as "not transparent, but is a construction that must be reached through the mediation of language and representation."[3] And, Wheatley, as a writer, mediates this language with her words. What she writes represents or speaks for not just her bodily form but also that which she can only feel and say in rhyme, in a sonnet or elegy, or even in an epistle. She authors a privacy, an intimacy that "builds worlds; it creates spaces and usurps places meant for other kinds of relation."[4] It demands a "reckoning."[5] As her cast-off eyes and the quiet melancholy of the engraving suggest, it's what's unspoken and, at times, what she imagines that inspires Wheatley's pen.[6] Hers is an interiority, like most, that lives inside her body, and it lives way into those poems and sites where the dreaming lovers of her poetic voice sigh and where language helps make sense of who she is and who we, her readers, are.

Surely, Wheatley is enslaved—until 1773—to the Wheatley family in Boston, and she is the poet, writer, and author of a world that is hers to read or write. Readers happen upon this inner life with every "I" that finds its way into her poetry and her writings. There's "I speak, while I speak sincerely and love" (line 37) in "On the Death of Rev. Sewell." In "On Imagination," she writes, "The monarch of the day I might behold, / And all the mountains tipt with God, / But I reluctant leave the pleasing views" (ll. 46–47). With every "I" that interrupts the poetic voice, there's a lot of feeling too. At times, she feels "less happy, cannot raise the song, / the fault'ring music dies upon [her] tongue" (ll. 46–47).[7] Sometimes, she strives. She snatches laurels off the head of Maecenas, "While you indulgent smile upon the deed" (line 47). Other times, in her letters, she writes that she is pleased to hear from or take a walk with a friend.

This chapter seeks after the many interiorities of Phillis Wheatley. I wrestle with these in her extant letters, in particular, though her poetry first introduced me to the very possibility of her inner life. I say "many" because interiority is either public or private and always variable and plentiful. Even as it suggests a particular "emotional weather system," its depths are unspecified, multidimensional, and its complexities are neither fixed nor certain.[8] Her letters lead me in pursuit of that which is inside her, because it's there that Wheatley delights in the pleasures of her living in spite of and because of the world-at-large. The poetic voice is turned into a real person when Wheatley writes to her friends and acquaintances in Boston, Newport, New Haven, Wales, or London. Wheatley writes letters (and about twenty-three or so are still extant) to many well-known and lesser-known men and women: namely, the Countess of Huntingdon, popular Newport minister Rev. Samuel Hopkins, John Thornton, and her friend Obour Tanner.

Wheatley's letters are neither too lengthy nor too short, but just long enough to evidence what matters most to her. And of course, what matters most depends upon to whom she is writing. For example, when Wheatley writes to Selina Hastings, the Countess of Huntingdon, she seems most concerned about whether or not her travel plans will hinder her ability to meet the countess. When she writes to John Thornton, Wheatley notes Susanna Wheatley's death and is thankful for his book recommendations and for her own return to better health. Her letters take us into her everyday life with its travels, its Christian worship, and its commitments to friends and acquaintances. In her letters, she is no longer a solitary young woman on a frontispiece or an enslaved teenager who is compelled to write poems to amuse and delight the Wheatley family.[9] Every letter takes us out of the confines of the engraved room of the poetry collection's frontispiece into geographies of community, worship, friendship, and eighteenth-century urban and revolutionary-era living.

Reading her letters, it's easy to see that Wheatley isn't just a lonely poet, but rather she admits to her various interiorities while in conversation with her interlocutors. She confesses to her likes, her desires, and to her Christian worship. Wheatley's letters have her admit to an interiority that is, at best, difficult to access because it is inward and personal. Yet, it is useful to pursue because it can, as Castiglia and Stern note, "register not the stasis or fixity of identities and social positions, but the moments where the phenomenology of life change becomes the basis for imaginative dissent and revision."[10] It's not only dissent and revision but also the site of those pleasures that make life's changes private, palatable, and possible.

Pleasure and what it means to be pleased, to enjoy, or to be happy happens inside of and because of the body. So, it is no surprise that Wheatley holds interiorities closely within her very public self and body. They are hers to know and to make do with as she pleases. Wheatley's interiority seems to possess the sort of "quiet" that Kevin Quashie argues is the "source of human action." Its quiet and subtlety do not presume a lack of "expressivity" but rather invites a consideration of living that does not depend solely upon publicity or demonstrative feelings.[11] Feelings and the interior space in which they are felt aren't always for everyone to witness. Rather, interiority is familiar and affective. It only seeks after itself and its desire for privacy and quiet.

This is the quiet of Wheatley—with hand on her cheek—on the frontispiece. The engraving is two-dimensional, yet it insists upon a depth that refuses to advertise what it knows—namely, "the full range of one's inner life—one's desires, ambitions, hungers, vulnerabilities, fears."[12] It leaves readers to wonder who this servant of John Wheatley really is and what or who else may govern or participate in her living.

To wonder who Wheatley is is to hope for a glimpse of a what writer Ralph Ellison speaks of as a very human "something else." Ellison reads this sort of inner life as the "something else" that he cannot name even though he can feel it as part of his everyday living; whatever it is—that "makes for our strength . . . for our endurance and our promise"—posits an alternative reading of living that does not privilege suffering as the only way to be. Both Quashie and Ellison pursue—in something other than the publicity of "grit" or "ruggedness," "hardship," and "poverty"—that which is "complexly and compellingly human" inside the experience of personhood.[13] By "compellingly human," Ellison gestures toward the kind of quietude that, Quashie argues, lays bare the varied inward and affective experiences that make meaning. For Quashie, it's those feelings that make everyday life pleasant or, at least, livable in spite of itself.

Wheatley reconciles her compelling humanity, and in so doing reminds us that, as Kevin Young notes, "for while corresponding to the outside world, the slave's map was chiefly an interior one—which all too often has left it unread, misplaced, or denied."[14] Even though it's easy to miss this interiority while hunting forms of public expressivity, the enslaved know how to read it, see it, and look for it. It is legible to those who know that reading is just as much a practice of living, faith, and religious enthusiasm as it is forms of schooling or book learning. For this reason, Wheatley doesn't have to advertise this interiority, and she shouldn't. It's hers to speak, write, or share with those who know how to read and listen to it. More importantly, it is where she can celebrate herself and praise her God. In this place, Wheatley's Christian faith belongs to her; God is hers. For Wheatley, God listens and acts "as the spiritual interrogator," as literary scholar Katherine Clay Bassard observes, who "asks questions that prompt a response from the 'heart'."[15] This response may take many forms, but Wheatley is often pleased and she speaks of her experiences of a faithful joy. Her interiority is where her pleasure is felt and experienced.

When I speak of this feeling, pleasure, I mean to suggest the affective experience that results from the satisfaction of a desire. Pleasure is fickle, mundane, radical or, sometimes, a kind of quest. Pleasure is an invitation inward into the sensorial experience of desiring, anticipation, and ultimately satisfaction. It is an intimate and bodily knowing that names the "complex, messy, sticky, and even joyous negotiation of agency and desire."[16] Periodically, it leans toward and takes on the ecstatic or that which "exceed[s] or transcend[s] the self" and language.[17] It feels good. It is an everyday kind of good feeling that names what it means, as James Baldwin describes, "to respect and rejoice in the force of life, of life itself, and to be *present* in all that one does, from the effort of loving to the breaking of bread."[18] Where this force lands—on the body or inward, beyond the physicality of the body—depends upon what has meaning or material significance.

I am often met with doubt whenever I mention Wheatley's access to joy or even its possibility as its recollected in her poems or letters. I am inevitably asked some version of this question: "Might this so-called joy actually be anxiety or a misplaced grievance?" The question in its many forms presupposes the inaccessibility of pleasure to Wheatley or enslaved women, more generally. It refuses to consider the many ways in which Wheatley represents or writes into being the stuff that might make her smile.

Even while enslaved or as a free woman, Wheatley lives those good feelings that are "not necessarily subversive," as historian Treva B. Lindsey explains of Black women's pleasures, "transgressive, or even progressive iterations" of her racialized or political subjectivity.[19] Wheatley tells jokes and imagines herself to be funny. She teases John Thornton when he invites her to go on a mission trip to Africa with Newport-based missionaries John Quamine and Bristol Yamma. Not only does Wheatley say "no" to Thornton's request, she calls out its absurdity and questions his good sense or lack thereof. She notes the obvious fact that if she can't speak the language, then she can't do the work. Wheatley's joke expects a laugh or a scholarly acknowledgment of her ability to laugh. Her jokes evidence the sorts of ungoverned feelings that signify joy and make life worth living. Because Wheatley neither hides her pleasures (or at least some of them) nor are they all lost in the archive, it seems to me that her various interiorities, subjectivities, and pleasures mean a lot to her.

Because Wheatley really does write about joy sometimes and even tells jokes, I'm looking for and after her pleasures because "such inquiries," to borrow from historians Treva B. Lindsey and Jessica Marie Johnson, "allow for the interior lives and erotic subjectivities of enslaved Blacks to matter."[20] Literary scholar Frances Smith Foster rids this point of its abstraction as she remembers that "Wheatley's letters made me realize that even though enslaved (and maybe most of it was only in her imagination), she did have a love life. Then I started to remember how often in her poems her 'bosom burns,' she has 'intrinsic ardor,' and her '*Fancy*' has 'raptur'd eyes'."[21] Foster gives us a short list of Wheatley's descriptive language of those ways of feeling that may matter to her. Wheatley gives us more. There's also Aurora rising out of Tithon's bed, with "Her cheeks all glowing with celestial dies" in "On Imagination" (ll. 44–45). Wheatley writes of her pleasures in God and in what she calls, "joy," "enrapture," "passion," or a kind of "happy." And, Katherine Edes Beecher, the wife of Obour Tanner's pastor, recalls Tanner's stories of the poet's mentions of "'Mr. John Peters,' 'a complaisant and agreeable young man,' 'an acquaintance.'"[22] Literary historian Julie Ellison argues that Wheatley "represents her own poetry as pleasure, adventure and moral opportunity; she experiences as pure gain the writing of poetry and the transatlantic vision it permits."[23] Her pleasures have asked us to observe how she experiences her joy. She leaves clues to it in her poems, letters, and the sleights of her penmanship—with its attention to its swirls, squiggly lines and grammatical flourishes—and she leaves readers to imagine those affective experiences that, simply put, make her life easier.

The fact of Wheatley's pleasures admits to the very possibilities of her "unrestricted, unpoliced, unbound, and unbossed" and quotidian desires and their satisfaction.[24] While Wheatley certainly desires often and widely, she speaks mostly through a language of her Christian faith. She invokes the language of God as a way to make meaning and as a way to understand herself and her feelings.

For Wheatley, desire, at times, is both an admission of a physical need (see, for example, her requests for the profits from the sale of her poetry) and a religious imperative that seeks its satisfaction in the pleasure of godly salvation.[25] Desire is an asking and an anticipation; its fulfillment is contingent "upon conditions which may or may not have been met."[26] This uncertainty invokes and demands faith in the possibility that God will satisfy and provide for her. For Wheatley, this desire for satisfaction is praiseworthy, but it must ask for and anticipate a godly response. Wheatley announces the satisfaction of her desire for God, in particular, with every mention of feeling and in so doing confesses to that which lies deep down inside her and avows God's access to this interiority. These are Wheatley's pleasures.

"On Being Brought"; Or, Lessons from Reading the "First Black Published Poet"

It's funny to think that I had missed her lover in Wheatley's *Poems* (1773). I don't mean "haha" funny but the curious kind of funny that must eventually admit to its error. I had read this poem often, but I had never noticed before, and I can't remember how I happened upon Wheatley's dreaming lover:

> When action ceases, and ideas range
> Licentious and unbounded o'er the plains,

Where Fancy's queen in giddy triumph reigns.
Hear in soft strains the dreaming lover
sigh to a kind fair, or a rave in jealousy—
(ll. 86–90)

But there her love is in "Thoughts on the WORKS of PROVIDENCE."[27] I had missed what mattered to this young woman. Her thoughts on God's providence include not only an imaginative and earthly bounty, but also a "dreaming lover" whose sighs "to a kind fair, or a rave in jealousy" wrestle with the materiality of feeling. The sleeping lover breathes in and out those laboring passions—pleasures and vengeance—while awaiting the onset of morning and the return to the glories of God.

Despite the insistent breaths of this dreaming lover, I had missed the sighs, dreams, and love in this poem and throughout Wheatley's volume of a poetry amid my expectation for authenticity and any bit of a reference to slavery or the Middle Passage. I read these verses for stories of a harrowing enslavement or a run to freedom because I hadn't yet learned that Phillis Wheatley, the "first" Black woman to publish a book of poetry and servant to John Wheatley, not only writes melancholic elegies but also poems that delight in the curious play of Fancy, Reason, and God.[28] I didn't yet know how to read her as she writes with her pleasures in mind. Because I hadn't yet read her letters or learned of her friendship with a woman named Obour Tanner, I still wanted her to represent the story of a linear and deeply racialized tradition that moved with ease from her poems to the narratives of Frederick Douglass and Harriet Jacobs and then on to the fiction of Toni Morrison.

I expected Wheatley to tell me again the origin story of this great literary tradition that begins, in Africa, with her "On Being Brought from Africa to America;" she declares, "'twas mercy brought me from my *Pagan* land / Taught my benighted soul to understand / That there's a God, that there's a *Saviour* too" (ll. 1–3).[29] It continues through the infamous Middle Passage, though an explicit reference to this fact is absent from Wheatley's extant writing, to Boston where she is named after the slave ship that carries her to colonial America. There, a precocious Wheatley writes subtle and ironic verses that mask her fight against oppression—like, "Remember, *Christians, Negros*, Black as *Cain* / May be refin'd, and join th' angelic train" (ll. 7–8).

I read into this poem a tradition that I needed to tell me stories of collective suffering (e.g., the physical privations of slavery) or resistance to white supremacy and heroic accounts of overcoming (see of course, Douglass's autobiographies). I expected Wheatley to discuss slavery and the very public matters of her existence all the time. I needed her to memorialize a past that

I presumed was dependent upon the suffering and resistance of her racial body—just like one that appears in her frontispiece. I read her poetry with, as literary scholar Jordan Alexander Stein explains, "an overdetermined interpretative frame that presumes that" what matters most to the enslaved is the public experience of enslavement.[30] My misreading privileged slavery and the master's gaze as the sole site of a racialized and cultural becoming. I expected Wheatley to serve as a "first" in the makings of a literary tradition made real—from the Revolutionary War to the present—by racialized suffering and a desire for literacy.

What I wanted to read and what I expected Wheatley to write were right in part if we are to assume that race and representation are Wheatley's only concerns. It is certainly the case that Wheatley is important to the history of African American literature. She and her book of poems are famous enough for Thomas Jefferson to cite her and for George Washington to thank her for her poetry, and there are many other notable references to Wheatley and her writing by the likes of eighteen of Boston's "most respectable characters," Long Island–based poet Jupiter Hammon and French Enlightenment thinker Voltaire. As a "first" in this so-called tradition, her famed poems might be read as proof that her experience of racial identity is part of a collective resistance to slavery or as evidence of her humanity.[31] Amid the brevity of "On Being Brought from Africa to America," it is easy to hear, in Wheatley's couplets and rhyme, protests of the misreading of her race's "sable" skin as a "diabolic die" (line 6). It seems she resists the admonition that "Negros, Black as *Cain*" cannot achieve the refinement of white Christians (line 7). It appears that she, in fact, exemplifies this refinement in her verse and her steadfast belief in a Christian God.

Just as it seems plausible that Wheatley resists her adversity and her enslavement, it also seems true that Wheatley experiences a very real suffering. Take, for example, her testimonial in "To the Earl of Dartmouth":

> I, young in life, by seeming cruel fate
> Was snatch'd from *Afric's* fancy'd happy seat:
> What sorrows labour in my parent's breast?
> Steel'd was that soul and by no misery mov'd
> That from a father seiz'd his babe belov'd:
> Such, such was my case. And can I then but pray
> Others may never feel tyrannic sway.
> (ll. 24–31)

Although she gives away no specific details of her capture or the Middle Passage, Wheatley remembers, in her poem to the Earl of Dartmouth, William Legge, the "cruel fate"—with its steeled soul, unmoved by the sight of human misery—that snatched her from an unnamed place in Africa. She recollects her profound sense of loss and her father's suffering. She returns to and imagines a longing for family that seemingly still haunts her. Wheatley professes the origins of her desire for freedom and admits to a past she no longer knows. It may be true that Wheatley knows suffering well and resistance too and uses both to attend to and compel the sympathies of her audience.

But this story is too simple, too easy. It assumes—cultural critic Irving Howe's mid-twentieth-century error—that "unrelieved suffering is the only 'real' Negro experience, and that the true Negro writer must be ferocious."[32] This simple story's pursuit of suffering or resistance privileges a sense of racial determinacy with which Wheatley does not always bother. Wheatley does not narrate her plan to escape to freedom even though she does admit to a desire for freedom sometimes. She laments the death of Susanna Wheatley, her beloved "mistress" even after she concedes to a "love of freedom" too in a 11 February 1774 letter to Mohegan minister Samson Occom. She writes, "God has implanted a Principle, which we call Love of Freedom; it is impatient of Oppression, and pants for Deliverance."[33] Even if we read for irony, in "On Being Brought from Africa to America" she often celebrates her Christian God, who, she explains, gives her the redemption that she "neither sought nor knew" (line 4) in the "benighted" (line 2) and unidentified region of her birth. Wheatley's extant oeuvre can't anticipate our present-day need for simple, resistive acts, and an obvious performance of a racialized subjectivity. Wheatley does not provide any obvious pronouncement of her racialized objectivity because she can't imagine the sorts of literary tradition making that would need her to prove her loyalty to freedom, suffering, and personhood.

As literary scholar Robert Reid-Pharr explains of Wheatley's racial subjectivity, her "particular idiosyncrasy is that she is not concerned at all with announcing a Black American singularity."[34] Even as an enslaved teenager and later, a grown woman, in the midst of a growing revolution for a certain kind of political freedom, Wheatley understands that her life is not without contradiction and paradox. What if we, her twenty-first-century readers, believe her? She can and does love freedom, and she says she cares deeply for Susanna Wheatley. She can mourn her parents and praise her faith. What Reid-Pharr identifies as idiosyncratic is actually a greater concern for something other than a cohesive racial identity.

For her subjectivity in its many forms, to matter to her, Wheatley must and does create meaning on her own terms, and these terms are not necessarily consistent or obviously racialized. Wheatley speaks of a concern for

God, Fancy's roving nature, writing, book sales, or living. It is these external concerns about her racial identity and enslaved status that prompt Wheatley to write and devise, as literary historian Joanna Brooks tells it, "the attestation as part of a months-long strategy to secure the London publication of her *Poems*, obtaining signatures from prominent Boston citizens at a town meeting on 28 October 1772."[35] Brooks argues that the attestation of eighteen of Boston's finest and wealthiest citizens, at the beginning of Wheatley's book of poetry, was not a public test of Wheatley's wit. Rather, Wheatley collects these signatures—from prominent Boston clergy, politicians in support of Britain or the colonies, and many acquainted with the Wheatley family—because she wants to publish a book. Wheatley seems to anticipate that there are some, in London, Boston, and elsewhere, who doubt that she can write or think well. Her aim is so often obscured by a desire for proof of her commitment to a particular kind of racialized subjectivity.

When Wheatley shares her sincerity or her pleasures with her readers she offers a glimpse into an interiority that delights and is, at times, pleasing and knows for sure what it means to be well pleased.[36] Consider the concluding stanzas of "Thoughts on the WORKS of PROVIDENCE," the poem in which her dreaming lover rests.[37] The poem—published in her first collection of poetry—sings its praises to a creative, unseen God that is to be "ador'd for ever" (line 11). It's a praise song that evidences just how much God matters to Wheatley and how much Wheatley matters to God. It honors the providential works of God as a creator of life and as a guide to the poet's soul and intention. The psalmic salute to God's generative creativity gives way to an allegorical conversation between two women, immortal Love and mortal Reason.

The dreams, lovers, and vengeance of the previous stanzas give way to a question, "What most the image of th' Eternal shows?" (line 105). It's the "mental pow'rs" (line 104) of the unnamed speaker that have asked. To whom is uncertain, but a dialogue ensues that seemingly responds in a parable form. The divine Love—the "celestial queen" (line 116)—approaches corporeal Reason with a different question that confesses their mutual strife: "Say, mighty pow'r, how long shall strife prevail / And with its murmurs load the whisp'ring gale?" (ll. 108–9). There is a conflict between them that may hold the answer to the aforementioned question. The nature of the conflict is unspecified, but it seems to have inspired gossip—"murmurs load the whisp'ring gale"—and suggests something (maybe, its affection or trust) is missing.

Love begs Reason to "Refer the cause to *Recollection's* shrine." Because she is powerful, divine, and worthy of affection, Love hopes to end their dispute. Wheatley's Love is also creative, infinite, and "where'er we turn our eyes appears" (line 122). Love supplies the wants of every creature. What Love explains to Reason are those reasons for her godly significance. She chronicles her love and godly exploits for Reason. She must prove herself because Reason seems to have lost her ability to see, find, or experience properly Love as love or God (see 1 John 4:8). Immortal and celestial Love dispels the doubt that has Reason miss just what "th'Eternal shows" because as Wheatley writes, "This most is heard in *Nature's* constant voice" (line 124).

Reason is persuaded by Love and responds, "my soul enraptur'd feels / Resistless beauty which thy smile reveals" (line 118). Reason speaks ardently in response to and at the sight of Love. Love's smile engenders Reason's soul to feel an intense pleasure. Love returns Reason to herself.[38] Love anticipates this reunion; it seems Love has always suspected that Reason would find her way back to love. Reason loves again. What Reason's senses take in—this "resplendent" (line 117) love—makes for an enthusiasm that prompts her to "clasp'd the blooming goddess in her arms" (ll. 120).[39]

Reason gathers Love up in her arms because she remembers her vital need to love and to hold this love. She understands fully "the human requirement to discern and declare God as Creator and God of love."[40] Reason's gesture or "hug" evokes "an embracing of the yearning for mutuality" and proper discernment.[41] Her clasping embrace reunites them and reconciles the strife that Love calls to an end. Reason praises Love with an affective and physical touch; Reason recognizes Love as that which makes her mortality worthy. Their heart-to-heart ends with their embrace, and a new stanza begins with the start of a new day. Love makes morning and evening rejoice as the immortal goddess ushers forth "to serve one gen'ral end / The good of man" (ll. 128–29).

With Love and Reason, Wheatley narrates an imagined and invariable friendship that reconciles reason to love and evokes her God as love. She conjures a friendship that compels both to realize the necessity of who they are as friends. Love and Reason set the terms of their affection, their conflict, and their reconciliation. This reconciliation remembers the friendship of God that Wheatley speaks of in the 30 October 1774 letter to John Thornton: "What a Blessed Source of consolation that our greatest friend is an immortal God whose friendship is invariable! from whom I have all that is *in me* praise worthy in mental possession."[42] God is her greatest friend, a consoler who gives her "all that is . . . praise worthy" in her. God loves her enough to make her, inwardly, praise worthy. She—as an enslaved, African girl (then, woman)—matters to God. Wheatley's God is Love, a "she" and a figurative source of her profound faith and, together, their "coupling is an alliance, a political and spiritual union."[43] A lover and friend, her God conspires to conciliate her reason and her love. This love has no bounds. God's friendship surrenders Wheatley to this companionship. With God, she can yearn toward and know the satisfaction of a mutual and self-serving love that fully accepts her as a child of God.

There's a lesson in her dreaming lover and in Love's reconciliation with Reason—that Wheatley can neither anticipate the racialized anxieties of the twenty-first century, nor does she write to prove just how "Black" she is because she is too busy living and loving. What I have learned to read instead is quite simply indicative of the leisurely exercise of dreaming and allegory. It is at the site of this play between Love and Reason, where day turns to night and dreams rove, that I hear first the "soft strains" that give way to eventual sighs. In the depths of the poem's restless sleep, the melodies of breath herald "pleasure now, and now on vengeance bent" (line 91). It's the pleasure—albeit alongside a bending vengeance—that begs me to wonder at the site of this dreamscape.

Wheatley writes a friendship that not only lives through the trauma of conflict but also the creativity, sweetness, and play of peacemaking. As Reason takes up her beloved in her arms, Wheatley seems to declare that she too plays with language, with possibility, within poetic traditions, and most importantly, with herself. Admittedly, her declaration isn't explicit because this is not an entirely public activity. Instead, Wheatley confesses in the sighs of her dreaming lover and the reunion of Love and Reason to the kinds of play that take place in an interiority that twenty-first-century readers don't often read onto or into enslaved women.

Wheatley, by way of her poems and her musings about the likes of Love and Reason, is willing to play and to show that love, God, and imagination matter to her. Wheatley's writing, in its many forms, discloses an inward landscape that she crafts and creates. Wheatley takes those who can listen rightly or read well enough into this inward space wherein she can write a friendship between women, remember a violent conflict on King's Street, or the face of a dreaming lover. Wheatley creates an intimacy with her real and imagined readers that realizes what matters. What matters for her is the heartfelt stuff: dreaming lovers, ideas, godly grace, and the shared experience of religious faith.

When Phillis Wheatley Writes Letters to her Friends

While her poetry uses metaphors, allegory, and neoclassical styling to hint at her poetic voice and its concerns, Wheatley, in her letters to various people, takes readers into what matters to her, into her interiority, and into the quiet of her prayers. Wheatley's letters move over land and waterways by way of persons, known and unknown. They travel in a series of hand-to-hand transactions. As is customary, Wheatley usually names the person who has carried the letter to her or to whom she is writing. There is Cato Coggeshall, Mr. Whitwell, Mr. Wooldridge, Rev. Samuel Hopkins and his son, "a young man of your Acquaintance," Mr. Pemberton, Mrs. Tanner, and presumably unnamed persons in between. With every mention, she contextualizes and places herself as a friend, servant, slave, and woman in New England and the greater Atlantic World.[44] Wheatley's letters locate her within communities of readers and writers within which ideas are discussed and traded as friends talk among themselves.[45]

Wheatley's correspondence bears witness to the ways in which she creates religious, reading, and "writing communities" made up of various religious converts, faithful followers, and fellow readers and writers brought together by circumstances: such as, enslavement, geography, Congregationalism, Methodism, George Whitefield, or the Countess of Huntingdon.[46] When Katherine Clay Bassard names this early "writing community," she remembers a productive possibility that unfolds as it seeks itself. It is a "potentiality" wherein writing moves language and ideas across time and geography toward those who can read its form.[47]

Writing presupposes a version of reading that understands how to make sense of what's written; writers need readers—with listening ears or discerning eyes—to generate meaning. I don't mean to limit reading to the book learned, but rather I mean to remember the kinds of reading that discern how to hear or see language. It's worth remembering that Wheatley's poems are most often spoken aloud and heard. She recites her poems in front of eager audiences that must know how to interpret her words. Her letters may have been read aloud to their recipients. This uncertainty suggests that reading is as much a practice of seeing, listening, and discernment; because—as Barbara Christian tell us—"writing and reading . . . 'bridge the joinings,' across differences not only of time and space, but also across differences between selves within and without any number of groups or categories by which we define ourselves."[48] And, every letter puts Wheatley, at the center of discourse and conversation, knowledge, and exchange. Her correspondence narrates what's of interest to her and, in particular, what's inside her, and what pleases her: God, household quibbles, her travels, her health and Wheatley family issues, poems to grieving widows or her everyday concerns.

Writing and reading in this manner make way for invention and conversation in a community or as part of communities. What results from

Wheatley's missives facilitates the discursive development of a smaller yet growing faithful community, in which she can and does worship together with friends and acquaintances. Wheatley actively participates in the making and revision of those boundaries that make her communities real. In so doing, she directs her readers to reading as an act of caring. Wheatley cultivates a self-affirming space wherein a loving God actively joins in these communities as they emerge. Her letters direct those private readers—a friend, political dignitaries, or an acquaintance—to what matters, and what matters demands that Wheatley share in the experience of faithful living. They privilege "not only Christian conversion and the literatures of slavery and sentimentalism, but more specifically . . . ecstatic, charismatic, 'enthusiastic' religious expression and power."[49] Amid what matters, Wheatley proffers a religious literacy wherein a true believer—one who possesses an open heart where Love and Reason coexist—can receive the Spirit and, subsequently, speak of the pleasure of this union. Wheatley's letters offer sites within which she might and does nurture this interiority by herself and while in conversation; they reveal her in ways that her poetry cannot, because the letter—as a form—serves her as a way into her private and public dealings with self, an interlocutor, and God.

Wheatley nurtures this interiority because she has learned that it makes a way for an understanding of self that knows what it means "to *'feel right'*"—to borrow from Harriet Beecher Stowe by way of Glenn Hendler—or "to have proper sentiments, an appropriate response to the scenes of suffering and redemption that the reader has witnessed."[50] To feel right is to answer "yes" to Stowe's question, "Are you in harmony with the sympathies of Christ?" For reasons of chronology, Wheatley cannot respond to Stowe's question directly, but she knows what it means to "Plainly dem[on]strate the sensations of a Soul united to Jesus."[51] Wheatley certainly knows that to feel right is to know this union with Christ. Such a soul must have an opened heart in order to experience the enthusiasm of the Holy Spirit through the Word of God. This open heart or right feeling happens in her body; she knows God in her body, and her faith is a bodily matter. A subject of a Wheatley elegy, minister George Whitefield explains it this way: "Followers might be united to him [God] by his Holy Spirit, by as real, vital, and mystical an Union as there is between *Jesus Christ* and the Father."[52] This affective and inward experience of this union evidences faithful living.

Because Wheatley has already accepted this union within herself, she prays for those who still need to create this union with God; "May the Lord bless to us these thoughts," Wheatley petitions, "and teach us by his Spirit to live to him alone, and when we leave this world may We be his: That his may be our happy case, is the sincere desire."[53] Her desire is to live in God alongside believers who can share in this faith because this union isn't available to everyone. It requires the cultivation of right ways of feeling and acceptance of what Whitefield calls the "indwelling of the spirit." Whitefield argues that "for they [our letter-learned Preachers] talk professedly against inward feelings, and say, we may have *God's* Spirit without feeling it, which is in reality to deny the thing itself."[54] A believer receives this Spirit inwardly upon accepting God with an open heart. What is felt are those enthusiastic sensations, wherein "grace in every heart might dwell," that affirm the body's union with God.[55] A believer knows that to feel rightly is to know inwardly a God that saves and delivers in spite of enslavement, distance, or a twenty-first-century scholar's contrarian expectations. If the believer feels rightly with eyes that can see and ears that can hear, she can then claim that she is a Christian who, as Whitefield explains, "in the proper Sense of the Word, must be an Enthusiast—That is, must be inspired of God, or have God in him."[56]

Whitefield offers a charge—the Christian "must be inspired of God, or have God in him"—and enjoins his listeners to welcome the Spirit and to make way to receive the Word of God inwardly. Wheatley's pleasure is faithful and because of it, Wheatley not only converses with God, specifically, or whomever but also feels deeply with God or whomever. Her inward self is united to God by a sincere faith because of which she knows the pleasures of salvation. She is pleased to know what it means to have her Savior die, so that she might live and worship with like-minded believers.

As a believer, God is hers to enjoy and to pray with. God is hers with whom to know a "freedom that was close to love."[57] "Yet I hope I should willingly Submit to Servitude to be free in Christ," Wheatley writes to John Thornton in her 30 October 1774 letter, "—But since it is thus—Let me be a *Servant of Christ* and that is the most perfect freedom."[58] Just a sentence before, Wheatley celebrates her manumission from the Wheatley family. After the publication of her poems and the death of Susanna Wheatley, the Wheatley family manumits her. She gives thanks for her freedom. Despite her gratitude, she goes on to assert the possibility of a freedom that exists whether sociopolitically enslaved or free. Wheatley revises the language of Apostle Paul's first letter to the Corinthians in order to picture the freedom that exists because God is, in fact, greater than man. Paul explains the freedom in Christ in this way: "For he that is called in the Lord, being a servant, is the Lord's freeman: likewise also he that is called, free, is Christ's servant."[59]

Because Wheatley feels "called in the Lord," as Paul writes it, this freedom offers Wheatley a way to delight in who she is as a child of God. Wheatley assumes her personhood despite the sociopolitical privations of former enslavement. She knows that there is a freedom inside her that cannot be touched by human laws, and she pays attention to the "free person" who lives inside of herself.[60] Wheatley can claim ownership of this inward self because she serves Christ, and her faith is greater than any person's political status as her earthly master.

Wheatley juxtaposes her inward selfhood—to be a servant *in* Christ—with a weakened exterior body that cannot, by itself, access this most perfect freedom. Wheatley's body is weakened not only in a religious sense, by its inherent sinfulness, but also by her unstable physical health; she is an asthmatic. While this interiority is sited within the body, this body is frail and sickly. Wheatley frequently laments her body's frailty: its flaws ("some view our sable race with scornful eye, / Their colour is a diabolic die," ll. 5–6); its tendency toward sin and earthly pleasures ("Let us be mindful of our high calling, continually on our guard, lest our treacherous hearts / Should give our adversary an advantage over us");[61] and its sickliness (viz., asthma and tuberculosis). She often prays on behalf of a body that cannot do for her what God can: "And O that when my flesh and my heart fail me, God would be my strength and portion for ever, that I might put my whole trust and Confidence in him, who has promis'd never to forsake those who Seek him with the whole heart."[62] Her prayer, in this 21 April 1772 letter to John Thornton, acknowledges the inherent fallibility of her humanity, its body, and her language. She must borrow language from the psalmist: "Whom have I in heaven but thee? And there is none upon earth that I desire beside thee. My flesh and my heart faileth: but God is the strength of my heart, and my portion for ever."[63] Where her body might fail, God does not and cannot. God's promise of salvation affords her a discursive or epistemological freedom—for example, to revise the Bible, to write letters, or read poems often.[64]

Wheatley creates in her letter writing, by way of Apostle Paul's letters and Old Testament references, a revisionist biblical framework with which she can renew and strengthen her inward self in spite of the weakness of her fleshly body. She repeatedly speaks of and juxtaposes her inward self and her outward body. In so doing, she identifies how much her faith matters to her living. She lives because she is faithful. This faith heals her body and protects her, and this fact matters to Wheatley. Wheatley writes in a 19 July 1772 letter, "while my outward man languishes under weakness and pa[in], may the inward be refresh'd and Strengthened more abundantly by him who declar'd from heaven that his strength was made perfect in weakness!"[65] As Wheatley's body languishes in various forms of pain and weakness, she juxtaposes her weak and sickly body against an unnamed interiority.

Revising the language again, this time from Apostle Paul's second letter to the Corinthians, Wheatley calls attention to the ways in which this unnamed inward self might be strengthened—namely, by receiving the Spirit (that which is eternal) inwardly through her senses of touch, smell, and sight. She invokes 2 Corinthians 4:16, wherein Paul writes "but though our outward man perish, yet the inward man is renewed day by day." Wheatley's declaration, "his strength was made perfect in weakness," borrows the wording of 2 Corinthians 12:9 and anticipates Paul's charge to "take pleasure in infirmities, in reproaches, in necessities, in persecutions, in distresses for Christ's sake: for when I am weak, I am strong." That is to say, her body or, as she describes it, her "outward man," no longer matters because she can access the interiority wherein she can feel strengthened by God.

Wheatley's prayer does not end with her criticism of her weak body. Rather, Wheatley continues "pressing forward to the fix'd mark f[or] the prize." Wheatley takes from Apostle Paul to write a prayer that honors a mutual pursuit of God. Wheatley doesn't say what the prize is. Paul's letter suggests that it is the "high calling of God in Jesus Christ."[66] Wheatley doesn't name Jesus. But she does paraphrase the Bible's language: "How happy that man who is prepar'd for that Nig[ht] Wherein no man can work! Let us be mindful of our high calling."[67] Though Wheatley doesn't say his name, Wheatley references the words of Jesus in John 9:4–5: "I must work the works of him that sent me, while it is day: the night cometh, when no man can work. As long as I am in the world, I am the light of the world." Wheatley asserts the promise of salvation and the potential for a healing and a freedom in Jesus Christ. Even while her body cannot save her, she must still admit to its ability to experience God inside it. This body serves as an intersectional site wherein spirit, pleasures, sickness, and sin happen. Wheatley doesn't solve this tension but rather creates a way to understand who she is as a God-fearing, enslaved (and then "free") woman, living in revolutionary-era New England. Wheatley seems to feel this freedom and its pleasures inside where her "'humble and contrite heart'" lives and where her love of God (and His love) is most decidedly felt.[68] Her letters prove that she doesn't do (or feel) this work alone.

Occasionally, Wheatley travels inwardly to God and takes up such faithful pleasures with a particular friend. Her friend's name is Obour (or, at times, Arbour or Orbour) Tanner. Wheatley's spelling varies. She is enslaved to James Tanner of Newport. She's just a bit older than Wheatley; even though the ages of both women are uncertain, literary historian Vincent Carretta speculates that she's about four years older if she is baptized, as custom requires, at eighteen years old in 1768.[69] She outlives Wheatley by fifty years.

Her name survives by way of her correspondence with Wheatley, but how these women meet does not. Their extant letters begin when both women are near twenty years old in 1772.[70] Wheatley writes to her in letters that don't always have the formality of her other epistles. She shares with Tanner. In these letters, both women conjure a space wherein they live out their worth, their humanity, and faith in a loving God. Wheatley's friendship with Tanner locates her within Tanner's Newport-based circles of acquaintance.

When Wheatley writes letters to Tanner, she makes mention of how she feels about matters of concern, such as political conflict, missionary work, or walking with a mutual friend. Admittedly, she does not bemoan her Black skin or her enslavement.[71] In what's left extant, she neither mentions slavery as a metaphor or a lived experience, nor does she belabor her sadness over how Black she is or is not. She doesn't talk about systemic oppression or white women's requests for an elegy or her obligations to the Wheatley family.

Rather, she is pleased to hear from her friend about whatever she deems important at the time: God, book sales, travels and sickness, or a "complaisant" man.[72] Wheatley's letters to Tanner—only a handful of them, from 1772 to 1779, extant—are decidedly ordinary glimpses into a friendship between women. Amid the growing conflict between the colonies and Britain as well as Wheatley's emerging stardom, Wheatley and Tanner chronicle their movements as young women and then twenty-somethings until Wheatley's death, in 1784, at about thirty-one years old. As Tanner's friend and correspondent, Wheatley moves between Boston and Newport with her mentions of the Reverend Samuel Hopkins, Mr. Zingo, Cato Coggeshall, Bristol Yamma, John Quamine, and as part of a community of women who "acted as sales agents for Wheatley's published poems in New England."[73]

Because the whereabouts of Tanner's letters to Wheatley are unknown, it's Wheatley's letters that tell their stories of belonging, friendship, and love.[74] Wheatley collects and remembers Tanner's words with passing references to what she's mentioned in earlier letters. Maybe Tanner, too, knows how to read the language of Wheatley's interiority and her profound relation to faith in God—with her many biblical references. Wheatley names who they are and what they mean to each other—sisters in God and friends. And together, their letters announce a friendship that seeks a mutual fellowship with God and an intimacy that strives for the pleasures of friendship.

"Dear Sister": Phillis Wheatley, Obour Tanner, and the Pleasures of Friendship

Wheatley's letters to Obour Tanner often begin the same way, with a familiar greeting: "Dear Sister," "Dear Obour," or, quite simply, "Dear friend."[75] She also signs off with an announcement of her affections for Tanner: "friend and humble servant," "your affectionate friend," "most affectionately ever yours," or "your sincere friend." And with every invocation of "friend" and "sister," Wheatley helps us understand that "Mammy, Jezebel, and Hagar," Frances Smith Foster writes, "were not the only names by which women of African heritage could or should be called." Wheatley has many affectionate and grateful names for Tanner that evidence those "names that she may have preferred and that may be more accurate."[76]

Even though Wheatley uses the standard, salutational conventions, she offers these greetings to no one else (in the extant archive). Her other letters refuse this familiarity. To everyone else, she is consistently "a humble servant" who greets her addressee—John Thornton, Selina Hastings, Madame Wooster, among others—with the requisite formality. But, when she writes to Tanner, Wheatley is not simply a "humble servant." She is more often an "affectionate friend," "most affectionately" hers, and "a sincere friend" or a "dear sister."[77] Her formality gives way to familiarity and the kind of affection that comes from a shared intimacy. Even her postscripts to Tanner— occasioned by the receipt of a shipment of three hundred books or a chance meeting with a "clever" and "agreeable" man—suggest familiarity and the secret keeping of a close friends.[78]

Both women pursue a way to, as Wheatley writes to Tanner, "adore the wonders of God's infinite Love" and to know God who teaches them to "live to him alone" in order to belong to God.[79] As Wheatley seeks to know Tanner, their intimacy "is a self-centered process."[80] It centers both Wheatley and Tanner at the site of a belonging where their "expression of love and affection from one woman to another [is] a necessary and even critical practice."[81] It allows both women to privilege who they are individually and together. By way of her letters to Tanner, Wheatley's story turns toward a friendship that cares for that which matters most to her (and Tanner)—God, family, nation, and friendship.

Theirs is an ordinary friendship; it is neither unique nor is it extraordinary. And, historian Erica Armstrong Dunbar is right to note that "friendship was not a luxury; for many, it was a necessity."[82] Because Wheatley knows who Tanner is to her, she never bothers to write answers to those questions that I ask whenever I read these letters. She never gives up too much of what she knows about Tanner. She does not mention how they've sustained their friendship or why Rev. Samuel Hopkins or his son sometimes carries their correspondence. She does not write of the last time she sees Tanner or under what circumstances. Wheatley's letters tell us instead that Tanner is a fellow Christian, a resident of Newport, and also a traveler. Wheatley keeps Tanner abreast of her book sales, her bouts of sickness and asthma, her travels to the country and out of the country, and even the death of Susanna Wheatley. Wheatley sends Tanner her proposal and her books, and Tanner sells Wheatley's book of poems around Newport and maybe elsewhere. Some years there are more letters than others, but in every letter, what Wheatley does reveal in these seemingly mundane occurrences serves a decidedly Christian end for both her and Tanner. Together, they share their mutual pursuit of God who died in the flesh so that they, two women, two friends, Africans and enslaved (at times), might live.

Their shared faith is not a single-minded acceptance of enslavement or a representation of assimilation by force. Rather, their faith acts as "an orientation, a basic turning of the soul toward another defining reality" where worship and friendship happen in letters between friends.[83] Religion allows both women "to 'mash out a meaning' of life" because the form of their worship "is not simply a doctrine of faith or the methods and practices of church, rather it is all the ways we remind ourselves who we really are, in spite of who the temporal powers may say we are."[84] Their friendship conspires to realize where two or three are gathered so is God.[85]

Both women worship on the page as they might have in person or at either of their respective Congregationalist churches: Tanner at First Congregational Church in Newport, and Wheatley at New South Congregational Church and later Old South in Boston.[86] Though both women are informed by the doctrine of their respective church homes, each governs the methods and practices of their worship. Wheatley and Tanner minister God's Word with ease and without a great concern for who may care. Their Christian faith realizes their shared humanity rather than the abstraction of a demoralized and racialized objectivity. Their shared belief confesses to that which writer James Baldwin observes in the twentieth century: "our humanity is our burden; we need not battle for it; we need only do what is infinitely more difficult—that is accept it."[87] Wheatley and Tanner have accepted their humanity and have shared in its burdens because together they pursue a collective worship and a mutual friendship that admits to the possibility of pleasure and fellowship. Each letter asks us to remember them as they are, as two friends, two women in love with their God.

Each letter offers the mundane as the beginning of mutual prayer for continued blessings and God's mercies on their lives. And together, they worship God and live a friendship wherein the promise of God's love creates the intimacy that inspires this epistolary space of mutual language and exchange. They love each other as they love God. Wheatley and Tanner, through a collective, letter-based faith and worship, experience God and, as a consequence, journey inward in order to experience the pleasures of an abiding friendship in God.

It is not often that we speak of Black women as friends now, and it is even less common to speak of friendships among enslaved women. I asked an audience once if enslaved people had friends. I can't remember what kind of audience it was—maybe students or conference participants. What I do remember is that no one said anything. I was met with silence. And I learned that the collective and initial silence confessed to a disbelief in the very possibility of enslaved friends. I learned later that no one was ready to picture friendship alongside the horrors of chattel slavery. That slaves had friends presumes a kind of leisure that may be misconstrued as a moniker for "happy slave" or a kind of normalcy that should not make sense in the midst of the horrors of enslavement.

Authors Toni Morrison and Gloria Naylor, in a conversation, agree that there is something unsettling and powerful about such a friendship between women (whether free or enslaved), even though it isn't always a topic for public or even scholarly discussion. Naylor blames the refusal to talk about women friends on a power that exists when women trust each other enough to love on and delight in their pleasures, intimacies, and interiorities.[88] Those women, who can trust and love one another as friends do, access the value that comes from loving one's self and another. These letters—between two women—leave us those stories, snippets, that ask us to wonder at the possibilities of friendship, in spite of enslavement or so-called freedom as well as varied forms of systemic oppression.

What their friendship offers is access to a deep satisfaction that Toni Morrison refers to as "pleasure deep down."[89] This deep-down pleasure bears witness to "the tangled relationship between 'thoughts' and 'felts'" that attends to that which lies deep down, inside.[90] There, in that space upon yet within this body, the act of feeling and loving occurs.

This "pleasure deep down" makes for what Audre Lorde describes more fully as "erotic": "a resource," "a power which rises from our deepest and nonrational knowledge," "an internal sense of satisfaction to which, once we have experienced it, we know we can aspire," and, quite simply, "sharing deep feeling" with another. I find the erotic useful because it bears witness to the pursuit of those intimate and corporeal experiences, which seek desire and its satisfaction. Lorde recognizes the many ways in which the erotic operates as: a way of profound knowing, an affectively driven creativity, a quotidian and sensory experience, and "a capacity for joy." It is not selfish either or specifically sexual. Lorde explains that the "erotic has often been misnamed by men and used against women. It has been made into the confused, the trivial, psychotic, the plasticized sensation." She juxtaposes the erotic with pornography or "sensation without feeling." The erotic is sensation with feeling. This experience of the erotic is powerful, informative, and enjoyable. It requires a deep engagement with sharing that remembers how to feel "that sense of satisfaction and completion."[91]

Wheatley writes into being Lorde's "erotic"—the "sharing deep feeling" or the sense of profound satisfaction, "whether it is dancing, building a bookcase, writing a poem, examining an idea"—with every letter to Tanner.[92] She likes to receive and read Tanner's letters and says so. She likes sharing her feelings and her faith with her friend, and so she does. What they do together is build community and determine what it looks and feels like as well as how it sounds and what language has meaning. Thus, the erotic names the language that mediates their distance as it accesses the power that comes from sharing with another. Wheatley shares deeply her pursuits, ideas, and troubles despite distance, illness, or the varied lapses in time between each letter (weeks, months, or years) in a way that is so "intimate and political, an act so powerful that it urges (each) self to love."[93] With Tanner as her friend and partner-in-worship, she admits to a personal desire for a mutual exchange with a best friend or a loving God.

And theirs is a friendship, like many, that isn't always consistent. Wheatley often laments the inconsistency of her writing and the busyness or illnesses that keep her from writing to Tanner. She mentions too Tanner's periodic ill health or the occasional lost correspondence. There are those letters that don't survive the transit. It's hard to know how often their letters were surveilled or lost because of a sloppy courier or intercepted during wartime.[94] Despite the complications, their friendship gestures toward what "friend" means; "friend" suggests intimacy, conveys love, and shares its root meaning with freedom. Wheatley's letters plot an intimacy that speaks love and grants a kind of freedom—to share, to feel, to conspire. Each creates a "woman-freedom" that has "ways of saying things" and those things they say admit to their mutual intimacy.[95] Tanner acts as "an interlocutor capable of understanding" Wheatley.[96] Tanner and Wheatley know each other well. This knowing makes for "the happiness that imbues this kind of friendship" which "comes from the simple belief and understanding that what one is feeling and doing is right."[97] Both women believe their friendship, their love, and their collective faith in God is right and worthy of sharing.

What they create together is a discursive and geographic place—at the site of the page and their interiority—in which they "can imagine safety without walls, can iterate difference that is prized but unprivileged."[98] It's the place Toni Morrison theorizes as "home." Wheatley and Tanner don't specify its location in this way. Wheatley concludes one letter with "Till we meet in the regions of consummate blessedness."[99] In the preceding lines, she requests that Tanner continue to write letters to her, and she ends with a desire to meet. But this meeting will not take place at a geographic location somewhere between their respective homes, Boston and Newport. Rather, they "meet in the regions of consummate blessedness," namely a space that hints at the reality of an afterlife in heaven and an earthly interiority where only God can enter and share his Word with each of them, both together and separately. Where Maya Angelou says that "nobody, kith nor kin, can take [them] beyond," Wheatley and Tanner meet with God, as only friends can, at this "someplace," or more specifically this "rhetorical meeting place."[100] This someplace—where God listens to them—serves as "a common lexical, syntactic, and semantic domain" wherein these two women make use and speak of those feelings that might otherwise go unspoken.[101] The discursivity of this meeting is not simply a conversation. It is a meeting of self (in this case, that of Wheatley or Tanner) with another that is "joyous, an act of mutuality that suggests that the human yearning for companionship is fulfilled in the meeting of a self that is one's self, but also not one's self."[102]

Both women pray with a faithful certainty in a God who protects, shelters, and secures them. "Join me," writes Wheatley, "in thanks to him for so great a mercy [a safe return to America], & that it may excite me to praise him with cheerfulness, to Persevere in Grace & Faith, & in the Knowledge of our Creator and Redeemer,—that my heart may be filld with gratitude." With God, Wheatley lays claim to herself and what this self feels. She includes Tanner in this reclamation. It is "we" who won't live in anxiety because this "we" pursues God with an "ardent fervor" because of what God has done in their lives. She praises how God has transformed their inward lives, how he delivers and, most importantly, how he offers salvation.[103]

God cures Wheatley of her afflictions and also heals Tanner. It's God who prompts Tanner's "Saving change" or baptism in 1768 about which she rejoices together with Wheatley.[104] They cannot help but testify to the greatness that is a transforming and saving God. When they praise Him, they experience the sense of satisfaction that comes from a profound faith and from sharing deeply this faith as friends.

In a 6 May 1774 letter, Wheatley is "animated" by Tanner's "kind & friendly Letter." While Wheatley admits to grieving the deaths of Susanna Wheatley (and Mr. Moorhead), it seems Tanner offers Wheatley prayers to which the famed poet responds with a call to prayer and with gratitude. "Assist me, dear Obour!," writes Wheatley, "to praise our great benefactor, for the innumerable Benefits continually pour'd upon me, that while he strikes one Comfort *dead* he raises up another." Wheatley's prayer acknowledges Tanner's "good advices" to "be resigned to the afflicting hand of a Seemingly frowning Providence." Tanner advocates for resignation in the midst of what seems like a "frowning Providence" because she expects a godly intervention, as does Wheatley. Wheatley offers it in the very next line when she notes the number of books that Tanner has sold and the amount of collected monies. Even as Wheatley mourns, she worships with Tanner a God who provides for her book sales and a friend who can listen and care for her "welfare." Wheatley, with Tanner's help, can refuse the "painful *anxiety*" and give "up to God, that which he first gave" them—life and love.[105] Wheatley underlines the anxiety as she strives toward her faith in and desire for betterment as well as being a good friend.

Their exchange is possible, and their shared intimacy, this erotic, lives in their mutual praise and their mutual love for each other. For these women, the erotic is spiritual, just as Lorde explains. It's an affective way of knowing. Wheatley and Tanner speak on this deep-down feeling and write it often. Wheatley claims this knowledge in the first extant letter to Tanner. Her 19 May 1772 letter starts with a pronouncement of gratitude. She thanks Tanner for her letter and then begins to rejoice together with Tanner "in that realizing view." What they make together—joy and pleasure—praises their "Crucified Saviour," for "in his Crucifixion may be seen marvellous displays of Grace and Love, Sufficient to draw and invite us to the rich and endless treasures of his mercy."[106] Their profound faith, biblical references, and Christian language provide commonality.[107] Wheatley acknowledges this commonality in the letter that not only gratefully thanks Tanner for her earlier "favour" but also celebrates the "Saving change which [Tanner] so emphatically describe[s]."[108]

What Tanner describes for Wheatley, in a letter that is no longer extant, is her "saving change" or, as Bassard notes, a kind of "important dialectical movement, calling forth, as it does both the continuity of salvation and the transformation of radical change . . . 'from sinner to saint.'"[109] This change unites them further in their conversion or "an experience of rebirth, of being made entirely new, of being filled with love for everything and everybody."[110] Wheatley commends Tanner's baptism and as a consequence, her conversion. She celebrates this radical change that promises, "here, the knowledge of the true God and eternal life are made manifest."[111] Wheatley knows for sure that what they share—as women who are saved by God—is a hopeful prayer, "to live the life, and we shall die the death of the Righteous. May this be our happy case."[112] Wheatley uses their common language to imagine a better kind of self that accepts what it means to depend upon her faith and her mutual friendship with God rather than the limits of her physical body. Salvation allows Tanner and Wheatley to feel the pleasures of a freedom in God.

Wheatley declares to Tanner: "Happy were it for us if we could arrive to that evangelical Repentance, and the true holiness of heart which you mention. Inexpressibly happy Should we be could we have a due Sense of Beauties and excellence of the Crucified Saviour." Wheatley names a happiness that she wants to feel on earth, not just in the after-life. She and Tanner strive toward an "evangelical Repentance" that is as much a part of the experience of their Christian faith as is the "Sense of beauties and excellence of the Crucified Saviour." This happy feeling promises an invitation "to the rich and endless treasures of his mercy."[113] Wheatley prays in the language of a self-affirming spiritual agency in order to minister a liberatory and love-based theology that evidences Frances Smith Foster's assertion that for Black women, "the work of the word was as much an outreach program as it was a self-creating process."[114]

Wheatley "privileges ecstatic, charismatic, 'enthusiastic' religious expression and power" and, in so doing, affords herself the experience of feeling into the "enjoyments" and "ardent desire[s]" of a mind fixed on God.[115] By way of this "self-creating" erotic fellowship, Wheatley preaches a theology that values and appreciates her ability to feel, to love, and to be pleasured by God. Wheatley reaches out to Tanner so that they might enjoy God together, and together, they do.

"Revive in Better Times": Remembering Phillis Wheatley

It seems fitting that Phillis Wheatley's last extant letter—dated 10 May 1779—is to Obour Tanner.

Dr. Obour,
 By this opportunity I have the pleasure to inform you that I am well and hope you are so; tho' I have been Silent, I have not been unmindful of you but a variety of hindrances was the cause of my not writing to you.—But

in time to Come I hope our correspondence will revive—and revive in better times—pray write me soon, for I long to hear from you—you may depend on constant replies—I wish you much happiness, and am

> Dr. Obour, your friend & Sister
> Phillis Peters.[116]

No extant letter to Tanner immediately precedes this one, and no letter to anyone follows. Here is the limit of Wheatley's epistolary archive. The letter finds Tanner in Worcester and Wheatley, now married to John Peters, in Boston. Phillis and John Peters, a shopkeeper and a free Black man, live together on Queen Street. Wheatley reports that it will be Cumberland who carries her brief note to Tanner. She doesn't say who Cumberland is or how she knows where Tanner is. This isn't the letter that includes any mention of her recent marriage to Peters or any reference to the second volume of poetry that she hopes to publish in the coming months. Wheatley reminds Tanner that she hasn't spoken to her friend in a while, and at this time, not only is their living with which to contend, the nation is still at war. She doesn't have to say how long it's been since they've last spoken. Wheatley only writes of her sense of urgency to hear again from her friend and her longing to speak and to revive their past dialogue. She begs a return to this particular friendship and correspondence. She wants to return to the pleasures of writing to and receiving a note from her friend.

Wheatley's urgency seeks after "a language which expresses [her] grasp of reality as present and immediate."[117] Wheatley grasps not only for fitting language but also for her friend, Obour. Wheatley admits to her part in the silence, "tho' I have been Silent, I have not been unmindful of you."[118] She doesn't concern herself with those "hindrances" that have prompted her lack of correspondence or her lack of response to Tanner's inquiries and even confesses that she is well. She seems to resist excuses. Urgency compels Wheatley to "revive" or return to life her correspondence with Tanner. Her choice to "revive" clamors for the discursive intimacy and mutual exchange that she seeks.

When her words fail, dashes intercede. What's not clear in the printed edition is their varied length in manuscript form. Wheatley's breaks are not consistent. Some are decidedly short while others linger. She seems to interrupt herself—to hold or catch her breath with a brief or lengthy pause that offers no word-based explanation. Rather, her short and long dashes reach toward what she cannot say aloud or what she must rush pass. When she doesn't specify the hindrances that keep her away, a dash of moderate length replaces her possible excuses. With every short or lengthy dash, Wheatley mimes the process of death and resurrection. Words meet pauses, then return to words again. Her words return her from the dead. The frequent movement from word to pause to word marks a restoration of feeling, a return to the pleasure she feels when speaking to her friend. Wheatley's revival of their correspondence asks to return to the profound and deep sharing, the erotic, that marks their earlier letters.

Despite her silences and dashes, Wheatley articulates her desire to feel deeply with Tanner again and to return to the pleasure of their mutual exchange. She seeks the shared language that allows to her delight in a varied kind of worship with a friend. She seeks to restore what she has missed—the eroticism of a friendship that allows life to feel itself out and to share what it knows.

No letter neatly closes the story between these two women. With no response or subsequent letter, there is no way to learn what happens next, but what these letters tell us for sure is that they have written of faith, exchanged money, and shared advice. By 1784, Phillis Wheatley has passed on. Her second book is never published, though a few of her poems appear in periodicals, here and there. The announcement of Wheatley's death remembers her as a celebrated poet.[119]

Obour Tanner outlives Wheatley by fifty years. She leaves behind her name in the census, on a baptismal registry, a record of marriage to Barry (sometimes Barra or Barrey) Collins, and correspondence as president of the Females Society in Newport.[120] She appears again, albeit briefly, in two provenances for a small batch of Wheatley letters and for a 14 February 1776 letter auctioned in 2005.[121] Both tell us that Tanner gives her Wheatley letters to Mrs. William Beecher of Northfield, a daughter-in-law of Lyman Beecher, who lived in Newport for a short while. Tanner may have given the letters to Beecher in 1833 or 1834—just before Tanner dies.[122] The provenance reveals not only Tanner's continued participation in and around Newport's religious and Congregationalist communities and her relationship with Beecher, in particular, it also evidences Tanner's desire to keep and to hold her friend close. Even though Tanner's words do not survive, Wheatley's do because Tanner keeps her close enough to protect her words and her memory. She passes her letters and a book of poetry on to Beecher for unspecified reasons, but I suspect she gives them away to a woman she knows will care for them, too. And Tanner is right. Beecher eventually hands off the letters to Edward Hale, who helps to secure a place for them at the Massachusetts Historical Society, where they are still part of the collection.[123]

What's left of these women as friends, together, is only this final letter, "favd by Cumberland" that hopes and prays for a response. What Wheatley seeks reminds us that "women must seek to become their own historical subject in pursuit of its proper object, its proper and specific expression in time."[124] These letters make subjects of Wheatley and Tanner in pursuit of various objects of their desire: love, fellowship, and God. The letters record the salvation, love, and friendship wherein both women feel and delight in the pleasures of a freedom in each other and God. Wheatley and Tanner, together, acknowledge the everyday materiality of life itself and narrate a shared way of being that bears witness to the intimacy, love, and freedom that makes living worthwhile and confesses to the good feeling that makes their intimacy, their love, and freedom so real. Even though Wheatley's and Tanner's letters can't tell us if their next meeting happens on earth or elsewhere, they aspire toward a final certainty—that together they will meet again.

* * *

I still wonder sometimes what Phillis Wheatley thought about as she brushed her teeth. At the time of this writing, there is no extant information about Wheatley's tooth-cleaning practices. (Historians have assured me that toothbrushes were not available in the eighteenth century.) I don't wonder because I actually care about Wheatley's teeth or dental hygiene. I care instead about the ways in which she experienced herself when no one was looking for a "servant" or asking for poetry. I suspect I wonder how Wheatley took care of herself or those various selves full of religious and moral subjects. When I speak of "self," I mean her body when it wasn't engraved on a frontispiece. I also mean the "self" that isn't for everybody—that self that lives deep down inside, into her interiority wherein she might speak in hushed and quiet tones to herself or to a friend or to a lover. I'm speaking of the "self" that knows to "listen to her body and love it."[125] It is the "self" that knows how to love another even in the midst of the uncertainty of everyday and in particular, revolutionary-era living.

Wheatley's letters and their resulting pleasures publicize the interiority that makes real what matters to her as a faithful believer, a writer and poet, a friend, and wife. Despite the prevalence of Wheatley's pleasures, it seems that what pleases her doesn't yet know how to fit the expectations of twenty-first-century readers. Wheatley's pleasures don't know how to please our contemporary desire for the fixity of "intersectionality," "resistance," or the certainty of "subjectivity." They can't anticipate the anxieties that compel us to keep watch over her intersecting subjectivities or to long for her resistance. Wheatley is just pleased to share what she likes with whom she loves, befriends, or does business. What she does expect are those letters from a friend that call her to the very matter of her living and loving. With her friend, Tanner, Wheatley can be the "servant of Christ" who is neither slave nor free but loved by her God and her friend. And she is not alone.

While Wheatley lives and writes her best life as a "servant of Christ," James Albert Ukawsaw Gronniosaw—a Methodist and a former slave who eventually lives free in England—publishes his *Narrative of the Most Remarkable Particulars of James Albert Ukawsaw Gronniosaw, An African Prince* (1774). It is believed to be the "first" text—printed in England—authored (or claiming to be so) by an African man.[126] Both Wheatley and Gronniosaw are writing or telling their stories at the same time and with the support of the Countess of Huntingdon and evangelical, Calvinist communities. Much like Wheatley, Gronniosaw's publication history is indebted to the Countess of Huntingdon. Gronniosaw authors a conversion narrative that is published in Newport (Rhode Island) and Britain. Gronniosaw tells the story of the transformational power of his religious conversion, and he seems to share eagerly the pleasures of a profound and transformative faith. His obligatory, Christian testimony may belong to him, but what Gronniosaw and Wheatley share in, by way of the Countess of Huntingdon's patronage, is a commitment to an enjoyable, religious faith practice. They love God, and God loves them enough to save and redeem them in spite of the privations of slavery or economic poverty. Their shared faith also locates Wheatley and Gronniosaw in a transatlantic print culture wherein they live and write as part of intersecting and creative writing communities where faith, friendship, and pleasure happen.

CHAPTER 2

James Albert
Ukawsaw Gronniosaw's
Joyful Conversion

When James Albert Ukawsaw Gronniosaw tells his story to an unnamed amanuensis, he is an older man with a story to tell about his Christian faith, his worthiness, and just how good God is. A native of "Baurnou" (presently spelled Bornu) in West Africa and the grandson of a king, Gronniosaw is about sixty years old in 1772. He has journeyed the Middle Passage (ca. 1727) as a young and inquisitive teenager to Barbados and has worked, for nearly forty years, as a former slave to the "Vanhorn" and "Freelandhouse" families in the greater New York City area. By the time he narrates his life to a young woman from Leominster, England, he is a free man, father, husband, and in search of steady work. In past years, he has worked as a butler and served aboard an English privateer. By 1762, he is an enlisted man in Admiral Pocock's fleet at the siege of Havana during the Seven Years' War.[1] He's traveled to Holland and throughout England and Wales to worship with and preach to his favorite ministers. He's lived a full and storied life. While living as a legally freed man in various locales, Gronniosaw has been consistently underemployed and not able to provide adequate food or shelter for himself or his kin. When his narrative is published, he is living in Kidderminster, England, without enough money to support his wife and children.

Gronniosaw tells his story because he hopes that the sale of its publication will earn him enough money to support his family. Because he hopes for his story's financial success, even his choice of a popular narrative form—the spiritual autobiography or conversion narrative—is meant to encourage readers to buy his story. And they do. *The Narrative of the Most Remarkable Particulars of James Albert Ukawsaw Gronniosaw, An African Prince* is his conversion narrative as told or as written by himself.[2] This pamphlet-sized, nearly fifty-page narrative is his testimony of faith and godly providence. Gronniosaw's *Narrative* is published—a year before Phillis Wheatley's *Poems on Various Subjects, Religious and Moral* (1773)—in Bath by printers Thomas Mills and William Guy and separately, by Samuel Hazard.[3] Subsequent editions of the narrative are published widely: in Newport, Rhode Island, by Solomon Southwick (1774) and in Dublin, Ireland (1790). The narrative is also translated into Welsh by W. Williams (1779).[4]

Nearly seventeen years before the success of Olaudah Equiano's *Interesting Narrative* (1789), Gronniosaw remembers his life as a curious boy in West Africa, an enslaved young man in Barbados, a new Christian convert in New York City, and an older, God-fearing man in England. As he looks back over his life, he returns repeatedly to his sense of wonder and longing to understand the world and how it was made. His wonder makes an aching in his spirit. It leads him, in his youth, away from his home and toward his religious conversion experience or that which theologian Yolanda Pierce explains as the "change in mind or a change in heart, which usually implies the abandonment of one set of beliefs (or lack of formalized belief system) and the adoption of a new set of beliefs."[5] It's his religious conversion though that orders his living. He experiences it physically and spiritually, in his body and in his way of being while enslaved in the Dutch Reformist household of Mr. Freelandhouse. ("Freelandhouse" is most likely minister and slaveowner Theodorus Frelinghuysen.)[6] He gives his life fully to Christ and undergoes a spiritual transformation. In the way of the biblical Saul on the road to Damascus, famed Great Awakening minister Jonathan Edwards, or countless cheaply published testimonies of salvation before him, he is transformed from a nonbeliever to a Christian with a subjectivity that consciously moves within transatlantic, transcultural discourses of Protestantism.

Gronniosaw's story is in no way singular or unique. It is, though, a story. I think of "story"—in the manner of poet Kevin Young—as a way of organizing experience that's shaped by "a vision based not on mere technical expertise, but feeling, purpose, presence." What the story invokes as a feeling is determined by what's kept and what's invented.[7] Stories are what "you choose to keep, and even more, invent: just because you need to invent it, or forge and find it, after all, does not mean it's not there." Stories make up a life or a larger narrative that "might be invented as much as lived, improvised as much as dictated, filled with struggle, rather than suffering—seeking among the weeds to find *what might be.*"[8] Stories are not always exactly true. And, because Gronniosaw's narrative pursues redemption, it is a kind of invention of the self. His intention is to demonstrate his faith and, to this end, it may not have truth telling in mind. His story—as part of this conversion narrative and storytelling tradition—works to imagine him as part of a religious and writerly community that celebrates and worships God together.

Gronniosaw's conversion narrative participates in specific trans-Atlantic cultural and literary traditions—for example, the religious errand, and the genres of the captivity and conversion narratives—that write him into a Christian selfhood. His titling likens his story to a writerly and readerly community of conversion accounts, such as Mary Rowlandson's *The Sovereignty and Goodness of God: Being a Narrative of the Captivity and Restoration of Mrs. Mary Rowlandson* (1682), Jonathan Edward's *A Faithful Narrative of the Surprising Work of God* (1737), and Briton Hammon's *Narrative of the Uncommon Sufferings, and Surprizing Deliverance of Briton Hammon, a Negro Man* (1760). He is part of a testimonial community of his biblical and literary predecessors as well as ministers of the gospel. Take, for example, his mentions of or hints at notable proselytizers George Whitefield, John Bunyan, Richard Baxter, St. Augustine, and Apostle Paul.[9] Gronniosaw's testimony is compelled, by doctrinal practice and custom, to remember the many ways that he experiences this new way of living and being. He must show his readers just how much he knows about God and the Bible. To demonstrate to his readers how well he knows God, he borrows and occasionally quotes directly from the Bible, including the books of Isaiah, Revelation, and Hebrews. At times he expects his readers to recognize how he's woven biblical stories and ways of living from the songs of Psalms and the stories of Paul, David, the books of John, and Jesus Christ into his own life's account. He structures his story as if he were a modern-day apostle, in the manner of a well-known subject of conversion, Paul. God matters most to Gronniosaw, and it's the godly word that gives his story meaning.

Gronniosaw is not just any kind of Christian or any kind of Protestant. He is a long-standing Calvinist. By the time he finds his way to England, he has lived among and worshiped at Calvinist churches in New York, England, and Wales. As a Calvinist believer, he understands himself to be among the elect and chosen few to be saved by the death and resurrection of Jesus Christ and to carry with him God's providence and favor. Despite his former political status as a enslaved man, he is converted and has a story worth telling because he is among the chosen. His narrative—note that the dedicatee, preface's author, and its earliest printers are tied to or part of England's Calvinist communities—is published with a Calvinist audience in mind. His audience expects his conversion. This conversion is not necessarily a one-time event. It's a lengthy and uncomfortable process, and it is, as Yolanda Pierce explains, "proof that God has divinely entered into an intimate relationship with an individual."[10] It is an iterative death and rebirth, and every iteration serves not only Gronniosaw's particular story but also as a Christian model of storytelling.

One of Gronniosaw's favorite Calvinist ministers and a man of his acquaintance, Rev. George Whitefield, in his sermon, *Sermon on Regeneration* (1739), explains the conversion process in this way: "So souls . . . yet are so purged and purified and cleansed from their natural Dross, Filth, and Leprosy, by the blessed Influences of the Holy Spirit, that they may properly be said to be *made anew*."[11] Whitefield borrows his idea—"to be *made anew*"— from the biblical language of Apostle Paul's second letter to the Corinthians. Paul characterizes, in his second letter to the Corinthians, what results from a conversion experience, "Therefore if any man be in Christ, he is a new creature: old things are passed away; behold, all things are become new."[12] Whitefield explains elsewhere that "what *St. Paul* calls being renewed in the Spirit of our Minds, and herein consists of that Holiness without which no Man shall see the Lord."[13] The convert is made entirely new and holy in Christ. Whitefield observes that there are particular affective and behavioral responses to conversion; he refers to these behaviors as the "marks of the new birth" in a sermon so titled. There are five: praying/supplicating, committing no sin, conquering the world, loving one another, and loving one's enemies. A believer's commitment to these faithful practices guarantees an intimacy with Christ. As the convert prays and begs for God's attention, he or she strives toward and is encouraged by an intimacy with God. Because of this intimacy, the convert refuses sin and conquers the world while loving humanity. For Gronniosaw (and any faithful believer), the fact of conversion—and the subsequent processes of rebirth—gives him a new way of being in himself. It calls him to share and to show himself and his marks in order to claim this intimacy with God as a believer who prays often, refuses sin, and agrees to love friends and enemies alike. Gronniosaw's narrative proves his relationship with God as he weaves a remarkable account of godly salvation and providence. His story begins with a confession of his sins and his spiritual transformation from a sinner to a Christian, from Ukawsaw Gronniosaw to James Albert, and from West Africa to Colonial America and eventually to England.

This chapter looks after and considers Gronniosaw's Christian faith and its resulting joys as he speaks of them in his *Narrative*. This story about a religious conversion is also a story about desire. Gronniosaw is constantly desiring. He wants answers to life's questions. He seeks after a god even before he knows there is just one creator. He desires to make books speak to him, to be saved, and to meet Reverend Whitefield. He longs to know himself as a child of a Christian God and to see his earthly parents again. He can't help but to feel this longing. His longing aims for its own satisfaction. It's in this pursuit that he learns not only who God is, but also what it means to be faithful in his belief. Gronniosaw's faith is real and meaningful to him too. Even as an enslaved boy and later freed man, he understands himself to be a "called and chosen" Protestant, Christian man who yearns for godly love. It's an aching that shows up as a need to pursue Christian faith and the conversionary processes of living and dying. He is called to it because it seems he takes seriously the idea of faith as the Apostle Paul speaks of it in Hebrews 11:1: "Now faith is the substance of things hoped for, the evidence of things not seen." He seeks after that for which he hopes and cannot see. This pursuit is built into his story and makes clear how faith allows him keep living. The structure of his narrative—from its title and preface to his choice of epigraphs—aligns with this repetitive cycle of living and dying.

While enslaved, he learns to pray and to submit to the Word and will of God. Because of his unwavering commitment to this process, his story carries in it the saving power that he hopes will bring salvation or this desire for intimacy with God to all those imagined readers—non-Calvinist Christians and nonbelievers—who read his life and decide to follow his faith. It's for this reason that his story honors his early lack of Christian faith and then progresses toward his growing need for a monotheistic faith. By telling his story in this linear way, he is proving that what matters most to him is his conversion and his love for God. This conversation not only transforms Gronniosaw's life, it also satisfies him. This satisfaction is enjoyable and delightful. It provides the sixty-year-old Gronniosaw with a greater and deeper sense of meaning about his life and the certain joy of knowing God's faithfulness.

Gronniosaw learns from the practice of his faith to fashion a self that is no longer degraded by the burdens of an unknown sin. Rather, his faith makes a man who learns the fallibility of his humanity even as he finds a way to claim the intimacy that makes him worthy and desirable. Gronniosaw seeks God as God seeks and provides for him. Gronniosaw challenges the limitations of his body—as a site of sin and enslavement—while also enjoying the enthusiastic pleasures of his Christian faith. It is the sort of good feeling that comes with the certainty of God's transformative work in his life.

What Gronniosaw learns for sure over the course of his living and his narrative is that his discomfort—in the form of his many spiritual deaths—give way to joy and also elicits the pleasures that come from a profound sense of satisfaction. What he has desired—namely, God—has satisfied him and as a consequence pleased him. His conversion "offers the deliverance of psychological healing, as well as supernatural intervention."[14] His life is a joy-filled testimony. He enjoys the truth of his worthiness in God, and he talks about it and delights in his faith and in his trust in God. Gronniosaw lives with a boundless joy, and it's so good to him that he speaks of it often. He remembers—after his conversion—his elation: "but this I know, that the joy and comfort it conveyed to me, cannot be expressed, and only conceived by those who have experienced the like." He can't help but to offer up praise: "I was one day in a most delightful frame of mind; my heart so overflowed with love and gratitude to the author of all my comforts."[15] He lives when death should have taken him. He finds favor even when none seemed available to him. He finds financial support even when it seemed no one would employ him. He is surely worthy, and his sense of worth gives him cause for celebration in spite of life's uncertainty or the surety of his political status.

Gronniosaw's Many Births

The requisite title page of Gronniosaw's *Narrative* includes an epigraph from Isaiah 42:16. There is a bit of disparity between the American edition's title page and its preface. The American edition—printed at Newport, Rhode Island, by Solomon Southwick—claims that Gronniosaw wrote his story by himself. The same edition's preface has a different accounting of the story's origins: "*THIS account of the life and spiritual experience of* James Albert, *was taken from his own mouth, and committed to paper by the elegant pen of a young Lady of the town of* Leominster."[16]

The frontispiece is followed by the narrative's dedication: "To the Right Honorable the Countess of Huntingdon, this Narrative of my Life, and of God's wonderful Dealings with me, is, through her Ladyship's Permission, Most Humbly Dedicated, By Her Ladyship's Most obliged And obedient Servant, James Albert." Gronniosaw dedicates his story to Selina Hastings, Countess of Huntingdon. Her patronage has sustained Gronniosaw at times. She later supports the publication of Wheatley's *Poems on Various Subjects* (1773), and the narratives of itinerant minister John Marrant (1785) and of the multifaceted, well-traveled Olaudah Equiano (1789). The countess's contributions to local church planting and colonial American missionary work are extensive. She extends her financial support to advance her proslavery faith against the doctrinal agenda of her rivals, John and Charles Wesley. The antislavery Methodism of the Wesley brothers is increasingly popular as Britain gains an interest in slavery's abolition.[17] Hastings is not only Gronniosaw's dedicatee, but her cousin, Walter Shirley, writes the narrative's prefatory remarks.

Shirley is a Calvinist believer too, much like his cousin, and he serves, at this time, as her chaplain. He takes his belief in predestination seriously and writes his preface to make clear his commitment to the belief that salvation is only for God's elect. His preface—when it's read alongside the dedication to Hastings and the printers' signature—assures the reader that Gronniosaw is also part of this particular England-based, Calvinist community. Shirley's preface affirms that this is a decidedly Christian story.[18] Shirley previews the story with his mentions of Gronniosaw's curious mind as a young boy, his journey as a teenager to the coast and his resulting enslavement, and ultimately, the manner in which a Christian god takes him "by a way he knew not, out of darkness into [the Lord's] marvellous light."[19] His summary of Gronniosaw's life also primes the reader to expect an account of conversion. Shirley's priming is important because it demonstrates the truthfulness of Gronniosaw's story and prepares the reader to expect the familiar story of a godly and faithful man.

Shirley regards Gronniosaw's narrative as an answer to a long-standing and perplexing question: "In what manner will God deal with those benighted parts of the world where the gospel of Jesus Christ hath never reached?" Just in case the reader doesn't understand his meaning, Shirley explains further: "Now it appears, from the experience of this remarkable person, that God does not save without knowledge of the truth; but with respect to those whom he hath foreknown, though born under every outward disadvantage, and in the regions of the grossest darkness and ignorance, he most amazingly acts upon, and influences their minds . . . he brings them to the means of spiritual transformation." Shirley's remarks suggest that this narrative provides a way to minister to those "benighted parts of the world"—that is, those communities comprised of individuals, "born under every outward disadvantage, and in the regions of the grossest darkness and ignorance." When Shirley speaks about the "benighted" and "outward disadvantage," he names a community of nonbelievers who are marked by their collective lack of faith. He hints too at a particular geography—namely, Africa—and a particular political status, an enslaved person. That Gronniosaw is an African and formerly enslaved matters to Shirley because it proves just how much God can provide for and transform a nonbeliever into a believer. Shirley recommends this narrative to an imagined reader who will certainly benefit from Gronniosaw's confession: "this Narrative to your perusal, and him who is the subject of it, to your charitable regard."[20]

Gronniosaw recounts a compelling story—"this little history contains matter well worthy the notice and attention of every Christian reader"—

that Shirley reads as discernable evidence of "an all wise and omnipotent appointment and direction."[21] Shirley's preface argues compellingly that Gronniosaw's story is a worthwhile read because his remarkable story bears witness to the very possibility of God's saving grace in his life.

Because Shirley's readers are prepared for a conversion narrative, they must expect Gronniosaw's life testimony to follow. And it does. Gronniosaw's story starts in West Africa with a bit of genealogy and the announcement of his physical birth. "I was born in the city of Baurnou," Gronniosaw notes, "my mother was the eldest daughter of the reigning King there."[22] He provides no birthdate (even though he must be born ca. 1712). He is born into a royal lineage in Bornu, a largely Muslim Empire; literary historian Jennifer Harris has argued convincingly that as elite members of an Islamic empire, Gronniosaw and his family must be practicing Muslims.[23] But Gronniosaw neither claims nor names a clearly defined religious practice. He hints instead at a polytheistic faith system with Islam-inspired rituals and a belief in the divinity of the sun, moon, and stars.

One of six children, Gronniosaw is unmistakably inquisitive and is "particularly loved" by his mother and adored by his grandfather. As a boy, Gronniosaw can't stop asking questions about how everything works and how life is made. Curiosity has troubled his mind from infancy, and it creates in him an ongoing and insatiable angst to learn what made the whole world. It seems to him no one has answers. He asks his mother, "who made the *first man*? And who made the first cow, and the first lion, and where does the fly come from, as no one can make him?"[24]

What Gronniosaw tries to pass off as a childlike spirit of inquiry is similar to the Lord's interrogation of Job. There, in Job 38, the Lord asks Job—who has nothing left after the devil strips him of his family, his employment, and his riches—questions about the origins of every living thing. The Lord poses nearly four chapters worth of questions to Job and awaits the man's answers. But Job can't answer the Lord's questions: "Where wast thou when I laid the foundations of the earth?" and "Who laid the corner stone thereof; When the morning stars stand together and all the sons of God shouted for joy?" He can only admit to his humanity in Job 42:2–3: "I know that thou canst do everything . . . therefore have I uttered that I understood not; things too wonderful for me, which I knew not." It's as if Gronniosaw, as a boy, knows to think and question as the Lord does with the humility that Job learns through this exercise. Gronniosaw wrestles with "the things too wonderful" of which he doesn't yet know, even as he does know to wonder and ask from whence these things have come.

Gronniosaw questions his siblings too, and they have no satisfactory answers either. His siblings suspect that he teases them with his unanswerable questions. They dislike his queries and deem him "foolish or insane." Despite their disdain, Gronniosaw wonders even more at the marvels of creation and its creator: "I often raised my hand to heaven, and asked her [my mother] who lived there? Was much dissatisfied when [she] told me the sun, moon, and stars, being persuaded, in my own mind, that there must be some SUPERIOR POWER." His mother tries to explain that the sun, moon, and stars govern creation, but he doesn't believe her: "'Twas certain that I was, at times, very unhappy in myself: It being strongly impressed on my mind that there was some GREAT MAN of power which resided in above the sun, moon, and stars, the objects of our worship." His wonderment leaves him feeling, as he says, "afraid, and uneasy, and restless, but could not tell for what." When neither his mother, siblings, nor his grandfather can assuage his "curious mind," his kin grow increasingly concerned about his well-being.[25]

Gronniosaw's anxious curiosity may seem odd for the reader who wants or expects his questions to admit to his childhood innocence. It might not make sense for Gronniosaw's questions to trouble him so much that he can't be a playful, little boy. There is nothing innocent or childlike about his storytelling or even his choice of questions. Gronniosaw experiences an intentional and decidedly Christian dissatisfaction, and it's a plot device and a useful literary tool for the aged storyteller. It's his Christian burden, which is familiar to his imagined, Christian readers.[26] Gronniosaw's burden evokes John Bunyan's protagonist in his allegory *Pilgrim's Progress* (1678). Gronniosaw seems to borrow of his sense of overwhelm and burden from Christian, Bunyan's pilgrim who cries out to his wife and children, "'O my dear wife,' said he, 'and you the children of my bowels, I your dear friend am in myself undone, by reason of a burden that lieth hard upon me.'"[27] For Gronniosaw, his burden—to question the origins of life—attempts to discredit and disrupt his cultural knowledge of a god and familial hierarchies—mother/child, older brother/younger brother, older sister/younger brother—that render him powerless. His childhood curiosity hints at what the elder Gronniosaw already knows—that his younger self is born into sin. He does not know Christianity yet. Because neither Gronniosaw nor his community know the saving power of Jesus Christ, he has no religion, and therefore, no salvation. No one can help him understand who this "superior power" is because, as the elder Gronniosaw recalls, none of his family or his countrymen know God. But Gronniosaw seems to have a vague and intuitive way of describing this godlike force that he calls "some SUPERIOR

POWER" or "great man of power." And he is certain that this "superior power" compels his siblings' dislike of him.

Gronniosaw's questions don't stop. His burden is made greater, in fact, by his desire to know who or what is greater than the sun, moon, and stars. Gronniosaw embeds the answer into his use of the "sun, moon, and stars"; he seemingly remembers the weeping prophet Jeremiah's prophesy: "Thus saith the Lord, which giveth the sun for a light by day, and the ordinances of the moon, and of the stars for a light by night, which divideth the sea, when the waves roar; the Lord of hosts is His name."[28] He is even more certain of this greater power after he is made even more distressed by "a remarkable Black cloud" that covers the sun and brings with it heavy rain and thunder. Gronniosaw remembers that he is "highly affected." He cries. He stands still and is overwhelmed by his fear of this divine "Great Man of Power."[29] The storm convinces him for sure that this unnamed superior power is real. This Great Man is greater than his family's objects of worship. It seems to haunt Gronniosaw, and it encourages his doubt and forces him to question further his world and his way of being in it. This Great Man creates a profound longing in the young Gronniosaw. He can't get away from this desiring after—who he understands to be—a greater, monotheistic god. Gronniosaw's desire serves his narrative's purpose—namely, to signal to the reader that his salvation is guaranteed and so are its joys—because he is chosen to be among the predestined elect. He foreshadows salvation and invites the reader to expect it. He uses "great man" and "superior power" to hint at an alternative worldview that needs a different kind of divine. Gronniosaw memorializes this desire and the ignorance that prompts it. He preserves this longing because without its sense of aching, his story has no god to seek.

When his questions feel too burdensome to ask and his desiring for truth are too great for him to bear, Gronniosaw realizes he can't remain at home. Even though his family tries to assuage his angst, he knows that he doesn't fit in: "I grew very unhappy in myself; my relations and acquaintance endeavoured by all the means they could think on, to divert me by taking me to ride upon goats (which is much the custom of our country) and to shoot a bow and arrow." But, their efforts don't work. He experiences "no satisfaction at all in any of these things." Instead, Gronniosaw is overwhelmed by what he describes as "a secret impulse upon my mind, which I could not resist, that seemed to tell me I must go." In the midst of this shared unease, Gronniosaw's life is interrupted by a merchant from the Gold Coast. The merchant offers Gronniosaw an opportunity to travel to "see houses with wings to [let] them walk upon the water, and should also see the white folks."[30] Gronniosaw agrees to go because this "secret impulse" has made enemies of his sisters, brothers, and servants. No one likes him anymore (even though he admits everyone is sad to see him go). He travels with the merchant for more than a thousand miles from his home to the Gold Coast.

At their arrival to the coastal city, Gronniosaw is welcomed by the sounds of trumpets and drums. "This account gave me a secret pleasure," recalls Gronniosaw, as it is a welcome made for a prince. Just as soon as he enjoys the sights and sounds, what might have pleased him—namely, the attention of a foreign king or the trumpets sounds—orients him in a wilderness among hostile and unknown persons. The merchant's sons let Gronniosaw know that despite the shouts of the horns and drums, the king wants to kill him. He is no longer joyful but instead quickly realizes that he is "without a friend and any means to procure one." He is alone, far away from his family. Gronniosaw is taken prisoner by the unnamed king and sentenced to execution because the king thinks that Gronniosaw is a spy. "The next day I was to die," Gronniosaw recounts, "for the King intended to behead me." He tries to explain that he means no harm and is really there to "play" and to "see houses walk upon the water, with wings to them, and the white folks."[31] The king does not believe him and is certain that Gronniosaw is there to start a war. So, he decides Gronniosaw must die.

It's curious though that when Gronniosaw recalls his great fear at this point in his story, he declares, "but still the Almighty was pleased to work miracles for me." The elder Gronniosaw intervenes in his story to introduce the reader to whom he calls the "Almighty" and to take up the story of John the Baptist's execution in Mark 6 and make it his own. To the biblically literate reader, Gronniosaw's possible execution reads similarly to Mark 6:27: "And immediately the king sent an executioner and commanded his head to be brought: and he went and beheaded him in prison." The king is Herod and the beheaded is Jesus's cousin, John the Baptist. John is beheaded because he's questioned King Herod's decision to marry his brother's wife. John the Baptist must die, but Gronniosaw does not. His body is spared. Left without the possibility of freedom, Gronniosaw begs for his life: "I went with an undaunted courage, and it pleased God to melt the heart of the King, who sat with his scymitar in his hand ready to behead me; yet, being himself so affected, he dropped it out of his hand, and took me upon his knee and wept over me." God shows up for the young Gronniosaw. The king can't bring himself to kill Gronniosaw because he is so affected by the presence of God: "[the king] dropped it out of his hand, and took me upon his knee and wept over me." Gronniosaw lives and writes, "I put my right hand around his neck, and prest him to my heart.—He set me down and blest me."³² Gronniosaw avoids execution because God does not will it for him.

Gronniosaw's God melts the heart of the king, and the king, in turn, lets the youngster live. Gronniosaw remembers this scene in this way because he is discerning just how God has intervened on his behalf and shaped him into the man who can tell this story. It's a godly impulse that has him journey away from home in order to—as Joanna Brooks observes—"confront death and to find in that confrontation a new orientation toward life."³³ Gronniosaw confronts death, but he does not die. He does find a new orientation toward his living. That he lives—because of a godly intervention—initiates the physical and religious transformation that eventually leads Gronniosaw to slavery and also a life in Christ. The king's only recourse is to sell the young man into slavery to a merchant heading across the Atlantic. Even as he has spared the youngster's life, the king takes Gronniosaw's adornments and his gold. Gronniosaw no longer looks like the grandson of a king and so begins his spiritual transformation. He sheds his wares in order to move toward and to learn God.

The merchant prepares to sell Gronniosaw and, together, they board ships to find a buyer. Gronniosaw grows increasingly concerned that no one will buy him, which will result in his being put to death. Fearing death yet again, he remembers, "and as soon as ever I saw the *Dutch* captain, I ran to him, and put my arms around him, and said 'Father save me.' (for I knew that if he did not buy me, I should be treated very ill or possibly murdered)."³⁴ Gronniosaw finds the words to remember this experience from John 12:27: "Now is my soul troubled; and what shall I say? Father, save me from this hour: but for this cause came I unto this hour."³⁵ Jesus offers up this prayer after he announces that it's time for him to make the final sacrifice. He must die in order to save humanity from collective and individual sin: "The hour has come that the Son of Man should be glorified."³⁶ Jesus is in Jerusalem and is certain that the time has come for God to be glorified. For God to be glorified, he knows truly that he must die and will be executed on the cross within a week's time.

Gronniosaw takes on Jesus's prayer, "Father, save me." His prayer hopes for a savior's intervention and for the earthly father that he's left behind. It hopes for salvation. He doesn't want to die and assumes that the Dutch captain can save him. He hasn't learned about his Christian father, and instead of God, he has chosen a man to save him. He's misunderstood who his father is. Gronniosaw makes no distinction between the Dutch man and God. Gronniosaw's revision of Jesus's prayer is meant to prepare him for his story's death and resurrection. This human "Father" won't save Gronniosaw. The Dutch captain won't return him home to Bornu, and he won't satisfy Gronniosaw's curiosity about the origins of the sun, moon, and stars. The Dutch captain can't save him because he is not divine and because Gronniosaw's story requires him to give up his life in West Africa. He must don European garb and leave behind the gold adornments of his home and head west. Because, when his former life is over, then he can find his way to a resurrected, Christian life while enslaved in New York. His "Father, save me" reminds the reader that God has already saved him variously on his thousand-mile trek to the coast, and God will save him again. His appeal "Father, save me" leads him to a kind of salvation. What the Dutch captain does do is introduce—with the help of a prayer book—the young Gronniosaw to Christianity as an idea, as a kind of world-making literacy.

The scene begins just after Gronniosaw is taken aboard the ship upon which he will travel the Middle Passage to Barbados. He spies his enslaver reading from a prayer book to the ship's crewmembers. Gronniosaw doesn't specify the passage that is read, and he doesn't say in what language the Dutch man is reading. But he does make clear that this sight produces a desire within him to perform the same act:

> And when first I saw [my master] read, I was never so surprised in my whole life as when I saw the book talk to my master; for I thought it did, as I observed him to look upon it, and move his lips. I wished it would do so to me. . . . I follow'd him to the place where he put the book, being mightily delighted with it, and when nobody saw me, I open'd it and put my ear down close upon it, in great hope that it would say something to me but was very sorry and greatly disappointed when I found it would not speak.[37]

He sees this reading, and he names it ("when first I saw him read"). And then, Gronniosaw says, he sees the book "talk to my master." He continues to watch his master as he looks at the book and "move his lips." Gronniosaw looks on as the words of the prayer book seemingly move his enslaver's lips. He imagines the book's words might speak to him too. And, though he claims to not understand book learning in this way ("I was never so surprised in my whole life as when I saw the book talk to my master"), he wants to "read" the book or have the book "read" him and move his lips. What Gronniosaw remembers is a desire to be moved by the words of his enslaver's prayer.

When his enslaver's reading group disperses, Gronniosaw sneaks to pick up the book and raises it to his ear. Quite literally, Gronniosaw attempts to hear, with his ear, the words of the prayer book. He waits for it to say something to him, yet the book does not speak. When he can't move his lips correctly or feel its words in his mouth, he assumes that the book refuses him. Despite his delight and his desire, it sits silently. Gronniosaw blames this silence on himself and his inadequacy. He believes the book would not speak to him because he explains, "this thought immediately presented itself to [him], that every body and every thing despised me because I was Black."[38] When Gronniosaw decides that the book would not speak because he is "Black," he is left with a silent book, a mark upon his person, and an unrequited desiring.

Desire, Refusal, and Silent Books

Gronniosaw is a teenager when he tries to make the book speak to him. Though Gronniosaw makes only a passing mention of the book and its silence, literary scholar Henry Louis Gates Jr. names this scene and uses it to tell another sort of literary origin story. He refers to it as the "talking book." He asserts that Gronniosaw is the "first" African author to describe a book's refusal to speak back to a Black face. Gronniosaw is not the last. Similar scenes are found in several early Atlantic world narratives by enslaved (and Native American authors): John Marrant's *A Narrative of Lord's Wonderful Dealings with John Marrant, a Black* (1785), Ottobah Cugoano's *Narrative of the Enslavement of Ottobah Cugoano* (1787), Olaudah Equiano's *The Interesting Narrative of the Life of Olaudah Equiano* (1789), and John Jea's *The Life, History, and Unparalleled Sufferings of John Jea, the African Preacher* (ca. 1816). Each subsequent "talking book" scene seems to revise Gronniosaw's misreading and suggests that these authors read each other's work. In each one, there is an individual (usually, an enslaved man or a Native American "princess") who spies his master or someone else reading a Bible or prayer book.[39] The sight produces a desire to hear the text speak. The inquisitive person picks up the book, looks into it, and, with ear or lips to it, waits for it to respond. But after touching it—either in the form of placing one's ear or lips to the text—the book remains silent. It never speaks back.[40] The silence prompts a great feeling of sorrow or disappointment that hints at a greater and, sometimes, unspecified inadequacy.

For Gates, this is an event about literacy, "the ultimate parameter by which to measure the humanity of authors struggling to define an African self in Western letters."[41] This "text of Blackness" makes a literary tradition, "the first repeated and revised trope of the tradition, the first trope to be Signified upon."[42] When the book doesn't talk back, Gates presumes that the book's refusal denies Gronniosaw the very possibility of literacy and his humanity. The book and its silence render Gronniosaw illiterate and unable to hear—even with his "ear down close upon it"—the book talk. Moreover, Gronniosaw, as a "first," marks a flawed way of being—that is, possessing an inability to hear the book as his master does: "I was very sorry and greatly disappointed when I found [the book] would not speak."[43] Gronniosaw's disappointment is not simply affective. The book refuses to speak because, as Gates explains, "texts can only address that which they see" and, without the right ways of book learning, the book cannot see or make sense of Gronniosaw.[44] It marks his body. He is made "Black" when the book refuses to speak to him.

Gronniosaw must suffer alone in his shame and disappointment until, as Gates understands it, Marrant, Equiano, and Jea try to read from their own "talking books." When Marrant, Equiano, and Jea revise Gronniosaw's words, they signify or share in "modes of figuration [that] only result when writers read each other's texts and seize upon themes and figures to revise their own texts."[45] Each revision acts as a form of intertextuality that creates "curious formal lines of continuity between the texts" that Gates writes together comprise the "shared text of Blackness."[46] They reproduce a version of Gronniosaw's suffering and in so doing participate in a collective experience of embodied and ontological suffering or the race making of African American literature. The resulting versions of this scene posit an idea of race "as a stable and trans-historical category of identity" that is lived as an experiential and collective way of being mediated through a collective feeling of great suffering.[47]

While Gates memorializes Gronniosaw's illiteracy and his racial formation, his "talking book" assumes that Gronniosaw doesn't know how reading works. It's easy to assume that Gronniosaw can't make sense of how reading books might work or that he really believes that books talk. But I question whether his suffering births a cohesive racial identity, literary category, or even if this scene marks a desire for actual book learning. To read Gronniosaw's misreading as a desire to read books assumes reading and making the book talk are the same activity, and it presupposes a need for this young man to prove his value through literacy. It also suggests that his story is wholly real and factual. But, this is a story that is meant to invoke feeling by organizing a spiritual experience into a meaningful one. Its interest isn't necessarily truth telling; what matters more is narrating Gronniosaw's faith. Truth and fact aren't necessarily the same, just as reading books and having the book speak aren't the same activity even though both, at times, require books, senses, bodies, and some form of literacy.[48] Gronniosaw seems to know this difference as he recounts his life even if we, at present, do not.

This isn't actually a story about talking books, silent books, or books that refuse to speak. Gronniosaw gives his readers a story about misreading and desiring. It is an intentional sleight and an easy one to miss if a reader assumes that Gronniosaw craves book learning or even doubts his humanity. What Gronniosaw observes in his enslaver's book literacy—the moving lips and listening ears, the book and its prayers—misreads how reading books happens. His error is not the result of a cultural difference. Gronniosaw doesn't want to learn to read books. He doesn't question his humanity or argue that book learning will make him "human" because he knows he already is. He makes a mistake for a good reason. Gronniosaw includes this scene because it primes the religiously learned (and likely, Calvinist) reader for his forthcoming conversion experience. What Gronniosaw understands (and what we miss) is that the book sets the reader up for the greatest kind of pleasure there is—namely, to acknowledge, for sure, that the reader is always worthy of God's love. Gronniosaw and his mute book fashions a way of Christian learning that begins with this desire to learn who God is and to be loved by God.

Because his conversion from sinner to saved is the story's impetus, Gronniosaw's every action anticipates his call to faith and his godly salvation. His initial failure sets up his inevitable success. That Gronniosaw can't make the book talk is a warning to his readers. The book's silence signals Gronniosaw's faithlessness. He can't yet experience God's Word inwardly or in prayer because he isn't saved. The book's silence announces a greater desire in Gronniosaw to feel the words of God and to have those words move him. When the book doesn't speak, Gronniosaw admits to his desire for what George Whitefield calls the "indwelling of the spirit" or the idea that "those who receive the Sacrament worthily, 'dwell in Christ, and Christ in them; that they are One with Christ, and Christ with them.'"[49]

Gronniosaw desires, for himself, an intimacy—with the book and its words—that presupposes a faithful kind of knowing, safety, and accessibility in God. He observes this intimacy between the book and his enslaver. The enslaver holds and touches the book, and he moves his mouth to it and is moved by it. Gronniosaw can't name what makes his master's lips move, but he yearns for it and to feel whatever it is within him. He desires God and the right ways of knowing God—through prayer and supplication, conversion, and a profound belief in God's saving grace. Gronniosaw is desperate for the familiarity that he reads between the sound of the words and the enslaver's lips. The reader must assume the enslaver knows the relationship between language, God, and a Christian self, and Gronniosaw wants to know it too.

Gronniosaw's desire stages an intimacy wherein he is no longer alone in his curiosity. He's no longer by himself because he is among those who can pray and speak to God's Word. When his desire is not satisfied and the book doesn't speak, his hope turns into the despair of seeing himself for the first time, just like the man of James 1:23, "beholding his natural face in a glass." The biblical writer James likens this man to someone who can hear the word but not do it: "For if any be a hearer of the word, and not a doer, he is like unto a man beholding his face in a glass." Gronniosaw can hear the words of the Dutch captain's prayers. He can't do the work of prayer, conquering sin, or loving one's enemies. He doesn't yet have Whitefield's marks of the new birth because he is merely a sinner. He is "blackened" with sinfulness, and he concedes, in his use of the term, to his sinful self and not necessarily to his racial identity. He "bends" language in a way that allows him to name his pre-conversion condition, but he does not single-mindedly represent his body.[50] He doesn't offer a "real" account of an overdetermined racial identity but instead sets up a kind of meaning for "Black" that is neither fixed nor determined. It's subject to change because race does not function as a stable or transhistorical category of identity for Gronniosaw (though this fact should not deny an emergent racial collectivity). As a youngster without faith or a sense of what his "black" self is, at this point in this story, Gronniosaw's misreading serves as a warning; it admonishes those who might attempt to "hear" rather than "do" the Word.

Gronniosaw's unrequited conversation is instructive because it models what's generative about desire. First, the book was never supposed to speak to those who want to touch it simply because it seems materially relevant. Second, the book only speaks to those who are moved and can be moved by its words. Third, the book and its silence reject the misguided desire for the materiality of the text itself, and, last, the book and its refusal to talk evidence a reading practice that is a faith-based, affective, and bodily experience. Gronniosaw's illiteracy inspires his readers to possess the requisite forms of desire and intimacy that engender a response from the text, and their desire is for God. The book refuses to speak to those who cannot feel and receive its message. Its rejection is telling. It is designed to prompt the right kind of desire in the imprudent reader.

Desire, in Gronniosaw's narrative, is not simply the very human longing for an unspecified someone or something. This desire functions as a deep yearning for a particularity, an inward experience of God and an intimacy with God's Word. It's a decidedly Christian yearning that requires a deepened sense of longing in order to achieve an ultimate satisfaction in God. "Real Christians, whilst they are among fiery serpents," as minister John Marrant—a writer who also experiences this misreading event—preaches in "A Funeral Sermon," "are waiting with desire, and holy expectation, for the good of the promise, which is yet behind."[51] Real Christians cultivate a desire for God that expects to receive "the good" of His promise. Without this kind of desire, books don't talk, and the satisfaction of living in Christ is unattainable. The reader is expected to discern that without this urge to hear the book speak or to be moved by its words, Gronniosaw might not have known conversion or life thereafter.

Gronniosaw's Joys

With every passing event in his story, Gronniosaw sets his reader up to witness his sin and to expect his conversion and his life thereafter. It doesn't happen quickly. The reader must first read through his mistakes and misunderstandings about who he is and to whom he belongs. When he finally happens upon the events that make for his conversion, Gronniosaw is enslaved in New York to the Vanhorn family after he's sold for "fifty dollars" in Barbados.

Literary historian Vincent Carretta notes that "Vanhorn" is, in fact, Cornelius Van Horne. He is a member of a family of well-established and politically influential Dutch slaveholders. Vanhorn, as Gronniosaw spells it, owns a large, 557-acre plantation in Somerset County, New Jersey, on the Raritan River and is a member of the Dutch Reformed Church.[52] Vanhorn takes Gronniosaw to New York City where he learns "to wait at a table, and tea & clean knives," and he learns English too. Gronniosaw admits, "but the servants used to curse & swear surprisingly; which I learnt faster than any thing, 'twas almost the first English I could speak." He swears often. He calls upon God to damn anyone who angers him. He tells the story of a maid who uses a freshly cleaned knife (Gronniosaw has just cleaned it) to cut bread. "I was very angry with her," Gronniosaw reminisces, "and called upon God to damn her." He calls on a god who can damn but who has no meaning for him. When Gronniosaw's cursing troubles another one of the household's older servants, he learns from Old Ned that "there was a wicked man, call'd the Devil, that liv'd in hell, and would take all that said these words and out them in the fire and burn them."[53] Old Ned introduces to Gronniosaw a way of seeing a world where not only do gods damn, but devils burn sinners alive.

When Mrs. Vanhorn learns of his cursing and his mention of the devil, she is upset by Gronniosaw's choice of words. She shares his language choices with a family friend, a Dutch Reformed minister whom Gronniosaw refers to as Mr. Freelandhouse. Mr. Freelandhouse (or Theodorus Frelinghuysen) is a popular local minister and a close friend of Rev. George Whitefield. Freelandhouse takes Gronniosaw in—after offering Mrs. Vanhorn £50 for his purchase—and, before doing anything else with the young man, he teaches Gronniosaw how to pray. Gronniosaw says, "He took me home with him, and made me kneel down, and put my hands together, and prayed for me, and every night and morning he did the same."[54] Gronniosaw asks Freelandhouse what these prayers mean, and Freelandhouse helps him "understand that he pray'd to God, who liv'd in Heaven." Freelandhouse explains that God is Gronniosaw's father and "*best* friend." Even though Gronniosaw tries to tell Freelandhouse that his father lives in West Africa, Freelandhouse—with tears running down his face—tells Gronniosaw "that God was a great and good Spirit, that he created all the world, and every person thing in it, *Ethiopia, Africa*, and *America*, and everywhere."[55]

Gronniosaw responds with delight. Freelandhouse confirms what he's always known—that there is a singular God who made the world. He describes his reaction to this knowledge: "But though I was somewhat enlightened by this information of my master's, yet I had no other knowledge of God than that he was a good Spirit, and created every body, and every thing . . . I was only glad that I had been told there was a God, because I had always thought so." He celebrates the truth of a singular God. He is obliged to go to school where he is taught to read and better hear God's Word. He hears it first when his schoolmaster, Vanosdore, reads from the Bible: "My schoolmaster was a good man, his name was *Vanosdore*, and very indulgent to me.—I was in this state when, one Sunday, I heard my master preach from these words out of the *Revelation*, chap. i. v. 7. '*Behold, He cometh in the clouds and every eye shall see him and they that pierc'd Him*.' These words affected me excessively; I was in great agonies because I thought my master directed them to me only."[56]

Vanosdore has chosen his text from the apocalyptic and final book of the Bible, Revelation 1:7, "Behold, he cometh with clouds; and every eye shall see him, and they also which pierced him: and all kindreds of the earth shall wail because of him. Even so, Amen." It anticipates "He" who is coming with the clouds to be seen by everyone. Gronniosaw doesn't cite the entire verse. He leaves out "and all kindreds of the earth shall wail because of him. Even so, Amen."[57] Vanosdore reads an expectant prayer that looks forward to the second coming of Jesus Christ. It warns of the reality of Christ's return to humanity to judge those believers and nonbelievers.

Rather suddenly, Gronniosaw senses God's judgment upon him, and he feels the Word directly as Vanosdore speaks. The Word has now pierced him and entered his body. Even though the "Him" that is "pierc'd" is God, it seems that Gronniosaw makes himself this "Him." An anonymous "they" has pierced Gronniosaw. Unlike God, though, this "they" is not a formerly unbelieving populace but rather God's Word. The Word finds the inside that

Gronniosaw has never had to consider or explore before. The Word gets in him, and it pains him: "I was in great agonies because I thought my master directed them to me only." It's as if the Holy Spirit has taken hold of the young man and what he hears is not the truth of the passage—namely, that God will return to judge those on Earth. What Gronniosaw hears instead is that he is to be seen and pierced because "I fancied, that he observed me with unusual earnestness."[58]

The Word isolates him—"I was farther confirm'd in this belief as I look round the church, and could see no one person beside myself in such grief and distress as I."[59] No one else seems to care. He is forced to wrestle with the Word and its meaning alone. Gronniosaw reads the force of the Word as an attack or a violation on his person. As such, this violation invokes a particular type of bodily "grief" and "distress." He cannot reconcile the intrusion of the Word into any part of his body. He feels compelled to think of his home in West Africa. He wants to return to what was because he's afraid that this Christian God is angry with him. He wants to avoid this godly wrath, but he can't.

Because he does not know Christ and fears that Christ cannot save his soul, he feels his "own corrupt nature" and his heart's misery. For this reason, he is unhappy: "I found myself so wicked and miserable that I could not come [to Christ]—this consideration threw me into agonies that cannot be described; in so much that I even attempted to put an end to my life." His grief grows, and he begins to wish for death. He has left his bed, distressed by the state of his soul. He remains a sinner who imagines that he cannot be saved. He has refused to return to his bed because he is overwhelmed by this sense of discomfort. God has displaced his self and allowed him to look upon his own body. Even though he cannot escape or deny the reality of its force upon who he is, Gronniosaw attempts to find relief by sleeping "in the stable upon straw."[60]

It is in this "place" that Gronniosaw begins to "feel all the horrors of a troubled conscience, so hard to be born, and s[ees] all the vengeance of God ready to overtake [him]."[61] The idea of place no longer refers to his location in the stable but rather to his body—the site of his affective response to his circumstances. His body allegorizes his spiritual distress, which names a space wherein night overtakes day and the darkness of ignorance displaces the light of salvation. Gronniosaw is no longer himself, and his expressions of agony admit to the fact that he must grieve over its loss as an outsider looking in. As he acknowledges this distress, Gronniosaw registers the possibility that the Word of God would transform him. Gronniosaw can only walk away with the knowledge that the Word has revised him, and it has made him uncomfortable.

God's word doesn't leave Gronniosaw alone. It confronts Gronniosaw again on another day. He hears Vanosdore preach from Hebrews 7:14: "Follow peace with all men, and holiness, without which no man shall see the Lord." The Word makes him tremble. He remembers God's judgment against the whole world. This judgment burdens him and makes him feel "excessively perplexed." He doesn't know what to do with his burdensome thoughts. The Word is in him, and it leaves him without a way to speak about what's happening within him. He "continued in a most unhappy state for many days."[62] When he does speak about his discomfort to his "mistress," she recommends reading Baxter's *Call to the Unconverted* (1658) and selected works of John Bunyan. Reading Baxter or Bunyan doesn't quash his distress but in fact increases his sense of burden. His books can't save him.

Reading Baxter and Bunyan can't help Gronniosaw understand his affective experience. He can't make sense of his distress, and instead, he contemplates his death and suicide. When he feels called to end his life—"in the midst of my distress"—he hears, "*Behold the Lamb of God.*" He hears the words of John 1:29, who, upon seeing Jesus walk toward him, says, "Behold the Lamb of God." It is Jesus who has come to save the people. He acknowledges the divinity of Christ who as the Savior has come as the "Word made flesh" to "dwell" among the people. Gronniosaw gleans John's words and their meaning because he's realized, "I was sensible that there was no way for me to be saved unless I came to *Christ*, and I could not come to Him: I thought that it was impossible He should receive such a sinner as me." He seems to understand that God is working within him, and God will deliver him out of this grief. He has learned for whom he should desire—God. Despite his fear, he knows that he must move toward God. Gronniosaw, uncertain and distressed, takes a seat under a tree to contemplate his fate. He offers his lamentations to the tree as if he is speaking to a friend. He begins to read Baxter and finds himself able to pray to God—"my heart lifted up to GOD, and I was enabled to pray continually; and blessed for ever be his holy name, he faithfully answered my prayers."[63]

While seated under this tree, Gronniosaw has the opportunity to take delight not only in his ability to pray—"I was able to pray continually"—but also in the possibility of God's ability to provide for him. Gronniosaw is freed from his burdens and declares, "I can never be thankful enough to Almighty GOD for the many comfortable opportunities I experienced there." Finally, Gronniosaw experiences conversion's power most fully. Because God answers his prayers, he achieves the ultimacy that allows him to find delight. He sheds the grief and distress of the disembodied sinner. As the faithful follower, Gronniosaw says, "I was so drawn out of myself, and so fill'd and awed by the presence of God, that I saw (or thought I saw) light inexpressible dart down from heaven upon me, and shone around me for the space of a minute."[64]

Gronniosaw soon experiences that which he describes as "a most delightful frame of mind" wherein he says, "my heart so overflowed with love and gratitude to the author of all my comforts." He has been reborn in Christ. Gronniosaw's conversion offers him the language of pleasure, and he uses this language to assure himself that he has freedom in Christ. Because his sins are forgiven, he can rejoice and enjoy living. His freedom in Christ anticipates his freedom from the political condition of enslavement. Freelandhouse, on his deathbed, frees Gronniosaw. What Gronniosaw learns—as required by the conversion narrative as a religious and literary form—is that he is freed into the troubles and discomforts of the world. This world inevitably teaches Gronniosaw to trust God. He reads his discomfort in this way: "The more I saw the beauty and glory of God, the more I was humbled under the sense of my own vileness."[65] He learns that discomfort and providence work together, just like death and living. He must come up against pain in order to experience the beauty of godly providence. This pain is useful because it compels him to pray and to maintain his intimacy with God.

Gronniosaw's faith only gains strength. He keeps living with the certainty of godly favor. He travels abroad after his master, Freelandhouse, and Mrs. Vanhorn die. He is impressed into the British navy and survives wartime battles. He finds his way to England, where he starts his life yet again. He marries and has a family. And, he ends his life's story with a mention of his present situation: "As Pilgrims, and very poor Pilgrims, we are traveling through many difficulties towards our Heavenly Home, and waiting patiently for his gracious call, when the Lord shall deliver us out of the evils of this present world and bring us to the Everlasting Glories of the World to come. To Him Be Praise for Ever and Ever, Amen." He's hit hard times again. He's lost a daughter to fever. No church will bury her except for Quakers, who refused to read the "burial service" over her.[66] He's moved his family to Kidderminster, a town that he hopes will provide him employment opportunities. Neither he nor his wife has any remaining money. Their only hope is his story and, of course, the power of God. There is no resolution for the reader. But I suspect the reader needs no resolution because of the certainty of Gronniosaw's faith. He knows that his God will provide because God always has. It's this certainty that informs Gronniosaw's life story. It is the story of a man—in particular, an African prince and a formerly enslaved man—who reimagines Christian stories in order to recognize not only his human fallibility but also the sorts of living that lead him toward the development of his faith-based intimacy. Despite the discomfort that seems to frame this season in Gronniosaw's life, Gronniosaw still waits patiently. He still can send along praise to his God and pray for grace and salvation. Gronniosaw knows to rejoice despite this difficulty. He knows to whom he worships and prays, and he feels good about his faithfulness. For Gronniosaw, his faith is both useful and pleasing. It carries him through tough times and into the possibility of a better future.

* * *

James Albert Ukawsaw Gronniosaw dies on 5 October 1775 in Chester, England, just a few years after the publication of his narrative.[67] He is eulogized in the *London Evening Post*: "Died, This Thursday se'nnight, at Chester, aged 70, James Albert Ukawsaw Gronniosaw, an African Prince of Zaara."[68] He leaves behind his wife and their five children. All of whom—including Mary, Edward, Samuel and James Jr.—are baptized at the Old Independent Meeting House in Kidderminster.[69] Gronniosaw's faith is part of a legacy. It locates him among an emerging community of writers and authors with a story to tell about their spiritual transformation and the goodness of God. It's a writerly community that will include Olaudah Equiano, Venture Smith, Chloe Spear, and John Marrant. A decade and a half after Gronniosaw's narrative, itinerant minister John Marrant follows Gronniosaw's lead. With the help of the Countess of Huntingdon, he publishes his *Narrative of the Lord's Wonderful Dealings with John Marrant, A Black* (1785). He, too, uses the conversion narrative form to celebrate his faith and his call to ministry.

Born free in New York, about forty years after Gronniosaw's birth in Bornu, John Marrant finds his way—after a revolutionary war, and a series of trials and tribulations—to the Countess of Huntingdon whose patronage ensures that he is ordained as a Methodist minister in her church at Bath, England. His *Narrative* is, in fact, according to literary historian Cedrick May, an ordination sermon that advances his call to ministry.[70] Marrant's faith carries him through the literal and figurative wilderness and into the certainty of godly salvation. His trials remind him of the joys of being saved repeatedly. His published ordination sermon publicizes the goodness of a Christian God in this life. Not only does his life story animate God's Word his sermons, but also his journal provides evidence of Marrant's commitment to his faith. Marrant's published and extant writing is prolific, and it has a story to tell about what matters most to Marrant—namely, religious faith and meaning making.

It's noteworthy that Marrant has opportunities that are not afforded to Gronniosaw. Marrant is born free in New York and never travels the Middle Passage. He learns to read and write at a young age—as a free boy—in East Florida and continues his schooling in Georgia. What they share is their allegiance to God and their belief in this God's liberatory power that does not depend upon the political whims of the nation-state. It's a lesson in how much they matter to God, and it's a mutual feeling. Because God matters to them too.

CHAPTER 3

Desiring John Marrant

John Marrant is preparing to leave England for Nova Scotia when he publishes his decidedly popular and decidedly Christian story of spiritual transformation, *A Narrative of the Lord's Wonderful Dealings with John Marrant, A Black,* in the summer of 1785.[1] The itinerant Methodist minister uses his *Narrative* and its popularity to guarantee his position as a preacher with a mission, as literary historian Cedrick May explains, to proselytize and found "a model Christian society."[2] "I saw my call," Marrant remembers, "to the ministry fuller and clearer; had a feeling concern for the salvation of my countrymen."[3] His sense of mission leads him to his ordination in England where uses the tools of his faith—testimony, preaching, praying, reading the Bible—to speak and write the story of his spiritual journey from a sinful boy to a faithful believer and powerful preacher among his countrymen in South Carolina, Nova Scotia, and in Boston.

His *Narrative* is, in fact, an adaptation of his ordination sermon at the Countess of Huntingdon's (Selina Hastings's) church in Bath, England. As he tells his story to a church audience, he narrates his life in a way that has him seemingly live the work of making a Christian self and founding a community of believers. He writes himself into the Bible's many Old and New Testament stories, particularly those of Apostle Paul and Jesus. As a captive in the wilderness, he gestures toward the tempting of Jesus. He becomes the prodigal son, resurrected, who returns to his family as a new man. He models what it means to be chosen by God and to live guided by a sense of a predestined salvation. For Marrant and for his audience, it's a profoundly Calvinistic way of being.

To prove just how chosen he is by God to be saved, Marrant opens his storied and evangelical sermon with his birth. Marrant is born free in colonial New York on 15 June 1755. His father dies when he's about four years old. Before Marrant turns five, his mother takes the family south to St. Augustine, Florida, the capital of Spain's East Florida colony, and eventually they travel to South Carolina's low country. Marrant leads his readers and his listeners not only to his salvation as a teenager in Charleston, South Carolina. He also lives the joy of his call to minister in England, Nova Scotia, and Boston. This is a praise-filled story that takes seriously just what he means when he says, "I was full of the Spirit of God, and felt a willingness to tell the world the love of God in Christ."[4] Marrant is often filled with the Holy Spirit. And he pursues a love of his Christian God and his life's work realizes just how much he enjoys God's love in return.

Marrant organizes his story within the familiar conversion narrative form. What he intends, as he says, is to "write a useful story," "encourage the fearful," "confirm the wavering," and, lastly, to "refresh the hearts of true believers."[5] Marrant tells the story of spiritual conversion. He explains how he is inwardly changed by his Christian faith, and his resulting conversion narrative—with its transitions between birth and sin, conversion and rebirth, and redemptive transformation—is meant to demonstrate just how much God can and does matter to the believer. Because he orates a story with these aims in mind, he remembers and fashions a self that lives, as does his Savior, to save those who don't have faith and to affirm the faith of those who already believe. Before Marrant can bring salvation to his imagined audience or reader, God has to find him first. God doesn't find Marrant immediately. Though Marrant is saved by God as a teenager in South Carolina, he must first journey with his mother and siblings from New York and East Florida to Georgia and onward to South Carolina.

Marrant doesn't say what prompts his mother's journey southward from New York to St. Augustine with her children amid an ongoing international conflict. He offers no explanation for his mother's desire to live in a locale with a sizable free or formerly enslaved communities—most notably, at the neighboring Gracia Real de Santa Teresa de Mose (hereafter, Mose).[6] He only tells his readers that the Spanish outpost is "about 700 miles" from New York.[7] But it seems noteworthy that Marrant's mother expatriates to a coastal community of formerly enslaved or free Black persons that has various sociopolitical protections—against England's pursuit of fugitive slaves—from the Spanish colonial government.[8] At St. Augustine and just two miles away, at Mose, Marrant's mother can provide her family with a particular kind of sanctuary from English assertions of colonial power and its imperial interests in slavery and the recapture of fugitive slaves. He goes to school in St. Augustine where he learns to read. But in what language—English, Spanish, French, or any particular West African or Native American variety—is not made clear.[9] Their time in St. Augustine is short-lived. The family leaves around the time of the end of the Seven Years' War (1756–63)—an ongoing and international conflict between European empires and in particular, Britain and Spain—just as Spain loses its Florida territory to Britain.

Though many people and families head south to Cuba at the war's end, Marrant's mother moves the family to Georgia, where Marrant continues his schooling until he's about eleven years old. Marrant doesn't identify the area or say much about his time in the English colony, but he does find it worthwhile to mention to his audience that "the Lord spoke to me in my early days, by these removes, if I could have understood him, and said, 'Here we have no continuing city.'"[10] Marrant recites the first part of Hebrews 13:14. He aligns himself with the epistle's author, who seems to laud the outcasted living of early Christians—namely, those who refuse to comply with the Levitical traditions of Judaism. Marrant's family, like those early Christians, seems cast out of New York, East Florida, and eventually Georgia. In search of a secure place to live, Marrant's family heads to the area around Charleston in South Carolina, where they stay until the start of the Revolutionary War. The family splits apart when his older sister and her husband opt to live in Charleston, while his mother and younger siblings live miles outside of town.

It's odd that Marrant doesn't give Hebrews 13:14 in its entirety. He leaves out its anticipatory clause—"but we seek one to come"—even though his is a story of seeking after a god who consistently comes for him. Despite what he doesn't say, Marrant, as the preacher, looks back and understands that his cast-out life is expectant and is in pursuit of God. Marrant goes to live with his sister in Charleston. His story takes off there, where his salvation is ahead of him. God is certain to come for the young and sin-filled Marrant. He experiences his Christian conversion as he hears the famed Rev. George Whitefield preach at a Charleston meetinghouse. Once he experiences fully Christ in him, Marrant feels compelled to live in Christ and to spread the Gospel's good news.

Marrant finds his way to minister to various communities: among the Cherokee, then to the enslaved on plantations seventy miles outside of Charleston, the formerly enslaved Loyalists in Nova Scotia, and later to churches and community groups in Boston and Britain. With every providential move, Marrant realizes the union that exists between himself and godly providence. Marrant learns that his religious faith serves him as a disciplinary practice and as an "orientation"—to borrow from religious historian Charles H. Long—"in the ultimate sense, that is how one comes to terms with the ultimate significance of one's place in the world."[11] He masters God's Word and in so doing, enacts a religious power that allows him to live out his faith as a kind of messianic figure or a type for Christ. Marrant strives not only for an intimacy with Christ but also to embody his Savior. Because Marrant mimes the life of Christ and is pleased to do his Savior's will, pleasure is a necessary consequence of his belief in God.

Marrant enjoys his faith and his relationship to God. He lives a life that expects joy on earth, and of course strives for the pleasures of an eternal life and fellowship with God. Marrant explains it in "A Funeral Sermon" (1789): "We are not to let drop the interest of Christ, though its defence requires the greatest application of the mind, the severest self-denial, and the most evident danger, of parting with dear friends, or feeling the resentment of cruel enemies, such as Christ has redeemed, by the price of his blood, and the power of his graces."[12] Because he refuses to "let drop the interest of Christ," Marrant lives the advantages that come from his unwavering belief. These advantages—to know God and to have eternal life as Paul writes of it to the church at Philippi—is the reason for Marrant's praise. His praises to God declare the good news of his faithfulness. It prompts his continued joy, and it expects the sorts of providential blessings that remind him of his worthiness.

This chapter, then, pursues Marrant's good feelings and his pleasures as he narrates this Christian life story. I mean for "pleasure" or "good feeling" to invoke various forms of enjoyment, happiness, and peace that Marrant uses to name his experience of creative faith in the midst of war, migration, and uncertainty. Because he is saved and a true believer, Marrant knows he is worthy of godly affection and salvation. He is pleased every time he meets God in prayer or worship. There is pleasure in his faith, and God's faith, in return, pleases him. It's the pleasure of knowing with certainty that God is faithful and consistent.

There's a pleasure in what Rev. George Whitefield—the minister who brings conversion to a young Marrant—refers to as the "indwelling of the spirit." Whitefield explains that, as Christians, "we must confess, that all who believe in *Jesus Christ*, through the Word of Ministration of the Apostles, are to be joined to *Jesus Christ*, by being made Partakers of the Holy Spirit." For the Christian believer, Whitefield argues that to have the "Spirit of *God*" is to feel it within. It is a way to experience more fully the entirety of the Trinity—the Father, the Son and the Holy Spirit—because, as Whitefield suggests, "For no one can say, that Jesus is my Lord, but he that has thus received the Holy Ghost."[13] What Marrant knows for sure is that the Holy

Ghost or the spirit of God dwells in him too. Not long after his conversion experience, there's a time while walking and living in the forest that Marrant feels so much, he writes, "nearness to God I then enjoyed, that I willingly resigned myself into his hands."[14]

It's in the act of desiring that Marrant experiences the affective pleasures of his faith. He feels joy—as a boy, a teenager, and as a grown man—when God provides him with whatever he needs: food, traveling mercies, or an escape from death. Marrant's pleasures, his enjoyment, and his satisfaction have much to teach us about the very possibility of those good feelings that happen to him in spite of his everyday trials or even his occasional physical discomfort, pain, and living.

As a true believer, the Bible serves Marrant—in the way theologian James Cone describes of the Word—as "a poetic happening, an evocation of an indescribable reality."[15] For Marrant, the Word is real, and it is creative and literary. It is useful. Because he makes its language and its stories his own, Marrant's stories of travel, salvation, and rejection don't simply admit to the facts of his life. He takes up these Bible stories as a way into his own life story. Marrant borrows often from the Bible, as James Albert Ukawsaw Gronniosaw does in his *Narrative*, and its stories—just see the biblical books of Revelation, Acts, Matthew, and John—gather meaning for his life. Marrant borrows and bends (with a nod to poet Kevin Young's definition of "story") this biblical language in order to lay claim to his Christian knowledge and to his life's story. Marrant is certain that his walk to and with God will call "strangers" to Christ. He has particular "strangers" in mind: "that Indian tribes may stretch out their hands to God" and "that the Black nations may be made white in the blood of the Lamb."[16] His biblical knowledge authorizes him to admonish the unconverted (or those who don't know the Bible) with stories of how God pleases him and is pleased by him.

Marrant invites his readers to hear in his stories the kinds of cast-out living that remembers Jesus in the wilderness and on the cross, Paul in prison with Silas, and the Lamb of the apocalyptic book, Revelation, among others.[17] Marrant takes on the stories of Jesus, Paul, and the Old Testament because their stories are (or should be) familiar to his imagined reader. Marrant's biblical revisionism serves these ends: it demonstrates his textual authority to read and to speak the Word of God to those who don't believe. His love of God's Word evidences the pleasing nature of his faith. Marrant has learned his Bible. He is a faithful and a model believer who can and does confess properly the Word of God. Marrant knows for sure that his story can do a saving work in the life of his readers. Marrant claims his authority as a Bible reader and as a believer. Christ is his Savior, and Marrant's salvation is proof of his worth and his prophetic and predestined power. Marrant, in this way, figures himself as the messianic hero, a modern Jesus whose word offers salvation to various unbelievers.[18]

In the years just after Britain's loss to the Americans, Marrant's ordination sermon (and later, published narrative) sketches a story that troubles truth telling and pursues narrative, discipline, and the pleasures of its art with a decidedly religious vocabulary. Marrant has little concern for the facts of his life because he wants to "get at a larger freedom—and truth"—in Christ.[19] Even though William Aldridge, pastor of the Jewry Street Church, in his prefatory remarks to the *Narrative*, assures readers Marrant's recollections are "facts, and facts like these strike, are felt, and go home to the heart," Marrant pursues this Christian desire for true intimacy with God and its resulting pleasures, and they serve this end.[20] In pursuit of this intimacy, he crafts a story in which he is the model man, much like his Savior, Jesus Christ.[21] He is not only the model believer but also the model reader. Marrant is literary scholar Hortense Spillers's kind of "reader." Marrant is the sort of reader who, as Spillers explains, "then, in participatory readership, is *given* a history at the same time that she or he seeks to fabricate one."[22]

As the possessor of a particular religious literacy, Marrant gives himself a biblical history that makes him the subject and purveyor of God's Word. Because Marrant believes so well, he is worthy of God's love. He is worthy of his call to preach, to live, and to be saved. Because he is worthy, he knows how to desire God and how to read God's Word properly.

Marrant makes his position as a reader most evident in his call to ministry and his revision of an event that also happens in James Albert Ukawsaw Gronniosaw's *Narrative*. Henry Louis Gates Jr. famously refers to this event as the "talking book." This refers to a scene in which a hopeful, albeit illiterate reader tries to hear a book speak, and the book refuses (see chapter 2). While aboard a ship, a young Gronniosaw tries to speak to a book. He is a hopeful reader, but in spite of his hopes, the book won't speak to him. Even though it's not clear if Marrant knows of Gronniosaw's story (at different times, both men work within and worship among the Calvinist ministry of the Countess of Huntingdon), Marrant recalls an event similar to that of Gronniosaw's "talking book."

It happens when a teenaged Marrant finds his way through the wilderness to a Cherokee village, not too far from his Charleston home. As Marrant remembers, the book refuses to speak too. In Marrant's version, he carries a Bible with him to meet the village "king." "King" is Marrant's moniker for this anonymous leader. At the request of the Cherokee king, Marrant reads from his Bible. That he can read God's Word is noteworthy because this

Cherokee man cannot read it. Marrant's reading matters to him because he has a story to tell about religious conversion and salvation, and it must matter to his audience. When Marrant reads, the king's daughter intervenes. She takes the book and tries to read it. But, she cannot make it talk back to her. She is not the book's reader because she is not yet a Christian. Because Marrant is the reader, the Native American woman carries the burden of illiteracy; this is not a book that she can read. As the literate and prepared Christian believer and subject of this conversion narrative, Marrant's ability to make sense of the book proves that he is a good Christian. It proves too that his salvation will help to save the young woman's Cherokee community. It won't be long before Marrant and his Bible bring Christianity and, with the help of the Native American king and his daughter, redemption to this community.

A French Horn, Rev. George Whitefield, and a Conversion Experience

It's likely 1769 or 1770 when Marrant begins his journey to Christ at a sizeable meetinghouse in Charleston. He is a teenager, working as a musician. He has learned to play the violin and the French horn. He finds himself most often playing for Charleston's wealthiest denizens. It's important to the story that at this point, even though Marrant has steady employment, he has no god. He is not yet a Christian. Marrant admits that his music playing "opened to me a large door of vanity and vice, for I was invited to all the balls and assemblies that were held in the town, and met with the general applause of the inhabitants." He is successful and is able to make a living as a musician. Because of his success, he does whatever he feels like doing, to include "fishing and hunting on the Sabbath day," playing music and disobeying God, and dealing in "pleasure and iniquity like water."[23] Marrant marks—what he understands to be—his sinful behavior in order to juxtapose his secular desires as he anticipates his pending conversion and Christian desiring for God. He has given in to his wanton and childish desires because he doesn't know who God is and he lives in the sin of his ignorance. It's in this misguided way that he finds himself at a revival with his French horn, ready to interrupt the proceedings with his bit of noise.

On this day, Marrant is on his way to play music "for some Gentlemen," and he happens to pass by a boisterous and crowded meetinghouse. He stops in front of it, and he asks his companion what's going on. When his companion explains "that a crazy man was hallooing there," Marrant gets curious.[24] He wants to know who's caused the ruckus. Even though his friend tries to stop Marrant from going in, he can't and instead offers to go in with Marrant. There's a catch, though. The unnamed friend will only go in with Marrant if the young musician would blow his French horn. Marrant agrees to make noise with his horn in the midst of the crowded meetinghouse.

Marrant's plans are foiled. He's walked into a church service, and celebrated minister George Whitefield is preaching. Marrant walks with his horn in hand as the minister reads his text from the Old Testament book of Amos. Whitefield is reading from the fourth chapter where in the prophet Amos foresees the Lord's vengeance upon the people of Israel. Because the people haven't taken God's various corrections seriously, Amos sees that God will meet Israel and make the "morning darkness."[25] Before the teenager can blow his horn, Whitefield directs his attention to Marrant—with a pointed finger—as he reads Amos 4:12: "Prepare to meet thy God, O Israel." Marrant is struck by Whitefield's words, and he falls to the ground.

What follows is familiar to the biblically literate reader. Marrant bends the Apostle Paul's conversion to fit his own call to God. Marrant remembers, "the Lord accompanied the word with such power." For the youthful horn player, it's not Israel that has met God or even Saul on the road to Damascus. It is he and his French horn who have met God. Whitefield's directive has him "lay both speechless and senseless near half an hour." Marrant can't speak or move his body. Marrant hears every word as though it "was like a parcel of swords thrust in to me, and what added to my distress, I thought I saw the devil on every side of me."[26] He doesn't explain how he is returned home. He can't eat or drink, and neither can Saul, who "was three days without sight, and neither did eat nor drink" in Acts 9:9. Marrant's family brings doctors to visit him, and their medicines don't heal him either. He is despondent until Whitefield joins him and prays over his stricken form.

When Whitefield asks Marrant how he feels, Marrant insists that he is not improving. After this series of prayers that don't seem to heal Marrant, the minister tells him, "you are worth a thousand dead men." Whitefield calls out Marrant's worth as a child of God. It is only after Marrant learns that he is worth a "thousand dead men" that Marrant says, "the Lord was pleased to set my soul at perfect liberty and being filled with joy I began to praise the Lord immediately; my sorrows were turned into peace, and joy, and love.[27]

When Marrant experiences his conversion fully, he transforms his despondency into an experience of joy. He reads the Bible often. Even as his sisters ridicule his newly found faith, he grows stronger in his belief. For Marrant, it seems conversion is—as Joanna Brooks explains the process— "about change: the sovereign intervention of God, the abolition of the natural man, the overturning of sin, the regeneration of the soul, the establishment of a godly society."[28] With every passing day, Marrant seems to take pleasure in knowing and feeling that he has changed. He is worthy of God and that God is real. What begins as a Word-inspired wounding and unspeakable despair turns into those good feelings that legitimate Marrant's faith and his sense of purpose.

For Marrant, his purpose is in his story. After conversion, he has a new story to tell, and like most conversion narrative authors, he has a story worth telling. Marrant's sense of purpose sends him into the forests outside of Charleston. He leaves his family because he can no longer live with their faithlessness. His conversion prompts, as Yolanda Pierce explains of a spiritual experience, "the abandonment of one set of beliefs (or lack of a formalized belief system) and the adoption of a new set of beliefs."[29] Marrant's change of heart calls him to abandon his family and his community in order to desire and turn toward God. What he gains from this loss leads him to the forms of Christian desire that compel his life's work as a minister and as a child of God. He gives up his sinful habits—playing the French horn and violin and all manner of "vanity and vice"—in order to adopt his new Christian life.[30] And he takes nothing with him, except his commitment to what Rev. Whitefield refers to as the "marks of the new birth." According to Whitefield's sermon, "The Marks of the New Birth" (1740), five "scripture marks" identify the true believer: praying and supplicating, not committing sin, conquering worldly temptations, loving one another, and loving one's enemies.[31] Marrant peppers his narrative with all of these signs of his belief. He makes certain that he prays, commits no sin, conquers temptations, and loves his friends and his foes while wandering various types of wilderness—as a prisoner among the Cherokee, as a soldier in the British navy, or an itinerant minister in Nova Scotia. As a true believer, Marrant possesses the requisite inward life of a follower of Christ.

According to Whitefield, the true believer feels inwardly the "indwelling of the spirit" at the site of this interiority (Marrant and Whitefield call it "heart" too) wherein lives those "feelings, fantasy, desire, and affect (. . . define[d] as the emotional weather system that is the expressive outside of one's imagined emotional states)."[32] For Marrant, this interiority performs a decidedly religious end—to affirm a relationship to God that is grounded in an affective propriety. As Marrant journeys farther away from his family and deeper into the forest, he treks into his inner life, which requires him to pray and supplicate more. With every prayer and supplication, Marrant hopes to satisfy his spiritual hunger. He commits less sin as he devotes his life to Christ. Marrant models the interiority that allows him to read God within his heart and confess the biblical Word to the masses. It's the interiority that is necessary to cultivate and inspire the religious, writing communities wherein he preaches. This interiority is the site of indwelling Spirit that makes for the requisite self-mastery, necessary to create the openness that allows the Word to enter into one's heart. The true believer must cultivate this inner life and ground his or her faith in an affective propriety or those right ways of feeling that gesture toward the legibility of faith and God's Word. As he travels through the wilderness and further away from his family, Marrant shows his reader just how committed he is to his walk with God with every one of his prayers for godly mercy. In spite of the possibility of his own physical death, he refuses his former sins and in so doing conquers his worldliness. He loves both his enemies and his friends even as they mock his belief. Only eating and drinking what food he can forage and praying often to his newfound God, he strikes out on his own religious errand.

Alone in the wilderness, Marrant describes his delight in God's continued protection and deliverance from wild beasts and unforeseen dangers. He recalls "descending from my usual lodging, a tree, and having nothing all this time to eat and but little water to drink, I was so feeble that I tumbled half way down the tree."[33] Marrant hungers and thirsts often while alone in the forest. Surely, he seeks food, but his choice of sensations—hunger and thirst—announces his lack and his desire to take in or consume what can satisfy him. Marrant desires food and drink because he cannot find either by himself. He also hints at the means by which God can and will satiate him.[34]

Marrant seems to live out Jesus's declaration: "I am the bread of life; he who comes to Me will not hunger, he who believes in me will never thirst."[35] Marrant's desire occasions the certainty of his faith; because of his desire, Marrant confesses to his humanity and its bodily weakness. His only recourse to his bodily frailty is prayer and belief: "there I prayed with my body leaning upon [a tree] about an hour, that the Lord would take me to himself. Such nearness to God I then enjoyed, that I willingly resigned myself into his hands."[36] This weak and worldly body cannot satisfy his literal and religious hunger. Marrant's reprieve is the anticipation and the certainty of a godly intervention.

Despite the bodily angst that Marrant faces as he searches for nourishment, he cannot help but describe the pleasure he receives as he discovers a "puddle of very muddy water, which some wild pigs had just left." Marrant explains further: "I kneeled down, and asked the Lord to bless it to me, so I drank both mud and water mixed together, and being satisfied I returned the Lord thanks, and went on my way rejoicing." Though his body acts as the larger site through which he understands this satisfaction, Marrant's interest does not only represent his body but also what's inside: his feelings and ways of being, such as "rejoicing." Even in the midst of uncertainty—namely, where he will live or how he will eat—Marrant has learned to live in the certainty of God's faithfulness. God spares his life as he passes two bears safely, Marrant "return[s] God thanks for [his] escape" and then "rose from my knees and walked on, singing hymns of praise to God."[37] Marrant is not simply alone in the wilderness, but rather he is realizing his right relationship with God.

With every prayer, every rejection of worldliness, Marrant grows in his ability to minister into the lives of those who do not believe. He has learned in this wilderness just who Christ is; he can and will introduce nonbelievers to his Savior and to the power of the Holy Spirit. Marrant seizes the opportunity to demonstrate his knowing. He is helped by a fellow traveler, to whom he refers as "Indian hunter." He remembers, "As I was going on, and musing upon the goodness of the Lord, an Indian hunter, who stood at some distance, saw me."[38] The hunter abruptly stops him. Even though Marrant doesn't recognize the man, the man recognizes Marrant and knows Marrant's family too. The unnamed hunter asks Marrant where he is heading. He threatens to take Marrant home. It's not clear whether the hunter's threat is meant to suggest that he might return Marrant to his mother or take him to where he might be sold into slavery.

Marrant offers this response to the hunter, "where the Lord was pleased to guide me." Marrant's curious response prompts the hunter to question him further. He asks to whom Marrant was speaking. And when Marrant tells him that he "was talking to my Lord Jesus," the hunter "seemed surprised, and asked . . . where he [Jesus] was? for he did not see him there." Marrant can't specify his Savior's location, but he does say "he [Jesus] could not be seen with bodily eyes."[39]

What follows Marrant's mention of Jesus again invites the hunter to ask those questions that led Marrant to respond with "Jesus" as his final answer. The hunter wants to know who provides for Marrant, protects him from wild beasts, and ensures that he is fed. Marrant has only one answer, Jesus Christ. When their conversation ends, Marrant doesn't make clear that he has converted the hunter. But, the hunter does introduce Marrant to his call to ministry. Marrant learns how his story can move (and save) someone else. The hunter is Marrant's first audience. He chooses to follow Marrant and share in this journey. The hunter is proof that God has not left Marrant alone in the forests of South Carolina. Together, Marrant and his hunter-friend travel the woods, hunting and collecting deerskins. Marrant teaches his companion about Jesus Christ as he learns his friend's language.

He remembers his time fondly even as he expects a forthcoming ordeal. "This together, with the sweet communion I enjoyed with God," Marrant remembers, "I have since considered as a preparation for the great trial I was soon after to pass through."[40]

"She Kissed It Again": Some Kisses, a Silent Book, and a Call to Ministry

Marrant's foraging through the wilderness with his hunter-companion sets the stage for the climax of his narrative or the "talking book" scene. The "talking book" famously names a story about a book that refuses to speak to someone who wants to read it. Henry Louis Gates Jr.'s talking book is a common "trope" or event that appears in various stories, including transatlantic narratives by John Jea, James Albert Ukawsaw Gronniosaw, Olaudah Equiano, and Ottobah Cugoano. According to Gates's reading of this event, Gronniosaw is the "first" among these men to write or speak of it. Because there is a "first," every author, after Gronniosaw, then, is understood to revise the scene. What Gates might argue "begins" with Gronniosaw's *Narrative* is reinvented in Marrant's 1785 narrative. In this act of intertextuality, Marrant places himself in a roving, religious, "writing community."[41] I use "writing community" because, as Katherine Clay Bassard argues, it suggests revision, renegotiation, and "a potentiality; an unfolding to be attended" by way of a shared collective experience.[42]

Despite the similarities, Marrant doesn't tell quite the same story. Whereas Gronniosaw is enslaved when the book refuses him, Marrant is free and already literate. Marrant already knows how to hear from the book and read it. For Marrant, it's a Cherokee woman who hopes to start a conversation. Both Marrant and Gronniosaw iterate a great sense of longing and invention, creativity, and possibility; both are stories about desiring. This scene is supposed to inspire a greater desire to create a shared affective experience with God's Word and a hopeful reader. When the book doesn't speak back, it initiates a new desire for the requisite intimacy with God that he or she observes between the book, the reader, and God. The hopeful reader who can't make the book speak sets the stage for the conversion experience that will bring this reader to God for the first time. It engenders in them a desire for the Word, as a spoken prayer or as a material object, to affect the reader in a deep and bodily way.

In Marrant's version of the not-so-talking book event, he understands fully what it means to desire God properly. Whereas Gronniosaw positions himself as a passive agent for the Gospel, Marrant leads his story as a teacher, maker, and purveyor of knowledge. Because he is his story's most knowledgeable character, Marrant is desired and desirable. The Word belongs to Marrant, and it's his message to carry and its stories are his to share. What Marrant borrows from Gronniosaw (and even more from the Bible)—his choice of the conversion narrative's form and the talking book—suggests an intertextual intimacy and a sense of shared belonging. It is a site of self-making and conversation across time and geography that privileges storytelling, expressivity, and right ways of feeling. Both men choose to profess their faith publicly and in so doing publicize the ways in which God dwells in them. Their belonging is made of the text's materiality. The book—as Bible, prayer book, or conversion narrative—matters to them. This materiality and its resulting intertextuality advance their faith and offers to them the intimacy of a collective desiring.[43] What these men share is how to feel rightly about God and how to talk about this right way of feeling.

What may be a revision of Gronniosaw's talking-book event is also a version of St. John's discussion of a worthy reader in the Bible's final book. In Revelation 5, St. John writes of a book that only those worthy enough can open and read. The worthy are called forth, yet "no man was found worthy to open and to read the book, neither to look thereon."[44] The saint weeps when he realizes that none are worthy, but it is a slain Lamb who can read from the book. And so it happens that the resurrected Lamb reads. St. John's teary account begins with the question: "Who is worthy to open the book, and to loose the seals thereof?"[45] It thus brings together the idea of literacy (the ability to read and write) with the seemingly unrelated idea of self-worth. Yet, the response, "No man was worthy," reveals the extent to which literacy is not simply the ability to read the alphabet and write letters. It is the ability to possess the worth necessary to understand the Word of God. That the Lamb is resurrected ("stood the Lamb as though it had been slain")[46] gestures not only toward the resurrection of Christ, but also the means by which the new birth occurs. The Spirit must enter into the heart of the true believer. Endowed with the Spirit ("the seven Spirits of God"), the Lamb "took the book out of the right hand of him who sat upon the Throne" and opened the seals.[47] The angels celebrate by "saying with a loud voice, 'Worthy is the Lamb that was slain to receive power, and riches, and wisdom, and strength, and honor, and glory, and blessing.'"[48] Worthy is the Lamb who feels right enough to die for humanity and the believer who reads and lives the Word of God.

Marrant proves—by way of the talking-book story—that he is worthy of God's love after he is imprisoned in a Cherokee town. He and his hunter-companion find themselves at the gate of the town and even though Marrant can speak Cherokee and means no harm to the residents, he is not welcomed. He is questioned and, when his answers are not sufficient, he is sent to prison and eventually, he is to be executed. After a prayerful night in prison that borrows from the experiences of Paul and Silas in Acts 16, Marrant is brought to the king.[49] Marrant's appointed executioner is recently converted to Christianity by the young man's demonstration of faith and prayer. Because the executioner has found God, he wants the young man to show the king who his god is. The king doesn't know Christianity and questions Marrant. He also—like the executioner, the watchmen, and the hunter—wants to understand who this Jesus Christ is. The king searches the room for him, and as Marrant remembers, he "said he did not see him [God]."[50] Instead, there is only Marrant and the name "Jesus." Only Marrant can claim the knowledge of God though. Because Marrant, with the Bible in his hand, is the bearer of the Word and Christian faith, only he can answer the king's questions. He knows for sure what the king can't fathom. God is not a thing or a person to see, but instead God is a presence to be felt inside. Because he is converted now, the executioner feels God. Even though he tries to explain the feeling to the king, the king still doesn't feel anything.

As the king looks around for Marrant's God, his eldest daughter comes into the room. She interrupts the scene. Marrant gives her an age, but he does not provide her name. She is nineteen years old. As the king's daughter, the reader understands her power (or lack thereof) among these men and the younger Marrant. When she enters the room, she claims a space right next to Marrant, at his right side. She has stopped the conversation, and without saying a word, she takes Marrant's Bible. Marrant recalls: "I had a Bible in my hand, which [the king's eldest daughter] took out of it, and having opened it, she kissed it, and seemed much delighted with it."[51] Marrant—as the author of his story and the Christian in this scene—determines where the king's daughter goes and what she wants. She seems to know that Marrant's book has inspired this debate. She opens the Bible as if to receive and to feel it just as Marrant does. And it's as if she wants his book to resolve the dispute between her father, the executioner, and Marrant, and maybe even to answer those questions she won't ever ask (in the story as Marrant tells it).

When the opening of the book does not immediately reproduce the feeling in her, Marrant has her kiss the book. She doesn't simply touch the book, like Gronniosaw does in his *Narrative*, with her ear.[52] She, instead, offers a kiss that she hopes will receive an acknowledgment. When she offers this kiss, she lends to Marrant's story a greeting that mimes Paul's salutary kisses in his epistles to the Corinthians, the Romans, and the Thessalonians.[53] Marrant needs her—by way of this action—to admit to her longing to attend to a literate, Christian young man and for the possibility of a Christian conversion. Marrant's use of the king's daughter, as the site of this longing, disrupts the desiring that sends Gronniosaw to the book to hear it speak. What was once a young man's longing for the attention of a book-learned master is now the action of a desiring nineteen-year-old woman.

Because this is Marrant's story, what the Native American princess desires most is him. He makes sure that she needs him. He doesn't make her able to discern the difference in God's Word or his flesh. She cannot experience the difference between Marrant and the text because she cannot read or interpret their materiality—namely, a human body and a printed book. She can't discern right ways of feeling or sensation because she is not a Christian believer and because she is Cherokee. It seems, as Joanna Brooks argues, that "indeed, within the space of worship, their very bodies became texts, manifesting the overturning and reviving powers of God."[54] Marrant makes his body into the sort of text that she desires (to speak to and to hear). Both can presumably satisfy her desire as a site of Word and flesh because she can't read the difference between the Word and flesh. It's his body—as book and flesh—that the princess yearns to kiss. When Marrant speaks of her "delight" at his book, he names her delight at him and his book, both of which (hopefully) possess the ability to requite her desire to speak to and to feel with another.

Marrant creates, in this woman, a desire for literacy because he wants her to imitate his desire for God. He needs her to desire a response or an affective experience that might reciprocate her unspoken desire. Her misdirected desire confesses her "capacity for sensation" that lacks a proper subjectivity and interiority at the expense of godly sensibilities, such as those of Marrant.[55] Because Marrant has her desiring after the wrong body (as book or flesh), he can and does mark her inadequacy as a reader and her faithlessness.[56] When she cannot reach for Marrant, as the prisoner or her potential lover, she reaches for him in the Bible.

Marrant doesn't question her humanity. Instead, he identifies her growing need for a godly salvation. Marrant must prepare her for an inevitable conversion and, in anticipation of this future saving grace, the princess must try to feel what he names, though she does not know what she is feeling exactly. She cannot yet know or feel Marrant's God. Marrant makes her wait eagerly for an answer. Briefly, she is willing to delight in the waiting. What he does, then, with the princess's delight not only articulates a hope for conversational intimacy that her delight seems to suggest but also gestures toward and anticipates his revision of Old and New Testament scriptures to tell this story. Marrant uses her attraction to him to anticipate her failure.

What the king's eldest daughter doesn't know yet is that she will fail. Marrant's story needs her to fail. Her failure begins with her desire for the book. Her kiss invites the same kinds of intimacy that Gronniosaw seeks. Her kiss is the only means by which she can start a conversation with the young man who can stand up to her father. When she returns the book, the king asks Marrant what it is. The princess's desire for it prompts her father to wonder about it and to ask Marrant to read from it. Not only does Marrant read from it because he can, his reading evidences his power to hear and read the Word. There is no white man to mediate the interaction between the book and the hopeful reader. Instead, there's only Marrant. His literacy validates his true belief.

That Marrant can read is evidence of his Christian aim—to bring God to those who do not know him—and to publicize his faithfulness. For this reason, he speaks often of reading God's Word even before he finds himself in front of the Cherokee king. He admits to his ability to read early in his story. Marrant remembers, learning to read in St. Augustine, Florida, "here I was sent to school to learn to read and spell." He confesses to the power to read God's Word. It saves his life, and Marrant says, "young in Christian experience, I was tempted so far as to threaten my life; but reading my Bible one day, and finding that if I did destroy myself I could not come where God was." When he leaves him for the South Carolina wilderness, he explains, I "went on all this day, taking my Bible out of my pocket, I read and walked for some time."[57] Marrant gives his readers a historiography of his reading practice to confirm his textual authority even while he stands as the king's prisoner, awaiting an almost certain execution.

Marrant specifies that he is book learned in order to articulate a self-awareness that situates him within specific American cultural and literary traditions—those of the captivity and conversion narratives, Methodism, and the religious errand—that merge to form a Christian self.[58] That is to say, Marrant writes of a narrative self that is neither single-mindedly African or Black nor, as literary scholar Rafia Zafar argues, is it specifically "the agent of a white, Protestant, colonizing power and the colonial subject adapting and mimicking the sign of the colonizer."[59] These are the tools of Christian faith that will save and have already saved Marrant. It's easy to read Marrant simply as a kind of mockingbird of Anglo-American hierarchy or patriarchy and certainly for the white man's Christianity. Marrant isn't just a harbinger of a white man's faith. He means to act as a preaching savior because Jesus Christ belongs to him. He is a believer. His belief and faith in God realizes how his communities—both Christian and free men—are outside of the simplified binaries of free or enslaved and white or Black. He can only legitimate his Christian self and his self-authorized, empowered position as subject and object through the conversion of those without the religious knowledge he possesses—namely, the Cherokee or later, a child named Mary, and his enslaved students on Jenkins Plantation in South Carolina.

Marrant seemingly espouses a religious literacy that names a way to make meaning and purpose out of the biblical Word and out of his life's experience. This literacy speaks to a true believer's ability to read, understand, and hear the Word properly and therefore create a meaningful interpretation of the text. This manner of reading does not describe the transaction between eyes and letters that then produces a translation of words, phrases, and sentences into understanding. Rather, religious literacy names an affective practice that comes only to those who can feel the Word of God—namely, those who as Whitefield preaches, "might be united to him [God] by his Holy Spirit, by as real, vital, and mystical an Union as there is between *Jesus Christ* and the Father." The true believer can properly see and hear the Word, as Whitefield makes clear when he begs the question—"But unless Men have Eyes which see not, and Ears which hear not, how can they read the latter Part of the Text, and not confess the Holy Spirit, in another Sense, which is the common Privilege of all Believers, even to the End of the World?"[60] The true believer, with seeing eyes and hearing ears, possesses the requisite scriptural marks of the "new birth," the regeneration of the self through salvation.

Marrant testifies to the truth of this Word when his various Native American interlocutors ask him to whom he prays and speaks. Marrant responds at one point, "he [God] could not be seen with bodily eyes." Marrant's eyes, unlike those of the Cherokee, belong to a believer so marked by his faith. For Marrant, the Word of God is not only legible. It feels good. This right feeling realizes the discursive exchange between a believer and God by way of an ability to feel the Holy Spirit inwardly.

When Marrant reads from his Bible for the king, he chooses wisely. He takes his reading from Isaiah 53 and Matthew 26. Throughout his narrative, Marrant doesn't always cite his biblical references. But in this instance, Marrant cites his biblical text, and he reads from it. His choice cues his reader to yet another coming of Christ. He speaks from the book of Old Testament prophet Isaiah and from Matthew, one of Jesus's twelve apostles, as a sermon—an opportunity for his hermeneutical interpretation of the scripture. In Isaiah 53, the prophet predicts the coming of the "Suffering Servant" who will be "brought as a lamb to the slaughter, and as a sheep before her shearers is dumb, so he openeth not his mouth."[61]

Marrant transitions seamlessly from Isaiah to the Gospel of Matthew. The Suffering Servant of Isaiah 53 anticipates Jesus Christ, who is the messianic

Suffering Servant. He will suffer and die for the sins of all, and he will rise on the third day. Marrant reads of this suffering in chapter 26, where Matthew, in a lengthy seventy-five verses, describes Christ's betrayal by Judas and his promise to resurrect from the dead. Matthew 26 begins, "And it came to pass, when Jesus had finished all these sayings, Ye know that after two days is the feast of Passover, and the Son of Man is betrayed to be crucified."[62] Marrant reads of his Savior's forthcoming suffering because it looks like his own. He is to be killed and betrayed (unjustly) also.

Marrant's reading—think of it as a sort of sermon—"offer[s]," as Spillers suggests of sermons, "an equipment not only for literacy, but a ground for hermeneutical play in which the subject gains competence in the interpretation and manipulation of systems and signs and their grounds for interrelatedness."[63] His reading choices not only speak to his competency at seeing and hearing the Word because this narrative is actually an ordination sermon. He must demonstrate his competency to his readers. He is the masterful reader of the text who is made into a version of a savior for the Cherokee people. It's actually Marrant who "hath borne our griefs, and carried our sorrows . . . was wounded for our transgressions, he was bruised for our iniquities."[64] He is imprisoned and mistreated. His life takes on the life of Jesus. It's Marrant who must bear the burdens of our shared iniquity and has suffered in the wilderness just as Jesus does. Marrant lives—the prophet tells us—as the suffering servant, "brought as a lamb to the slaughter."[65] Just as Judas betrays Jesus with a kiss that identifies him, Marrant is kissed too.[66] He, as Jesus-like character, is the worthy sacrificial lamb as well as the oppressed, afflicted, suffering Servant. Even though this Cherokee audience may not understand fully what he means to do, Marrant's imagined reader—as a literate Christian—understands that he is there, in this village, to save the Cherokee.

After Marrant finishes reading from Isaiah 53 and Matthew 26, the king questions him again. He wants to know why Marrant spoke Jesus's name with "so much reverence." Marrant explains, "because the Being to who those names belonged made heaven and earth and I and he."[67] The king refuses to believe Marrant. He refuses to believe Marrant's God is real. As Marrant debates the king, he lures the king's daughter into action. Her desire is so compelling. She seems able to see Marrant as "a bearer of the Book and Speaker of the written Word" and so endowed with a text-inspired charisma.[68] In Marrant's story, she reaches for the book again. "She took the book out of my hand a second time," Marrant says, "she opened it, and kissed it again."[69]

With her second kiss, she restates her desire for reciprocity—a return to conversation—and an intimacy with Marrant. When the Bible does not respond or return her kiss, Marrant remembers that she speaks "with much sorrow, the book would not speak to her."[70] She speaks for the first time and says out loud what Marrant already knows. The book will not speak to her. She admits to her lack of salvation. She is not worthy yet to read from or hear the book. She is left desiring that which she cannot access. If only Marrant would speak to her as he does to the Word. She longs for the Word to enter her as it does Marrant. Not only does the book refuse her, but Marrant does too. Marrant and his book refuse her because her desiring for Marrant misunderstands the religious feeling that she hears when Marrant speaks the Word. What is actually religious literacy or the marks of a proper Christian faith looks to the princess like the conversation, the touch, or the intimacy that she desires. Reading suggests the promise of companionship. The book speaks to Marrant because he can read it correctly.

The Cherokee woman's kiss no longer acts as a greeting or an entry into a hopeful dialogue but rather serves, like that of Judas, as the marker of an imminent betrayal. Her kiss betrays her ignorance, and it also tells us who Marrant is. By way of her kiss, she learns the book cannot satisfy her desire to have a conversation because she has not yet learned to believe. But the princess is not yet worthy to read or feel God's Word, much like St. John in Revelation 5. And according to Marrant's account, she hasn't been saved by his Christian god.

The Cherokee woman does not know the scriptural marks of conversion that are required of the faithful. She does not have the properly seeing eyes or hearing ears that, so enthused by the Holy Spirit, can read the Word of God. By Marrant's account, she only has the story that he gives her. And hers is a story of an unrequited kiss and a series of misses: a misunderstanding, a *mis*seeing, or a *mis*hearing. Marrant uses the king's eldest daughter, and what she misses—the Word, the book, and its meaning—to invoke Revelation 5. Marrant places her in his story at his right hand and in so doing summons Revelation 5:7: "And he [the Lamb] came, and took the book out of the right hand of him that sat upon the Throne." In both instances, the language of the "right hand" is meant to cite the Son of Man who sits on "the right hand of the power of God."[71]

As Marrant's "right hand" woman, she momentarily stands in for the resurrected Lamb, chosen to read the book. Marrant has her accept this role in order to build an intimacy with Marrant whose power and will to live inspires her take the Bible out of his hands. Marrant gives her this role precisely because she will fail. Her failure signals her lack of faith and her inability to receive the Word properly.[72] The Bible—Marrant's taciturn book—refuses to speak to those who can't hear its word rightly. The princess will not read from the book, as her positioning suggests because she has not risen. She is not saved, and the Bible's silence betrays her lack of salvation. Marrant is saved. The Bible does speak for Marrant. He can hear its words and delight in it and in his experience with God. Marrant can read the text because he is literate in its words and in the inward experience of God's Word. He can read the Word because he knows God, and she does not. Marrant is the Lamb and, therefore, he is worthy. The book talks to him because he reads it and is moved by its Word.

The princess's failure informs Marrant's pleasure—namely, his right relationship with a Christian God and his position as Savior and purveyor of the gospel. What marks his pleasure is the princess's sorrow. When she can't make the book talk, Marrant has her admit to her failure. The sorrow of the princess gives way to a genuflecting Marrant and executioner. Together, they fall to their knees in prayer and worship. The princess's sorrow weakens her body, just as sorrow and fear weakened the body of the young Marrant upon his conversion. Marrant professes to his God's power to create the sun, moon, stars, and His greater glory. While he lifts his praises, the king threatens him again with death. He is returned to his prison cell where he, again, finds God and celebrates the pleasures of his faithfulness: "Though I was weak in body, I was strong in spirit."[73] As Marrant strengthens in spirit, the king's daughter weakens.

Marrant doesn't have to name what ails her, because he already knows that her mysterious sickness is brought on by her inability to read the Word. She is sick with sin, and her sickness frightens the king. The king realizes that he needs Marrant to fix his daughter. He needs Marrant's prayers and that name, "Jesus," to whom Marrant prays to save his daughter's life. Marrant complies with his request to save her. When Marrant, just as George Whitefield does years before, prays over the body of this sinner, he calls on the Holy Spirit—the indwelling spirit—and entreats the Lord to enter into her and restore her body. And the Lord complies. Marrant writes: "the Lord appeared most lovely and glorious; the king himself was awakened and the others set at liberty. A great change took place among the people; the king's house became God's house; the soldiers were ordered away, and the poor condemned prisoner had perfect liberty, and was treated like a prince."[74] Marrant saves the king's daughter. He doesn't just cure her of her unnamed illness. He lifts the burden of her sin. He gives her the gift of salvation. Her salvation makes possible the transformation of her entire community.

Because he saves the princess as well as reads and confesses the text, Marrant has saved this Cherokee community and introduced Christian faith to these nonbelievers. As such, he serves them as a kind of pastor. He is made a leader among them and "assumed the habit of the country, and was dressed much like the king, and nothing was too good for me [Marrant]. . . . Here I learnt to speak their tongue in the highest stile."[75] Dressed "in the highest stile," Marrant begins to proselytize. He journeys across Native American communities and carries the Word with him. Endowed with right ways of seeing and hearing, Marrant takes on a biblical history and is transformed into a preacher whose ability to minister inspires conversion in this Cherokee community and elsewhere.

This scene and its nineteen-year-old Native American woman are instructive. Even though the princess commands the attention of the reader for less than a paragraph, her unrequited gesture hopes for Marrant's story. Marrant needs her to do for him what he can't do for himself. He needs her to long for his textual authority. It's this longing that Marrant uses to compel her to reach for him. What she reaches for—his faith, his body, his book, and toward his desires—has something to tell Marrant's reader about reading, desire, and self-making. Because of her misinformed hope, readers are supposed to pursue God and to learn what's important: God speaks to those who can hear and see his Word properly and to know God is to experience his Word inwardly. The faithful should feel God deep down and know the pleasures of a profound faith.

Books refuse to speak because they aren't supposed to say anything to just anyone. The book chooses its discussant, and Marrant chooses his book, the Bible. The joke is on those of us who want either the truth or for the book to talk back. We've made the mistake of the Cherokee woman and hankered after the wrong thing. The king's daughter teaches readers how and what they should desire. Marrant calls the reader to God. God is the desired object, and this lesson is learned by way of the princess's failure. And she fails because she goes after the material object, Marrant's book, and misses how the Word moves within and as part of Marrant's body. Marrant gets it right.

And what follows this scene is proof of a life that lives the pleasures of faith, itinerancy, and ministering to those who for whom the book won't talk. Marrant takes what he has learned and leaves the Cherokee village. He heads back to Charleston, armed with biblical knowledge and the success of his proselytizing. He returns with a sense of purpose as a "self-possessed agent of God, whose perseverance and accomplishments rival those of John Smith and Daniel Boone."[76] Despite his successes with the Cherokee, Marrant's return home lacks the celebration of a proper homecoming and, in fact, those who once knew him don't even recognize him. His mother doesn't know who he is. Because she believes he's dead, she can't fathom this man to be her son. He's older now and dressed in the manner of the Cherokee who have cared for him. Not only does his mother deny him, so do his brother and one of his sisters. Marrant remembers they even go so far as to "contriv[e] to get me out of the house, which being overheard by me, I resolved not to stir." But his youngest sister, despite his adornments and his adult face, does know him. Marrant explains that she, "eleven years of age, came in from school, with a book under her arm. I was then sitting in the parlour, and as she passed by the parlour door, she peep'd in and seeing a strange person there, she recollected me."[77]

The youngster tries to explain to the adults that her brother has returned. No one believes her. Her older sister "called her a foolish girl, and threatened to beat her." The child insists despite their doubts, and they respond to her insistence with a charge: "If it be your brother, go and kiss him, and ask him how he does."[78] And with a kiss, she identifies him as her brother. She can see what her mother and siblings cannot in manner that seemingly revises Acts 12. In Acts 12, King Herod imprisons Apostle Peter, a disciple of Jesus. King Herod aims to persecute the followers of Christ, and Peter is next on his list. While in prison, the church prays for him, and an angel rescues him. Peter heads first to the house of Mary to praise God for his successful escape, but no one can recognize him. A servant named Rhoda does, "and when she knew Peter's voice, she opened not the gate for gladness, but ran in and told how Peter stood before the gate. And they said unto her, Thou art mad."[79] No one believes her despite her insistence. Marrant's sister, unlike Rhoda, finds a way to get her family to believe her and with her kiss Marrant writes, "I was then made known to all the family, to my friends, and acquaintances, who received me, and were glad and rejoiced."[80] His sister's kiss, much like that of the Cherokee woman, marks Marrant. It admits to a desire that Marrant has placed upon his sister. In Marrant's story, she too hankers for the intimacy that she seems to have lost while her big brother lived in the forests. But her kiss won't mark her failure.

Marrant doesn't question his youngest sister's literacy or faithfulness. He distinguishes her from the Cherokee woman with his passing mention of her return from school and the book under her arm. Her book has no name, but it suggests the literacy that the princess cannot have. She can speak to and hear Marrant in a shared language. Hers is a holy kiss, like the kisses Apostle Paul recommends in his letters to the Corinthians, the Romans, and the Thessalonians. It is a salute, a greeting that makes clear the siblings' relation to each other. Because of its salutary function, she can pursue his affection with the certainty of their shared intimacy. Marrant responds to her affectionate question, "Are not you my brother John?" with recognition: "I answered yes, and wept." Marrant needs his sister to recognize him so that "the dead was brought to life again; thus the lost was found."[81] So it seems her desire is to remember her lost brother, to know him, and feel with him.

With her kiss, she returns her dead brother to life. He is resurrected, or, at the very least, recognizable to his family. He is yet again made anew or, as 2 Corinthians says, "therefore if any man *be* in Christ, *he is* a new creature: old things are passed away: behold, all things are become new."[82] His sister's kiss carries with it a desire to mark her brother's various conversions: to adulthood, to Christianity, and to an "Indian stiled" preacher, or to a new man in Christ. Marrant is found again. Her kiss finds him, and it marks him as chosen. He is chosen to live, to be raised (in the way of Jesus), and to talk about it. He is the chosen brother who is returned from the dead yet again. Because death is not cumbersome for Marrant.

Desiring Home, Desiring Sierra Leone

John Marrant's story keeps on, and he never stops preaching or hearing from God. He continues to bring salvation to communities wherever he travels in South Carolina, on the high seas, and elsewhere. As he tells his story, he returns again and again to those times when he saves people with God's word. He proves his call to ministry and to Christ repeatedly. Take as example what happens when he joins his brother at the Jenkins family plantation on the Combahee River in South Carolina. Both Marrant and his brother work as carpenters there. Despite his daily work obligations, Marrant starts up a Bible study for enslaved children, women, and men. It's not his intention to minister. But after the plantation's children find him singing Isaac Watts's hymns and reading scripture to himself, they get curious about this free carpenter. He is joined by the children first, and he promises to teach them the Lord's Prayer and the catechism. Later, his students bring their parents, and even more adults join him. His classes grow in size to about thirty students.

About three or four months later, Marrant's classes are discovered by the plantation's owners. He remembers how Jenkins—at the behest of Mrs. Jenkins—and a team of others violently disrupt one of their prayer meetings. Jenkins and others gather up Marrant's students and beat them. Marrant takes care to tell the story of the attack and the resulting threat on his life. Jenkins doesn't kill or beat Marrant. He's too scared to kill a free man, as Marrant explains it. Jenkins does offer Marrant an explanation for his violence: "[Jenkins] told me afterwards that I had spoiled all his Negroes." Marrant is, of course, not satisfied with this explanation, and he questions Jenkins's thinking by asking "him whether he did not think they had Souls to be saved?" When Jenkins concedes that his slaves have souls, Marrant asks a follow-up question that Jenkins can't answer. He asks him, "whether he thought they were in the way to save their Souls whilst they were ignorant of that God who made and preserved them." He asks Mrs. Jenkins the same questions, and it seems she can't answer them either. Marrant quickly realizes that he can't keep working for the Jenkins family. It's as if he's learned that he can't be where the God's Word has no place. He leaves his students with an encouragement "to call upon God as well as they could."[83]

Marrant announces the start of the colonial war with a brief mention of "those troublesome times." Marrant doesn't offer much other detail about what would quickly escalate into the Revolutionary War except that he is, "pressed on board the *Scorpion* sloop of war, as their musician."[84] That he names the *Scorpion* is noteworthy. The *Scorpion* is a part of the flotilla of South Carolina's royal governor, William Campbell. Just before and after Lord Dunmore's proclamation (1775), the sloop of war harbors a number of fugitive slaves and free persons who are willing to claim loyalty and fight for the British. Marrant joins the loyalist ranks and serves the crown for nearly seven years. He fights for England during the Revolutionary War, the fourth Anglo-Dutch War, and at various conflicts in the West Indies. He's there for the battle at Sullivan's Island (1776) and the Anglo-Dutch War's Battle of Dogger Bank in the North Sea (1781).

While in the military, he loses his "spiritual vivacity, life and vigour." It seems he keeps worshipping because of his doubts and disbelief and not despite them. While his journey seems rife with discomforts, he often delights in godly providence. At one point, he sees his "old royal benefactor and convert, the king of the Cherokee" and the king's daughter. Marrant learns that the king and his daughter are happy in their faith and "glad to see" him. He is later at sea and Marrant celebrates how he is saved, after being thrown overboard, despite the ocean's hungry sharks and violent waves. Instead of dying at sea, "he who heard Jonah's prayer," he writes, "did not shut out mine, for I was thrown aboard again; these were the means the Lord used to revive me, and I began to set out afresh." Marrant serves in the North Sea battle at Dogger Bank (1781) against the Dutch. Marrant thinks back on the brutality of the clash that leaves six men dead and three wounded: "my head and face were covered with the blood and brains of the slain." Marrant survives even with his wounds and "was happy during the whole of it."[85]

He travels on a warship to the West Indies and later, journeys to England, where he is discharged—at the request of a doctor—from his military service. Marrant goes to London to work for a "respectable and pious" merchant, and there he feels further called to ministerial service. Marrant reaches out to his brother, and his brother confirms for Marrant that there is in fact a need for good ministers. Marrant learns how to pray and exhort better at Monday evening services and is eventually ordained at the Countess of Huntingdon's church at Bath. His ordination leads Marrant to Halifax, Nova Scotia, where he is tasked with ministering his brand of Calvinism—with its emphases on predestination—to the recently arrived and mostly Wesleyan Methodist, loyalist communities along the coast at Birchtown, Shelburne, Cape Negro, and Barrington.

Marrant journals his ministerial efforts and notes his chosen scriptures and his travels throughout the countryside. He publishes his *Journal* in 1790 in London, just five years after the publication of his *Narrative*. He chooses to have his journal printed in order to dispute and to "give a strict and honest account" to those—in the Countess of Huntingdon's network of patronage—who suggest that he has mishandled the countess's monies in Nova Scotia.[86] He itemizes his expenses and his travel around Nova Scotia, and at every location, he preaches and worships together with the people. He prays for godly provision continually because the landscape doesn't lend itself to farming or easy living. Despite England's promises of land and joys, there isn't adequate, arable land or employment. Marrant's prayers matter more than ever, but his stay in Nova Scotia is short-lived. Not only is he confronted by an ever-present interdenominational conflict (Wesley Methodists versus Huntingdonian Methodists), racial tensions, and a growing interest in an emigration movement to Sierra Leone's newest settlement, Marrant runs out of money and falls ill. He leaves for Boston in January 1789.[87] In Boston, he meets Samuel Beans, who brings him together with Prince Hall, founder of a local and thriving African-based freemasonry organization. Marrant serves as chaplain to Prince Hall's Freemasons and then returns to England, with a mind to carry on his work and to go onward to the settlement at Freetown in Sierra Leone.

But Marrant never makes it to Sierra Leone. On 15 April 1791, he dies in a London suburb.[88] He's almost thirty-six years old and prolific. Marrant has published a narrative, a journal, and two sermons, all of which are extant. Marrant lives by Apostle Paul's promise that to live is Christ and to die is gain. Even though Marrant doesn't see the earthly Zion at Sierra Leone—which the British government promises to those formerly enslaved, Loyalists communities, looking for respite away from Nova Scotia's racism—Marrant gains his due in death. What he gains in eternal life he anticipates in his every action, from his sinful wandering to his ministerial efforts in Charleston, Nova Scotia, and Boston. Marrant lives and writes with his legacy in mind. He makes himself better in order to advance his decidedly Christian mission—namely, to proselytize the Word of God. His narrative, journal, and sermons are meant to bring the unconverted to Christ. At one time, the Word of God acts as a parcel of swords upon his body, but once converted, he is made a new man, a true believer in Christ. What he knows for sure as a believer and a preacher are the pleasures of faithful living. Marrant's pleasures don't deny his suffering or his discomforts. Rather, for Marrant, pleasure is what he gets when he loves God in spite of his circumstances. What begins, in part, with a failed prank or an unrequited kiss leads Marrant on a journey toward his godly love and a greater sense of his worth.

Marrant is never alone on this journey. He travels alongside those who aid him in his mission. They are his "countrymen," "brethren," or "kinsmen." They are also those who carry his words when he can no longer speak them. They print his story yet again in subsequent editions into the nineteenth century. Prince Hall remembers Marrant to an audience of fellow masons in his 1792 *Charge* when he says that "it is required that we should on these public days, and when we appear in form, give some reason as a foundation for our so doing, but as this has been already done, in a discourse delivered in substance by our late Reverend Brother *John Marrant*, and now in print." His passing reference to Marrant—as a fellow Mason and in print—establishes an emergent genealogy of men who are Christian and who know the duties of a Mason and the "first thing is, that he believes in one Supreme Being."[89] When Hall memorializes Marrant, he not only acknowledges a deceased brother but also affirms his brotherhood's tradition of faithfulness and affection.

For Hall and his brethren, Marrant leads by example, even in death, with his real-life words and as printed matter. Marrant lives on as part of this print culture and a particular Masonic writing community. His legacy is meant to help his Masonic brethren, his congregants, his friends and family, and his readership understand just how much they matter to God. It's meant too to teach them how to read and to feel God's Word better inwardly and in spite of life's privations.

His storied life and affective sensibilities offer a bit of context to a nineteenth-century pamphleteer and fellow Mason, David Walker. Walker doesn't and can't meet Marrant in person; Marrant dies a decade before Walker is born. But it seems he's met Marrant in print. Nearly forty years after Marrant's death, David Walker writes his *Walker's Appeal to the Colored Citizens of the World* (1829, 1830). His brief pamphlet implores his readers to understand why they matter and to whom they matter. He appeals for an affective literacy in order to parse those sites of ways of reading that admit to and compel the reader's interpretative sensibility and affective responsibility. His goal is simple—namely, to remember to his "coloured citizens of the world"—that they are not slaves, and their lives are worth their freedom. To convince his audience of its worth, he calls them into the very "heart" of the matter, into the inside stuff of feeling and the experience where the dance of imagination realizes the creative possibilities of living.[90] Because they must feel slavery is wrong in order to imagine a better and more joy-filled future. What matters has David Walker happy to think of an American nation where he and his imagined brethren—namely, the colored citizens of the world—belong and live as citizens.

CHAPTER 4

David Walker's Good News

David Walker is angry. And, to prove just how angry he is, in September 1829 he writes and publishes a pamphlet-sized appeal, *Walker's Appeal in Four Articles Together with a Preamble to the Colored Citizens of the World, But in Particular and Very Expressly to Those of the United States of America,* in Boston. In less than a hundred pages, the North Carolina–born and Boston-based clothier and antislavery activist explains his many reasons to be angry. Born free, near the end of the eighteenth century, Walker has journeyed throughout enough of the United States to learn just how evil slavery is. And, Walker explains, in his appeal's preamble and four articles (with a nod to the U.S. Constitution and the Declaration of Independence), how angry he is at slavery and its westward expansion.

He's raging about slavery's continued degradation of those women, men, and children who he calls "colored citizens" or his brethren. They are the enslaved or formerly enslaved "Coloured People of these United States" who must live without the protections of freedom or U.S. citizenship. As a consequence, they are, as Walker often reminds his readers in his preface and throughout his appeal, "the most wretched, degraded and abject set of beings that ever lived since the world began."[1] Walker is enraged not only by the condition of his brethren but also by the rising popularity of colonization schemes that intend to and do remove free and formerly enslaved men, women, and children to settlements in Liberia sponsored by the American Colonization Society with the promise of land, employment, and equality. He calls it the "colonizing trick" and, as Walker sees it, it's meant to deny his brethren's claims to personhood, U.S. lands, and citizenship.

Walker lays out his truth—that because of slavery, his brethren are "the most degraded, wretched, and abject set of beings"—in his four articles: on slavery, on ignorance, on preachers, and on colonization.[2] He endeavors in each to narrate a historiography of freedom, selfhood, and citizenry. He juxtaposes histories of enslavement against those of his antebellum era in order to prove his thesis and tells a story, across time and geography, of a people chosen by God to live in a chosen place.[3] Walker opposes slavery in order to appeal for freedom. He chastises ignorance to advocate for education. He damns so-called preachers in favor of a Christianity that treats his brethren well too. He argues against an increasing interest in West African colonization schemes (at the behest of the American Colonization Society and various state governments) because surely, the United States of America is, Walker writes, "as much ours as it is the whites, whether they will admit it now or not."[4] The United States is home.

Because Walker is so angry, he prints and distributes fourteen hundred copies of his *Walker's Appeal*, with the help of subscription agents, sailors, churches, and African Masonic Lodges throughout the United States.[5] And immediately his "incendiary" pamphlet is deemed too angry for those who fear that his "free" and "Black" rage will spark an insurrection or widespread defiance. But his anger works to encourage the appeal's sale and distribution, even as various state and local governments—for example, in Georgia, South Carolina, North Carolina, and Louisiana—struggle to prohibit the pamphlet's circulation and thereby the growth of its readership.[6] Between the end of 1829 and 1830, Walker publishes two more editions of his pamphlet, and in all three of his self-published editions he appeals, with ever greater feeling, for slavery's end. In each version, Walker invokes the form and language of the nation's founding fathers to foresee a nation wherein men and women eagerly delight in knowing their collective humanity and affective responsibility to another. It seems that—to borrow from literary critic Marcy Dinius—every "typographically radical" revision is a kind of prayer or invocation of this future even as it's meant to inspire more rage.[7]

This chapter acknowledges Walker's anger and its many uses as well as the pleasures that his anger engenders. It's easy to miss Walker's pursuits of happiness—namely, a world where his brethren are no longer enslaved—because his anger is so loud. That Walker is angry seems most obvious amid his appeal's grammatical choices and various modes of exclamation. He litters his appeal's preamble and four articles with italicized words, dramatic and lengthy footnotes, pointed index fingers (or manicules), and exclamation points. He sets the type in a way that allows readers to—as Dinius explains—"virtually hear his rising voice and anger in his text's italics, capitalized words, and multiple exclamation points."[8] When he can't use his words for emphasis, he uses punctuation and typography to say and emphasize the unspeakable. Take for example his use of exclamation points. Walker rarely uses just one exclamation point. Instead he uses several at a time. He doesn't just indent a paragraph but rather uses manicules to point out what's most important. Taken together, his words, punctuation, and typography allow him to yell from the page. It is clear that his noisy anger is well-intentioned and purposefully excessive. It is, in part, his affective remedy against the ills of enslavement.

Walker's demonstrative anger serves his activist and pedagogical ends. First, he intends to teach the kind of affective sense that his brethren, the "colored Citizens of the World, But in Particular and Very Expressly to Those of the United States of America," need in order to rid themselves of their enslaved or outcast, "wretched" condition. Second, he intends to rally a creative and collective activism—prayer, courage, truth telling, and if necessary, violence—among "colored citizens" who must demand a new and freer kind of American nationhood and citizenry. Third, he intends to point a finger, in a literal way, at those who have enslaved and degraded his community of readers.

Walker gathers his preamble's "we Coloured People of these United States," in their wretched condition because, if his brethren accept their wretchedness and can feel against their "wretched" condition, then they can be saved. Wretches do, in fact, get saved (think John Newton's "Amazing Grace" or Romans 7:24). "The God of the Ethiopeans," Walker writes, "as been pleased to hear our moans in consequence of oppression." Because if his readers accept the truth of their wretched living, they can and do feel what seems to lie at the heart of the matter—that "we are *men*, notwithstanding our *improminent noses* and *woolly heads*, and believe that we feel for our fathers, mothers, wives, and children, as well as the whites do for theirs."[9] When Walker's "we" accepts and is freed of their wretchedness, they can—as Christopher Apap observes—"rhetorically reshape" their nation.[10] Walker means to inspire—with his emphases on feeling—the dissolution of a slaveholding United States and its slave system. What he imagines thereafter is that his brethren, or the title's "coloured citizens of the world," might live as part of a free, unburdened citizenry with the right kinds of care and feeling for each other. Walker's brethren might better direct their anger toward slaveholding "tyrants." As a result, they can secure a new way of being citizens in this country.

Because Walker believes this way of feeling is the right response to slavery and its degrading effects, he wields his pamphlet and its anger as a kind of reading primer. Its lessons are meant to teach and to awaken a religious faith and a desire for freedom within his readers. It's a primer for, as he says most fully in his third and last edition (1830), "coloured men, women, and children of every nation, language and tongue under heaven" and, in particular, those "coloured men, women, and children . . . who are not too deceitful, abject, and servile to resist the cruelties and murders inflicted upon us by the white slave holders, our enemies by nature." He writes his appeal "in language so very simple, that the most ignorant, who can read at all, may easily understand."[11] With his easy reading in mind, Walker models a reading practice for an affective sort of literacy. It presupposes godly salvation and his brethren's moral superiority. It's a way of reading that promises a better future where freedom and happiness are guaranteed by God.

Walker's "Wretched" Citizenry

David Walker minces no words when he declares that "we, (colored people of these United States,) are the most degraded, wretched, and abject set of beings that ever lived since the world began."[12] And he knows he's right because he's traveled throughout the United States and has witnessed firsthand the experiences of this "we." He has lived in Wilmington, North Carolina. Later, he moves to Charleston, South Carolina (even though how or why he moves there is not clear) where he may have known Denmark Vesey or others who took part in the "African Society."[13] He eventually settles in Boston, where he sells used clothes and works as a subscription agent for the New York–based newspaper, *Freedom's Journal* (1827–29), published and edited by Samuel Cornish and, for a time, by John Russwurm. In Boston, Walker is a founding member of the Massachusetts General Coloured Association.

By 1829, Walker is a well-traveled, thirtysomething observer of this failed American experiment. He has, as he says, "taken the most accurate observations of things as they exist."[14] He has gathered the nation's news, as both a reader and a subscription agent, providing proof of this "we" and its collective wretched condition. He has the citations to show for it. He cites newspaper accounts, from near and far, of slavery's sleights and abuses with names, dates, and places. What he gathers proves who his "we Coloured People" are. "Wretched" is one of Walker's favorite descriptors for his imagined citizenry. For Walker, "wretched" is not just hyperbolic sentimentalism. To name the wretched is, for Walker, a first step toward a future without slavery. That his "we" are the most "wretched" signals their affective familiarity and their ability to understand his thesis as distinct from the so-called "white" American ideals of nation and citizenry. He juxtaposes their condition against the U.S. Constitution's "We the People."

Instead of a "more perfect union," Walker constitutes a different kind of community. His "we" is neither a perfect union nor the imagined "we" of James Madison and the founding's slaveholding politicians. He names this "we" and its collective wretchedness in order to create another sort of union. His use of "wretched" is an important and unifying descriptor. He uses it often and in every form. It is a reference to a particular biblical ailment. It is a condition of the fleshly body that is mentioned in the Apostle Paul's letter to the Romans as well as in the books of Numbers and Revelation.

The wretched are those who live in a bodily misery that resists or does not pursue God's grace. "O wretched man that I am! who shall deliver me from the body of this death?," writes Paul in his letter to the Romans.[15] Apostle Paul laments the weakness of sinning flesh and declares that the wretched man accepts the misery of the unsaved, fleshly body. The wretched, in Revelation 3:17, speak of what they have even when they have nothing of substance. St. John writes in Revelation to the church people of Laodicea, "Because thou [the Laodiceans] sayest, I am rich, and increased with goods, and have need of nothing; and knowest not that thou art wretched, and miserable, and poor, and blind, and naked."[16] The wretched boast without perspective, understanding, or quite simply, an ability to read what they see and hear because they lack the right kinds of seeing and hearing. The Laodiceans do not know they are wretched; they do not know that this wretchedness has left them steeped in a deep ambivalence without sight or clothing. In Revelation 3:18, St. John's letter offers a way out by way of a word from God: "I counsel thee to buy of me gold tried in the fire, that though mayest be rich; and white raiment, that thou mayest be clothed, and that the shame of thy nakedness do not appear; and anoint thine eyes with eye salve, that thou mayest see. As many as I love, I rebuke and chasten: be zealous therefore and repent." The wretched may suffer, but the certainty of God's love and a deep abiding faith in His love make possible an alternative life where wretchedness cannot dwell or linger. God delivers the wretched from their condemnation.

When Walker gathers this "we" and names their wretchedness, he speaks to what this "we" shares and must fight against. To be "wretched"—for Walker's brethren—is an experience that names the enslavement, disenfranchisement, and degradation that strips Walker's brethren of a collective sense of agency and personhood. It is, as literary scholar Phillip M. Richard explains, to live "a worldview that undermines Black humanity," and it is "the source of the breakdown of civic virtue."[17] What Walker knows for sure is that theirs isn't a unique condition. That they are wretched ties them to Apostle Paul and a human sort of physical condition that requires godly salvation. Walker invokes Paul's wretched condition as evidence of the fact that wretches are saved: "Whether you believe it or not, I tell you that God will dash tyrants, in combination with devils, into atoms, and will bring you out from your wretchedness and miseries under these Christian People!!!!!!"[18] In their salvation, they can reject the shame of this collective misery, and as literary critic Fred Moten explains, use their wretchedness as "a standing against a kind of subjectivity that [Walker] unsuccessfully embodies." Moten hears Walker's use of "wretched" as an identifier of community, a "formulation about us and the righteousness of being against them that can only have emerged from or in the condition of never having to be with us."[19] The wretched suffer together. The wretched can act out, feel, and do whatever is necessary to thwart their degradation and, in turn, imagine a better future.

There is value in this suffering, and it presumably helps people to realize unity. Because the "wretched" suffer together, Walker suggests they can feel together. They have a heart for one another. "I call upon you therefore to cast your eyes upon the wretchedness of your brethren," Walker appeals, "and to do your work utmost to enlighten them—*go to work and enlighten your brethren!*" What they see will "indeed rage to such an alarming pitch."[20] Walker uses suffering as an affective experience—at the site or sight of his particular truth—that helps the reader discern what it means to access the affective sensibility that comes from feeling rightly for another.

Walker has long understood unity's power. As a founding member of the Massachusetts General Coloured Association, Walker understands that unity builds nations, and he calls this "we" together in order to engender a collective potentiality, a possible creative activism that emerges when they feel for someone else. Because "we must and shall be free and enlightened," his activism creatively pursues a disruptive independence and national revision and guarantees—because God said so—access to a worthy citizenship in the United States of America.[21] Walker's "we" are citizens.

Walker insists that this "we" are citizens in spite of the privations of enslavement, perfunctory forms of freedom, or even what legislation might say. They are citizens because of their own insistence upon—as literary historian Derrick Spires notes—"the kind of political world in which they would not have to make such an argument."[22] As Spires further argues, theirs isn't a simple argument for inclusion. Rather, Walker's "we" seeks to dismantle America's whites-only, slaveholding citizenship. He wants to found a new United States of America where this "we" isn't removed—with the American

Colonization Society's help—to settlements in Liberia. He is certain this citizenry makes its home in the United States.

Walker does not support the American Colonization Society (ACS) or its mission, and he is, in fact, part of a larger community of naysayers, including Samuel Cornish and *Freedom's Journal* as well as Rev. Richard Allen. He discredits the ACS and its "colonizing trick"—to send freed and formerly enslaved men and women to Liberia—because its intentions are insincere. The organization's founders and leaders are not expressly abolitionists, but rather are, more often, slaveholders and racists who intend to keep the United States racially "white." What Walker refers to as the "colonizing trick" is, as he explains further, "not for the glory of God, but on the contrary the perpetuation of slavery in this country." Walker understands colonization schemes to be part of a racist plot, and he is in no way fooled by the ACS and its propaganda. Walker minces no words when he condemns those willing to join the ACS and leave the United States for Liberia: "those who are ignorant enough to go to Africa, the coloured people ought to be glad to have them go, for if they are ignorant enough to let the whites fool them off to Africa, they would be no small injury to us if they reside in this country."[23] Walker's "we" is not fooled by the tricks of the ACS.

Rather, Walker writes a constitution for a reimagined United States that refuses slavery and colonization. Walker's "we" are not "hard hearted, unmerciful, and unforgiving" in the way of those who make slaves of and degrade them.[24] Walker's citizens, as part of what Spires calls a "self-reflexive, dialectical process of becoming," share a common language of community or "nation talk" that Walker's appeal reinforces with its "putative national genealogy stretching back to ancient Egypt and a sense of destiny."[25] He believes in the possibility of a national community "with mutual duties and obligations among far-flung members, through his invocation of a shared religious model (even if it was a model to be transcended or broken) and the exhortation against a common enemy."[26]

Walker believes his imagined citizenry would know well his fellow Mason John Marrant's 1789 charge "to be kindly affectioned one to another, with brotherly love in honour preferring one another."[27] And citizens, in Walker's reading public, feel what it means to be free, to feel fully, and to experience feeling freely. Walker's citizens feel their humanity. For Walker, to be human with a heart that so loves God and his fellow man is to feel excessively for the plight of the enslaved. "Freedom is your natural right," Walker writes. "You are men, as well as they, and instead of returning thanks to them for your freedom, return it to the Holy Ghost, who is our rightful owner." No man, not even his *natural enemies*, can do what God can.[28]

Reading *Walker's Appeal*

Walker primes his readers for the affective sensibility that they need to read his words, to awaken to their plight, and to get angry enough to take inspired and revolutionary action against slaveholders and this country's government: "I appeal to Heaven for my motive in writing—who knows that my object is, if possible, to awaken in the breasts of my afflicted, degraded and slumbering brethren, a spirit of inquiry and investigation respecting our miseries and wretchedness in this Republican Land of Liberty!!!!!!" Walker prays for an affective awakening in his brethren. He prays for them to feel the wrongs of their enslavement because he is certain that this affective response has a transformative, even divine, power to alter their lives. Because he is certain of the *Appeal's* ability to awaken his readers to this inward transformation of the self, Walker expects that his audience "will try to procure a copy of this Appeal and read it, or get someone to read it to them, for it is designed more particularly for them."[29] Walker imagines the appeal as a community reading. Walker urges his readers to read his appeal out loud and together, and he prints it—with its manicules and exclamation marks—in a way that reads like spoken words.

It's as if Walker needs his readers to know where to shout, where to tarry, and where to lean into his words in order to make any community of listeners feel rightly for each other. How these men, women, and children take in Walker's words—whether by book learning, sound, or sight—does not matter. What matters is that they understand his words. What matters for Walker is that they are changed by their ability to feel into their rage. For this reason, Walker's request—"get someone to read it to them"—is instructive.

Because Walker neither insists on nor presumes book learning at all, this reading practice isn't tied to the stuff of print—books, ephemera, pamphlets, and printing presses. Walker doesn't even espouse a belief in the liberatory power of book learning. For Walker, book learning cannot guarantee the moral credibility of the reader; book learning can't serve Walker's brethren if they don't know what his words mean. "I pray that the Lord may undeceive my ignorant brethren," Walker writes, "and permit them to throw away pretensions, and seek after the substance of learning."[30] This "substance" of learning hints at an inward kind of reading practice, a heart-centered way of reading.

Walker culls this way of reading from his particular religious, political, and Masonic genealogy of free (or recently freed) men who undertake this practice as a way into a greater self.[31] Consider the example of Prince Hall, founder of African Freemasonry and of Boston's African Lodge No. 459.

It's noteworthy that Walker is no stranger to Prince Hall, Freemasonry, or the African Methodist Episcopalian churches that help spread Freemasonry. He is a Mason in the way of Prince Hall too.

Walker's reading practice is reminiscent of what Prince Hall refers to as "the means of meditation." Nearly forty years before Walker's pamphlet, Hall, in his "Charge" (1797), addresses an audience of fellow Masons at Menotomy in Massachusetts. "Although you are deprived of the means of education," Hall preaches, "yet you are not deprived of the means of meditation." When Hall speaks of meditation and its means, he names the practice of "thinking, hearing, and weighing matters, men, and things in [one's] own mind."[32] What Hall specifies is reading, in the way literary scholar Hortense Spillers describes, as a "process, encounter, and potential transformation."[33] He accepts and heartens his audience "to recognize their powers of divination as a source of political strength."[34] For Hall, those who take up this meditative literacy can do that which book learning cannot always teach or can never guarantee: correctly forecast storms as well as recite sermons and conversations without the help of books or almanacs: "This nature hath furnished you with, without letter learning; and some have great progress therein, some of those I have heard repeat psalms and hymns, and a great part of a sermon, only by hearing it read or preached and why not in other things in nature: how many of this class of brethren that follow the seas can foretell a storm . . . without any other means than observation and consideration."[35] Hall's means of meditation claims a reading practice that imagines reading, without formal education, as a kind of meditation. What Hall cannot and does not specify—the exact means of this meditative practice—expects the reader to trust the experience of feeling: the sound of a sermon against their ears or the bend of the sun's rays in their eyes. For the reader, this affective experience offers him an interpretative and active knowing that informs his experience of the self and the world at large. Hall offers his audience a way to value their feelings and to experience community. He demonstrates not only their humanity but also the way feelings and the ability to feel the signs and wonders create meaning and possibility.

Walker is teaching his brethren how to read, as a kind of discernment or a way to make meaning, and in so doing, how to feel in the right way. "I am after those who know and feel," Walker writes, "that we are MEN, as well as other people." To feel rightly, Walker's readers need to have a feeling heart that allows them to take in his truth. What Walker wants is for the reader to have an inward and affective experience that leans on a Christian God who, as Walker reminds his readers, "has been pleased to give us two eyes, two hands, two feet, and some sense in our heads as well," to read or make affective sense of the shared experience of oppression.[36] Walker seems to imagine reading as an everyday practice of discernment and a sensory experience that correlates often (albeit not always) with a spiritual faith. Readers experience what's read as heartfelt and interior in a way that echoes the enthusiastic means by which the faithful receive godly word and insight.

This manner of reading requires a belief in a Christian God whose manner of salvation opens the heart of the believer to the Word of God. Walker doubts the humanity of those who can't take to heart what they've read and experienced in his *Appeal*.[37] Reading in this way demands an affective, heart-centered, and experiential practice engagement not only with the book but also with the affective meaning of words as they are heard or seen. Walker writes of hearts often, and he differentiates them too. There are hard hearts, bleeding hearts, faithful hearts, and true hearts. Walker needs his readers to have an "open" heart to understand the truth of their condition and their certainty of their freedom. When he invokes "heart"—as a condition of humanity—he names the site of this inward experience of feeling. At the site of this "heart" is the interiority that literary theorist Kevin Quashie explains, "could be understood as the source of human action—that anything we do is shaped by the range of desires and capacities of our inner life."[38] He speaks directly to the kinds of hearts that know God well enough to carry in them the godly love necessary to understand the privations of enslavement and the very certain of its end in the United States. To feel rightly—after reading every part of his appeal—is to have an open enough heart to be angry, and it is to feel love, affection, or even anticipation for an America that's to come. To feel in this way (on behalf of someone else or one's self) promises to teach Walker's readers what it means to access the sensibility that comes from admitting to one's abject condition and also from feeling right for another.

Walker's "Natural Enemies"

Walker directs his anger and its resulting, expressive grammar at many, and particularly at those he calls "tyrants." According to Walker, tyrants are the slaveholders, pro-slavery advocates, hypocritical Christians and racists who—as he argues—"are so happy to keep [us] in ignorance and degradation, and to receive the homage and labor of the slaves, they forget that God rules." He identifies them further by their religion and their racial identity. He accuses and condemns with specificity the "white Christians of America." Even though Walker names them in this way, Walker mocks their self-identification as Christian. He insists theirs is not Christianity at all. In fact, they misuse and misunderstand Christian doctrine. The "white Christians of America" espouse a belief in a faithless religion with no obligation to one's fellow man. Walker questions their willingness to enslave "us and our children": "I ask, O ye Christians!!! who hold us and our children in the most abject ignorance and degradation, that ever a people were afflicted with since the world began—I say, if God gives you peace and tranquility, and suffers you thus to go on afflicting us, and our children, who have never given you the least provocation—would he be to us a God of justice?"[39] As Walker sees it, they claim to know God, but they keep slaves. Or worse yet, they refuse to take a stand against slavery or to recognize the feelings of the enslaved.

Walker argues that these white Christians are "hypocrites" because they have no sense of morality and no obligation to their fellow man. "The whites have always been an unjust," Walker explains, "jealous, unmerciful, avaricious, and blood-thirsty set of beings, always seeking after power and authority." Walker accuses slaveholders of not knowing how to feel with his brethren. They don't know how to understand the suffering of another person even when that suffering is obvious. "Any man who is curious to see the full force of ignorance among the coloured people of the United States of America," Walker writes, "has only to go into the southern and western states of this confederacy, where, if he is not a tyrant, but has the feelings of a human being, who can feel for a fellow creature, he may see enough to make his very heart bleed!"[40] Walker declares them the "natural enemies" of his title's imagined citizenry.

And Walker can't help but to be angry at those men and women who, he tells readers, are "ignorantly in league with slave-holders or tyrants" or "too deceitful, abject, and servile to resist" slavery. He chastises the people— Christians, the politically enslaved or free—"who acquire their daily bread by the blood and sweat of their more ignorant brethren—and not a few of those too, who are too ignorant to see an inch beyond their noses."[41] Walker despises their allegiance to white, Christian slaveholders and their acceptance of this collective wretched and abject condition. Because of this allegiance, these women and men, as Walker explains, can't feel rightly on behalf of the enslaved, and therefore, just like slaveholders, they too are morally bankrupt (even if they were once enslaved). Walker's vitriol attacks not only white, Christian slaveholding "tyrants" and their free or enslaved allies. By way of his criticisms, Walker models right ways of feeling—such as, anger or care—and offers his readers evidence of his ability to feel, to see, and to witness the abjection of his enslaved or freed brethren.

For Walker, his feelings and his expressed anger toward slavery and slave-holders are proof of his affective superiority over any slaveholder, pro-slavery advocate, or "ignorant" person who could say otherwise. It's proof of the superiority of his imagined, diasporic audience—the "colored" citizenry to whom he speaks directly—and their collective ability to feel and to know rightly that slavery is wrong. Walker publishes a moral and prophetic argument for proper ways of feeling and for right ways of Christian belief, "under the God of the *Blacks*." Those who believe in this God are assumed to be the real Christians or forthright "lovers of the Lord" because they care for and tend to one another.[42]

For Walker, this distinction—"the God of the *Blacks*"—is important. Because this god knows how much Walker's audience matters to themselves and to this nation, the "God of the Blacks" can and will do what the unnamed and irreligious god of the whites cannot. Walker explains: "Fear not the number and education of our enemies, against whom we shall have to contend for our lawful right; guaranteed to us by our Maker; for why should we be afraid, when God is, and will continue, (if we continue humble) to be on our side?"[43] Walker's God will win, and he means to teach his "colored citizens" that, because of their God's power, they are not at the mercy of slaveholders or misguided, pro-slavery politicians. They can get and must get angry too because their collective ability to feel, Walker suggests, is the way to ensure their liberation, their better future. This collective and inspired anger—as he represents it with his use of exclamation points, capitalized letters, and manicules—takes Walker and his readers somewhere into this realizable future: a decidedly American future without slavery. Walker promises their liberation if they can get angry enough to go after it. Walker trusts his anger and his God enough to call his "colored citizens" to revolutionary and, if necessary, violent action. Walker's anger serves his prophetic ends. His promise of freedom is ordained by God. His faith and his anger seem to prove it true.

Walker teaches his readers that it's not enough to just witness his anger. Because he is certain God will win, he offers his readers a guarantee of a successful and better future where they will all enjoy citizenship and belonging in a newer and freer version of the United States. It's a future where citizenship and national identity are not limited to who a person is or even what someone looks like. Rather, Walker believes in a future where citizenship is lived out as a practice of good will toward another person.[44] This future is happier because no one is burdened by enslavement; instead, living within and as part of a shared community are this future's priorities.

He anticipates the possibility of a different kind of affective and heart-filled future where his brethren are neither "wretched" nor "abject." The future's certainty is what seems to matter most to Walker. "And there is not a doubt in my mind," Walker writes, "but that the whole of the past will be sunk into oblivion, and we yet, under God, will become a united and happy people." This is Walker's good news. "The Americans may be as vigilant as they please," Walker writes, "but they cannot be vigilant enough for the Lord, neither can they hide themselves, where he will not find and bring them out."[45] Walker believes in a redemptive victory for the "wretched." And Walker means to see his appeal realized on earth. His commitment to the very certainty of liberation pursues the possibility of feeling joy or happiness, not just anger. Even as he iterates his present concerns—"degradation," "abjection," and "wretchedness"—Walker's future is a joy-filled one.

There is a redemptive pleasure for Walker in his faith-filled knowing that something better—akin to freedom, citizenship, and a sense of belonging—is on the way. Pleasure, in this instance, presupposes desire and longing for satisfaction. It is expectant and ever willing to enjoy the pursuit of its satisfaction. For Walker, there is pleasure not only in its certainty, but also in his literal and figurative appeal for it. There is pleasure in this yearning, in his anger, and in the knowing that he is a man with sense enough to know the truth of slavery's evils.

Fred Moten explains Walker's "capacity for joy" as a "condition of possibility of a necessary unhappiness, an indispensable critical destructiveness."[46] Walker's capacity for joy doesn't depend entirely on this "necessary unhappiness"—the result of the degraded conditions of enslavement—but his appeal makes joy and unhappiness inextricably linked and a necessary requisite to the liberation of his imagined community and readership. His joy, his pleasure relies, in part, on the very moral and redemptive possibility of slavery's abolition and proper citizenship in a free society. It's for this reason that he publishes a new constitution. Because Walker can see this future, there is joy for him in the very idea of dismantling this nation, as it is. With every exclamatory gesture, Walker seems to rejoice in the godly condemnation of "white Christians" and hypocrites too. There is a pleasure in this activism, in the hope for this citizenship, and in vengeance.

His readers should have no doubt that there is certain joy in this future. Even its anticipation is worthy of celebration. He writes: "Be looking forward with thankful hearts to higher attainments than wielding the razor and cleaning boots and shoes. . . . For I believe it is the will of the Lord that our greatest happiness shall consist in working for the salvation of our whole body." For Walker, this happiness is not just in salvation as a kind of missionary work. Walker hints at the salvation that comes from knowing freedom from enslavement, degradation, and various forms of systemic oppression. This kind of salvation must and will give way, as he explains, to happiness.

"What a happy country this will be, if the whites will listen," Walker appeals.[47] Walker conceives a citizenry that can and will know the happiness of living with greater ease, legal freedoms or "dependable companionship."[48] He promises his citizenry (viz., those who used to be "wretched") a new possibility, a new way of living and being—because when his readers can learn how to read their circumstances and feel their individual and collective experience rightly, then a godly joy and a new kind of national belonging await them.

Walker revels in the surety that his God will prevail against slaveholders and spiritually awaken his brethren to the truth of who they are. For Walker, there is joy not only in the process—of reading, writing or the possibility of decisive, revolutionary action—but most importantly, in the outcome of this reading, writing and action.

Walker's Futures

If his preamble and articles are a sort of reading primer, Walker's concluding pages are a syllabus. He closes his *Appeal* with a reading list. First, he directs readers to read history. Because if they do "search the pages of historians diligently and see if the Antideluvians [*sic*]—the Sodomites—the Egyptians . . . or devils, ever treated a set of human beings, as the white Christians of America can do us the Blacks, or Africans," he is certain that no one will find anyone treated worse than "us, the Blacks or Africans." Second, Walker "asks the attention of the world of mankind" to read the "declaration of these American people, of the United States." Walker ends article 4, "Our Wretchedness in Consequence of the Colonizing Plan," by excerpting from the two opening paragraphs of the Declaration of Independence. Walker ends his treatise against the American Colonization Society and its emigration schemes to Liberia with a reprinting of the familiar and decidedly American declaration. If his reader misunderstands his intention, his use of the declaration evinces his pursuit—to make the nation anew. He starts at the beginning of the Declaration: "When in the course of human events" and ends with "it is their right it is their duty to throw off such government, and to provide new guards for their future security." His rebuttal against the American Colonization Society and its settlements in Liberia concludes with a pronouncement of independence. Walker offers a reading—with italicized words and exclamation marks to add clarity of intention—of several key sentences, including "all men are created equal," "life, liberty, and the pursuit of happiness," and "it is their *right*, it is their *duty* to throw off such government."[49]

Walker reads Jefferson's Declaration of Independence, and to make clear the origins of his quotation, he titles and footnotes "A declaration made July 4, 1776." Walker doesn't bother with the "facts" that Jefferson "submitted to a candid world" but instead concludes his reference this way: "But when a long train of abuses and usurpations, pursuing invariably the same object, evince a design to reduce them under absolute despotism, it is their right it is their duty to throw off such a government, and to provide new guards for their future security."[50] He contests, throughout his appeal, the intellectual viability of Jefferson's arguments against the humanity of his brethren. Walker challenges Jefferson's morality, "while," as Gene Jarrett explains, "citing *Notes* line by line, to identify the self-contradiction that Jefferson shares with those who advocate religious egalitarianism even as they without hold it for Black slaves."[51]

By the end of his appeal, Walker no longer needs to disprove Jefferson's idiocy or the validity of his humanity. Instead, he needs to declare the collective freedom of those unnamed brethren who have worked to build Jefferson's country. For this reason, Walker takes up the country's pronouncement of freedom. What Walker invokes—by way of his choice of text, namely the Declaration of Independence—is "the 'right' of American citizens to independence."[52] Not only does Walker name his chosen text repeatedly, he lays claims to its call for rebellion and independent citizenship and asserts his positionality as an American.[53]

Walker dramatizes Jefferson's words with directives: "See your Declaration Americans!!! Do you understand your own language? Hear your language."[54] To encourage the proper hearing and seeing, Walker adorns and dramatizes the text by adding creative typography. He rewrites it just how he wants his readers to hear and see his revision.[55] He returns his reader to those self-evident truths with a pointed finger. "We hold these truths to be self evident," Walker writes, and the dash in the official version gives way to a capitalized "ALL MEN ARE CREATED EQUAL!!"[56] Walker seems to argue that Americans cannot understand their own language. He poses a rhetorical question. It's not the Americans who need to know the answer, but instead, it's those colored citizens of the world to whom he appeals. When they hear and see this truth, then they will have accepted the certainty of their shared humanity. Walker uses exaggerated typography because he must make his brethren hear its truth. For this reason, Walker capitalizes "all" and "equal"— as Marcy Dinius argues—to "visually distinguish the two most important words in the most important sentence of the document; setting 'men are created' in small capitals heightens the significance of the clause without diminishing 'all' and 'equal.'"[57] Walker doesn't stop at equality. He reminds his readers of the declaration's mention of "life, liberty, and the pursuit of happiness," "all men are created equal." He quotes at length: "that when ever any form of government becomes destructive of these ends, it is the right of the people to alter or to abolish it, and to institute a new government laying its foundation on such principles, and organizing his powers in such a form, as to them shall seem most likely to effect their safety and happiness."[58]

And with Jefferson's words, Walker declares independence. Walker has rejected the tyranny of the present system and has claimed his right to "alter or to abolish, and institute a new government." He ends with the declaration that begins American independence. He iterates the freedom that he has created in his preamble and four articles. Walker seems to suggest that he knows—better than Jefferson—just what this declaration means.

When Walker offers his reading of this American declaration, he makes clear that he understands its words better than the "tyrants" who make wretches and slaves of his brethren. What Walker knows for sure is that his brethren are citizens of this country. They are no longer slaves or enslaved. This "we" is a citizenry of readers and writers, former slaves and actively enslaved, women, men, and children. With his "we," Walker strives "to alter the land itself (and the body politic)."[59] And, he does alter it with a new constitution and return to the founder's words. Taken together, Walker compels readers to reimagine this "American space." What he imagines is a country that, as Charles Long explains, "will indeed have to become a radically different one, an-*other* place.[60] "I say that the day is fast approaching, when there will be a greater time on the continent of America," Walker prophesies, "than ever was witnessed upon this earth, since it came from the hand of its Creator."[61] Walker sees a future where his brethren enjoy the privileges of sociopolitical freedom, national citizenship in the United States. He's clear that this future should take root on American soil because it's the blood, sweat, and tears of his imagined audience that has made this country's prosperity. The United States is home, and Walker refuses to have his people displaced or "removed" to elsewhere. He is certain that it will advance God's glory and rid his brethren of their "wretched" or "abject" condition.

* * *

Even though he declared a new kind of national independence and constitutes a new nation on an autumn day in 1829, David Walker never sees his appeal's imagined United States. He'll never know how God intervenes on behalf of his brethren. His story ends with his untimely death in 1830, only a year before Nat Turner's rebellion in Southampton County, Virginia. He dies in Boston at the age of about thirty-four, just months after he publishes the third and last edition of his appeal. It's not clear how Walker dies. Rumor has it that Walker dies from consumption, or maybe he is killed by his enemies.

Walker seems to anticipate his murder. By the publication of his last pamphlet, he knows that he can't guarantee his own safety: "I write without the fear of man, I am writing for my God and fear none but himself; they may put me to death if they choose—(I fear and esteem a good man however, let him be Black or white.)" Walker is right to feel this way. There are many reasons for him to suspect foul play. In the summer of 1830, his enemies in Virginia, Georgia, and North Carolina put a bounty on his head. They've promised $3,000 for his murder and $10,000 to anyone who can capture and bring him alive to a slave state. And I wonder if it's in anticipation of his inopportune end that he concludes his 1830 edition with this explanation: "It may not be understood, when I say my Third and last Edition, I mean to convey the idea, that there will be no more Books of this Third Edition printed, but to notify that there will be no more addition in the body of this Work, or additional Notes to this 'Appeal.' THE END."[62] His closing remarks and the proverbial "the end" seem to suggest that there is no more left to say, and the finality of its capital letters hints at Walker's death.

Despite how Walker dies, what he constitutes—with his noisy anger—in his preamble and four articles is a morally awakened nation. He appeals for a nation that pursues, with fervor, the pleasures of its awakening into a slavery's end. Walker and his anger write a joy-filled and happy country into print. The way to it is to feel rightly. This is why Walker feels so much and so compellingly—because his anger, in particular, is a call to proper ways of feeling. It's a call to those who can listen to, see, or read his words properly and make sense of his various forms of rhetorical gesticulation. It's a call to those who can be goaded—with the help of his marginalia, extensive footnotes, and his many "pay attention!" manicules—into anger at the sight or the experience of enslavement. Walker's anger articulates what kind of affective sense his brethren need to read his words and to rally a creative activism that calls his "we" into the truth of their shared, affective experience—punctuated by action and reaction to the potential of slavery's end and the promise of a new way of living.

It's not for everyone, and it can't be for everyone. Walker expects and anticipates the illegibility of his anger. He writes his appeal to those who can understand it. Walker specifies his target audience—the "coloured citizens of the world"—and he criticizes those who cannot hear or read him correctly. He names and rejects those who are "too deceitful, abject, and servile" because he understands that they cannot receive his word.[63] Walker refuses to accommodate those who cannot make sense of it or the very simple fact that the lives of his brethren matter and are worthy of local and national concern. He needs readers who can experience feelings with him—and, really, the intimacy of his rage. He needs readers who can understand that his exclamations and pointed fingers express those unspeakable and seemingly angry kinds of feelings. Together, they must anticipate slavery's end and the real certainty of victory against slaveholders and "tyrants."

Walker, with his anger and his joyful future, invites his readers to feel and share even more closely with him. He invites readers into his interiority, into this heart space, and in so doing asks us, as his readers, his listeners, and his brethren, to feel this collective (and individual too) wretched condition. Feeling—inwardly in this way—is a shared burden. Those who know this truth in their heart—at the site of an inward experience of feeling—experience the kind of suffering that admits to the sick and twisted nature of our collective humanity and the depths of our human sympathy. Twentieth-century writer Ralph Ellison observes "that American Negro life . . . is, for the Negro who must live it, not only a burden (and not always that) but also a *discipline*—just as any human life which has endured so long is a discipline teaching its own insights into the human condition, its own strategies for survival."[64] Ellison does not specify the terms of this burden, but he refuses to accept it. Author James Baldwin suggests that humanity itself is the burden.[65] Literary scholar Peter Coviello tells us the burden lies in the very possibility of feeling.[66] It seems to me that Walker admits to those burdens too and accords a discipline by which his readers might understand their very human condition.

And there, Walker tells the good news and offers a hopeful truth: "For I believe it is the will of the Lord that our greatest happiness shall consist in working for the salvation of our whole body. When this is accomplished a burst of glory will shine upon you, which will indeed astonish you and the world."[67] Walker's anger is meant to make change happen. It encourages a creative activism that leads to the very possibility of Walker's imagined, collective resistance and, ultimately, to feeling good. To feel in this way promises his readers access to a kind of spiritual and political transformation that can rejoice in the possibility of a new way of being in a new kind of nation. What Walker teaches readers about affect and anger realizes the truth of fellow Freemason John Marrant's 1789 command "to love another sincerely . . . to sympathize in the good or evil that befalls our brethren."[68] When they learn Walker's lesson, then his brethren can enjoy the fruits of their anger. They can live, as citizens, in the country that they helped to build. Walker's good news is, ultimately, that God will make sure his brethren are free as well as happy.

Coda; Or, Reading Pleasures

Looking for Arbour/Obour/Orbour

(October ? 1809)

Gentlemen—

We received your address dated April 14 by our President, which address was very gratifying indeed. We thank you for the approbation you seem to express of our Society and we hope that by our forming this Society like that of yours in substance will give you not only our approbation of yours, but encouragement to persevere, surely nothing could induce us to form this Society but the good of our posterity, which we trust you have in view, and we receive into our Society all good and moral characters.—

We cannot forbear to inform you the encouragement we have in seeing so many of our sex coming forward and joining us, to the support of this institution beyound all our expectation. We also received your three committee [men?] namely Newport Gardner, John Marvatt, Tunbridge Hammond, whom you sent to enquire of us what prospect we have of affording the school assistance, with regard to expenses. We have voted that ten dollars be taken out of our treasury at this time and to be carried by three of our Directors, Viz—Patience Marvatt, Catherine Sheffield & Sarah Malbone, to your treasury, and we hope it may be accepted as the Widow's mite.

Finally—may the Lord enable both Societys to persevere in supporting this Institution is the Sincere wish of your Humble Servants.—

By order and in the behalf of the Society

Orbour Collins President
Sarah D Lyma Secretary pro term[1]

I'm looking for Obour Tanner, and I've come to Rhode Island to find her or to see where she might be. I know her as a friend to poet Phillis

Wheatley, whose letters name this enslaved, Newport resident, and as an abstract signatory on letters that I've never read. I'm looking for any way to make her real to me—maybe a word or something left behind or any passing mention of what or who might matter to her. I'm looking to remember her. I admit I didn't think I would find any such thing, because it's easy to misread, misunderstand, or simply miss what's left to read in a special collections' library or archive. And I've also learned how little the library and its collections has to say about or by formerly enslaved women. I don't have much of what she's left behind.

I know too Wheatley and Tanner used to correspond frequently about quotidian matters, and Wheatley's letters to her friend place both women between 1772 and 1779 in the midst of war, worship, and marriage. Their last bit of extant correspondence is a very short 10 May 1779 letter. I've learned from their epistles that, by 1779, Wheatley has returned to Boston. Tanner is living in Worcester, Massachusetts, a likely response to the British occupation of Newport—not much is left of Newport during and after the occupation. Wheatley's letter is noteworthy because it admits to a sense of urgency that seems to anticipate and even prays for an unspecified ending and a return to order in the wake of the American War for Independence. I can't say if Wheatley gets her desired ending because I find the proverbial dead end. There are no more letters left to read (at present), despite my sense of anticipation for what's yet to be found. When Wheatley dies in 1784, she leaves behind even less about her life, particularly those wartime years between 1779 and 1784.[2] And, in this last extant, springtime letter to Tanner, Wheatley doesn't say enough to give me much detail, and she doesn't bother to mention where Tanner will go after her time in Worcester or how her friend might feel about her wartime displacement. There is only uncertainty. It's this sort of uncertainty that has me fearful that I might find nothing of Tanner on this trip.

In the face of what I don't know about her or my fear that she might be nowhere, I do find Tanner. There she is in the special collections library at the Rhode Island Historical Society. I read her name in an October 1809 letter as its transcribed and collected in *The Proceedings of the Free African Union Society, 1780–1824*, edited and transcribed by William H. Robinson, a literary historian and a professor at Rhode Island College. I know it's hers because she has signed it just beneath a closing remark, "by order and in behalf of the Society" and just above the signature of Sarah D. Lyma, the organization's secretary. But she does not use the name that I've come to know well, Obour Tanner. This time, she signs her name, "Orbour Collins." She is no longer Tanner, but rather Collins. She has married Barry Collins, a member of the Free African Union Society in Newport and has been married since November 1790.[3]

I see her first name now has an extra "r" in it. It's yet another spelling. It's an inconsistency that I've come to expect because standardized spellings are not yet commonplace. Wheatley often spells her Tanner differently. In 1772, she writes "Arbour." By 1779, it's "Obour." But now, in 1809, the woman I've known as Obour Tanner is Orbour Collins. Thirty years have passed since the extant 1779 letter from Wheatley. Tanner is nearly sixty years old now and has lived so many different kinds of war and loss: a revolutionary war, the formation of a new nation, postwar resettlement efforts in Nova Scotia and the Caribbean, and several failed attempts to repatriate to colonial sites in West Africa. She's lost friends and must have lost kin, too, but she is still writing letters in and around Newport, Rhode Island.

William H. Robinson gathers this letter from Sarah D. Lyma and Tanner among the notes, letters, and lists of the Newport's Free African Union Society (later the African Benevolent Society). The Free African Union Society (FAUS) and its iteration as the African Benevolent Society (ABS) are a Rhode Island–based community of artisans, readers, and Christians. The FAUS is a members-only organization, founded in 1780, that serves Newport (a chapter opens later in Providence) as a religious and mutual aid society with the expressed purpose to provide financial and social support to the city's nominally free communities. Its outreach is not limited to Rhode Island but extends to Boston, Philadelphia, Nova Scotia, and Sierra Leone by way of friendly correspondence, travel, and affiliations with Masonic lodges and emerging church denominations, such as the African Methodist Episcopalian and the African Baptist.

At the start of the nineteenth century, the FAUS changes its name to the African Benevolent Society (ABS), but its commitment to various provisions and shared worship does not change. It continues to offer faith-based and financial relief services as well as burial rites to members and their spouses. It does open its membership to anyone.[4] By 1809, its members start a school "for the benefit of the Africans" and together, with women from the community, initiate the founding of an auxiliary women's organization, the African Female Benevolent Society (also known as the Females Society). The Females Society serves the community's women, "for so good a cause as to benefit the African race."[5] Tanner is one of its founding members and serves as president.

As the Females Society president and on behalf of its members, Tanner pens this letter with the Sarah D. Lyma, the organization's secretary. Because there is much discussion about the happenings of the society and its emerging community-building work, it is one of several formal letters between the society and the ABS in 1809. The ABS, in an earlier 14 April 1809 address to the society, salutes their work and encourages them "to be united, to lay no bar in the way so as to hinder any person from becoming a member of the society" and "to ask direction from Heaven of that God from whom all blessings flow." Their address admits to a collective need to unite, to come together in fellowship and in community. The ABS concludes with a bit of prayer, "that every blessing may attend you and may the Lord bless you all and make you an instrument in his hands of doing much good."[6] In subsequent months, the ABS writes again to ask the Females Society to help defray costs for their school for girls, boys, and adult learners, and it will be the first school funded and managed exclusively by Black persons in the United States.[7] They don't specify any particular amount, but they do send along long-time members Newport Gardner, John Marvatt, and Thomas Hammond "to wait upon them" and report back their decision.[8]

By October, Tanner and Sarah D. Lyma have an answer for the gentlemen of ABS. The women begin their letter with gratitude and laud their collective sense of purpose in this way: "we hope that by our forming this Society like that of [the African Benevolent Society] in substance will give you not only our approbation of yours, but encouragement to persevere, surely nothing could induce us to form this Society but the good of our posterity, which we trust you have in view, and we receive into our Society all good and moral characters."[9] It seems both organizations are united in their efforts to create a community within which to share, pray, and worship together too. Theirs is a purpose inspired by, Tanner writes, the "encouragement we have in seeing so many of our sex coming forward and joining us, to the support of this institution beyond all our expectation."[10] Tanner honors the community-building efforts of the Females Society and is encouraged by their success. She is encouraged by the increasing participation of women in her organization and what's unspoken is their shared impact upon their community. Society members collect clothing to give to those in need and teach those children and adults who want to learn.[11]

I am reminded that Tanner seems to have always believed in the value of encouragement and in the shared fellowship among women. Even in her letters to Wheatley, she is never without a prayer or two for her friend. Wheatley acknowledges—with thanks—the power of Tanner's healing prayers and the importance of their correspondence.[12] Even years later, because of her undeniable, Christian faith, Tanner is encouraged to persevere with the help of, and maybe, because of this fellowship of women.

The women of the Females Society are named by the letter writer's use of a collective "we." "We thank you," the letter says, "we hope" or "we have voted" or "we receive." Tanner, as society president, seems guided by a "we." It is a "we" that is led to serve and to give. Together, this "we" decides that their shared cause is fundraising for the free school for boys and girls. The women's auxiliary has decided to give a gift of "ten dollars" toward the school. It's unclear how the women have amassed this large sum of money, but it is theirs to give. The gift is to "be taken out of our treasury at this time and to be carried by three of our Directors, Viz—Patience Marvatt, Catherine Sheffield & Sarah Malbone to your treasury and we hope it may be accepted as the Widow's mite." Their letter ends with a prayer: "Finally—may the Lord enable both Society to persevere in supporting this Institution is the sincere wish of your Humble Servants."[13] It is a prayer that imagines a future for this school as it prays too for the longevity for the ABS and the Females Society. There is a desire here to share its gratitude, encouragement, and a certain belief in a godly and shared supply. The collective excitement of Tanner and her members bespeaks the work of the society and the good feeling that must come from this sort of giving.

Their donation reminds me that Tanner—just like Wheatley, in past years—and every woman, doing this work alongside her, knows what it means to be pleased. This is the pleasure of faith, of community, and the very possibility of sharing something together. On this day, Tanner and the Females Society share in the pleasures of giving money to support this school. Surely, Tanner's pleasures don't have to look like those of Wheatley or of Patience Marvatt, and with only one extant letter, it's not easy to make a lengthy list of what might please her. This letter is suggestive. It hopes for and believes in its encouragement, its community, and its commitment to faithfulness. With its hoping and believing, this letter hints at what it means to be pleased and to live in the uncertain joys of one's faith.

As quickly as the letter begins, it ends, and Robinson does not include any more letters that Tanner has signed. Orbour Tanner seems to disappear elsewhere and into an uncertainty that I've learned is always a part of any archival story. Even as she seems to disappear, she leaves behind Patience Marvatt, Catherine Sheffield, Sarah Malbone, and Sarah D. Lyma, but with little explanation. Marvatt, Sheffield, and Malbone serve the society as directors. No one says what they direct, and there are no notes about who voted for Lyma as secretary. I am left with my lingering questions. Where are the rest of Tanner's letters? How long does she serve as the society's president? How many children does she have? Was her husband nice? But these are *my* questions. What I know for sure—because I've read Tanner's letter—is that I can never know all of the answers. These are not questions that she has to ask because this is still her story even as I find its pieces.

Reading for Arbour/Obour/Orbour

Even though Tanner's letter is there—in the library, in its holdings—to be read, hers isn't always a story that we know to seek or to read. It's her sister-friend Phillis Wheatley who garners our attentions. But Wheatley's life is brief relative to that of Tanner. She dies fifty years before Tanner does. Despite the various ways that Tanner will keep living until about 1835, Wheatley—with her letters, poems, and advertisements that help mark her "firstness"—is presumed to warrant further consideration. And maybe, most importantly, Wheatley seems to have enough material to tell a more interesting story. Her story includes the United States' founding fathers, an attestation of her writing ability, a published volume of poetry, a proposal for a second volume, and some letters too.

It's true that Wheatley is easier to find because she has fame in her own time and at present. She is talked about and frequently anthologized in print. Her archival whereabouts are well-documented and likely digitized. She has her own Library of Congress subject heading. Because she is canonized and catalogued rightly, her print and manuscript writings are just a quick online search away.

Tanner doesn't have Wheatley's accessibility. It's far easier to read or imagine her as Wheatley's silent reader, a name in a letter's header or a writer of now-lost letters. Because Tanner doesn't have enough stuff—ephemera, letters, records, or artifacts—her story (or lack thereof) seems to prove a scholarly assumption that there is not enough, and there is never enough in the library to remember the stories of Black women. See, what we can't find—and the resulting urgency, disappointment, or angst—fits neatly into the scholarly expectation of the so-called "archive" as a problematic and limited site of either recovery or disavowal.

I understand why we read the "archive" in this way. Despite those glimpses of her life, it's still true that even Wheatley, much like Tanner, still has a story with few answers. Both women's extant snippets glimpse not only what there is to know but also those silences that seemingly prove that the "archive"—as a site of institutional power and legal force—cannot serve the enslaved (or formerly enslaved).[14] While it's true that "archive," in its simplest terms, means a collection of stuff that has belonged to someone, some group, or to some place, it's also true—as scholars often note—that the "who, what, and where" of remembering often belongs to those in power. The work of memory may choose not to remember everyone or everything. In place of memory, there is oftentimes silence, absence, or, sometimes, just a great sense of dearth. For this reason, scholarly discussions of the archive and its holdings imagine a place where eighteenth-century Black persons go to be missed: misunderstood, misread, or misplaced. We lament the institution's refusal to collect or recollect what might matter to Black people; in this way, the "archive" represents a limitation, a lack, or an ongoing site of recovery or unspeakability. Saidiya Hartman observes that the archive, for enslaved, Black women, as a repository of the unrecoverable, as "a death sentence, a tomb, a display of the violated body, an inventory of property, a medical treatise on gonorrhea, a few lines about a whore's life, an asterisk in the grand narrative of history."[15]

Even for the likes of Wheatley, the silences of her archive—for example, when or where she is born, what her favorite song is, or what she wore on the day she married John Peters—seemingly proves just how much we can't know or won't know.[16] Wheatley and Tanner might be read, then, among the dead or forgotten as proof of the archive's failure and its power to ascertain the materiality of Black life—because presumably Black lives don't matter in the archive.

Because we've learned that the "archive" doesn't concern itself with Black living, Tanner's name is certainly unfamiliar. It is assumed that because she isn't the right kind of "first," she isn't there to be remembered. She doesn't engender nearly as much curiosity. She must not have an extant book of poetry, a memorable patron, or digitized letters and poems. There can't be a frontispiece to mark her literary achievements, even though she, too, is a reader and a writer. But Tanner doesn't die with her friend; she is not simply erased from the record.

Rather, she keeps living in a census mention, a bit of correspondence, and a baptismal registry even though she doesn't have Wheatley's celebrity. In 1793, Tanner will be listed as "Obour Tanner" in the "Free Blacks" subscribers of Rev. Samuel Hopkins's *The System of Doctrines* (1793). As part of this intentional list of readers and activists, Tanner will announce a real interest in an emigration plan to Sierra Leone, spearheaded by her local chapter of the Free African Union Society and her pastor, Rev. Samuel Hopkins. She will write and read more letters. And she will be remembered by another Newport resident, William Beecher's wife, Katherine Edes Beecher. And those mentions and memories—even as footnotes or in their brevity—teach us, present-day readers, that Tanner is alive, and she leaves behind those bits of living that have me read her 1809 letter even more closely.

Surely, I am left holding my unanswerable questions. I am reminded of those questions that literary historian Lois Brown also asks, "how do we grapple with the seeming silences—these rhetorical ruptures and biographical caesuras—that all too often define the early African American canon and history."[17] Historians Marisa Fuentes and Brian Connolly iterate Brown's query by asking yet another version of it: "are these archives places of lack, absence, loss and silence or are they marked as much by excess, noise, and life, by 'an excess of meaning, where the reader experiences beauty, amazement, and a certain affective tremor?'"[18] Because I've read Tanner's letter at the Rhode Island Historical Society, I can't help but to wonder if there is a way in which Black living—and not simply Black death—is, in fact, an archival concern. I wonder still if the illegibility of Black living in the archive is a misreading or a misunderstanding of what's there, especially within a colonial American or U.S. context. How do we read when the stuff of the archive belongs to Black women during slavery or in its wake? How do we read stories when they are not made for or by the white enslaver? Tanner's letter isn't necessarily part of the scandalous and excessive archive that Hartman remembers for its "raw numbers of the mortality account, the strategic evasion and indirection of the captain's log, the florid and sentimental letters dispatched from slave ports by homesick merchants . . . and the rituals of torture, the beatings, hangings, and amputations enshrined by law."[19] Tanner lives through this sort of storytelling and offers us yet another story with a month, a year, and two signatures.

And it's what Tanner leaves behind, what's present, which is curious and compelling. Because Tanner has not died yet in 1809, but she leaves behind a "death-defying testimony" that is at times a Kevin Quashie kind of "quiet" and a Lois Brown kind of "riotous, symphonic, insistent national, international, pan-African noise."[20] She converses not only with the library that keeps her but also the men and women whom she names. Tanner reminds her reader that she participates in the makings of her memory, and her very presence alters the makings of this archive as a futurist or historical institution. She is living her story as it is, and I only have a glimpse of a life. This fact is my burden. And if I'm to read her life properly and closely, I must remember that we don't share the same curiosity. Tanner doesn't have to because her life is hers to know. If I'm to read or learn it, I have to accept what she can and will never tell me.

What I can know is that Tanner, as president of the Females Society, donates ten dollars to the free school. Under her leadership, Lyma is secretary. Tanner compels me to ask of my assumptions: What if silence or even death aren't the limits of the archive? What if silence can beget new ways of reading, new points of entry into a reading practice that takes up this silence and pictures its resulting pleasures? How do we read for the living in places that we have decided are for the dead? What if there are ways for Black living to matter amid those imagined, archival silences that are meant to render stories unmemorable?

There are stories in this 1809 letter that demand the kinds of close reading that teach and beg us to ask compelling questions and sit expectantly with those questions. Not only is Tanner living, she begs us to read in new ways, to reconsider what's already there, in the archive or the library. Her letter must remind us that what is misread as a lack or an absence is in fact generative if we read for what's present, if we admit to the pleasures of reading for those who still live, and if we believe in the many ways these authors are pleased. This is reading pleasure and reading for pleasure. It's an exercise in potential rather than certainty. Its practice is imaginative and committed to what's possible and what's pleasing in a text.

The Pleasures of Reading

Reading in this way—for pleasure and with possibility, in mind—is not an exercise merely in speculation but in the very practice of reading for what a page, an image, or a simple list might say. Poet Kevin Young is right to imagine reading as "not simply literary or even literate, but a matter of folk-faith."[21] What he calls "folk-faith" literacy supplants the tactility of the book with the materiality of fleeting or unspeakable feeling and understanding. Folk-faith literacy presupposes a relationship between the text (in words, place, personhood, or body), the reader and what she or he has hoped for or evidence of that which cannot be seen or heard. It is assumed that the reader can discern the text properly. The reader has learned how to understand its language and how to respond correctly to it because he or she has learned how to hear, see, or feel what the words or, more generally, an experience means. The reader finds meaning by way of his or her feeling and the experience of those sights, sounds, colors, and textures in the text. It's reading closely and a reading into uncertainty and into an interiority that does not always seek a way out, or the publicity of an expectant escape, or a decidedly racialized selfhood. Neither good nor unpleasant feelings can be measured by a fixed or quantitative unit such as, deaths, lynchings, bodies sold, or lives stolen. It's a reading practice that privileges what's possible amid textual uncertainty. The uncertainty rests in not knowing what's there or even in what it means.

This reading practice understands the "archive" not just as a scholarly euphemism for library but also as a site of interiority and uncertainty. The archive is an inside and what's inside it is, at times, chaotic and affective or, at other times, opaque and illegible. It's quiet. Nonetheless, it invites us to share in its intimacy, to search for and find what it possesses. This interiority, too, is its power and the site of its pleasures. This pleasure, like most, is fleeting and is the result of a pursuit rather than endings and answers.

Let me say, this way of reading is not necessarily recovery, reclamation, or recuperative work. "Recovery" is a term that best describes a return of what's lost, such as money or good health. Neither Wheatley nor Tanner, among persons known and unknown, is lost. Tanner and Wheatley know their life stories and neither have to remember in those obvious ways that might help us, presently, tell a story. Tanner's story belongs to her. It is us—as scholars, readers, and thinkers—who can't find or remember who and where they are. This is the burden of those who can't remember with Tanner (or Wheatley, Gronniosaw, Marrant, and Walker for that matter). This is our shared burden. For this reason, this is the work of desiring after that which we don't know. The pursuit is or, at the very least, can be, enjoyable. It's a joy to read into and to seek after what Tanner can take for granted—namely, her husband's favorite food, how much she might have missed Wheatley, or the location of her extant correspondence. There's a joy in the certainty that Tanner will never ever give up too much what she knows.

Even if led by truth, uncertainty serves as life's guiding principle. It's the joy that comes from remembering just how human these eighteenth-century persons are. They keep secrets and trade secrets with friends. Some of their stories are meant to remain unspeakable and unknown. And it's the uncertainty, the not-knowing of Tanner's story that makes reading her story and those like hers pleasurable because pleasure is just as much about pursuit—unrequited or not—and satisfaction. In my pursuit, I am certain though about how much her living matters. It matters, in a real sense, and has meaning in her letters to and from Wheatley. It's what's left of those letters that offer a glimpse of Tanner's faith and her commitment to friendship, fellowship, and those communities in Newport and Providence that will remember and keep her name. These are the faith-based communities that connect her—by way of her acquaintance or affiliation—to the Countess of Huntingdon's network of preachers, Prince Hall's Freemasons, and burgeoning free settlements in Nova Scotia and Sierra Leone. And this is the work of creatively remembering that Wheatley and Tanner are always there if we take seriously the idea that their lives matter enough to look and read for. This is the work of reading for or alongside what's left unsaid and what's left inside a letter, a bit of manuscript, or printed texts in the library.

* * *

This is a book about reading and its pleasures. It's about reading for fun or, simply put, for the pleasure of reading, for its own sake. It's a book that believes in reading as a practice of going in search of and with uncertainty in mind because reading—as it happens in early America and as it serves Black living—isn't just about making sense of words on a page. Reading inevitably names those kinds of social literacies and interpretative possibilities that result from familiarity and intimacy with a text or an object and its stories. This book appeals for an uncertain and unsettled reading practice that compels a reader to forego expectation and instead tend to and look after what is there in the text. It isn't the same as reading for answers or even reading for questions.

When reading in this way, with pleasure, joy, and Black living in mind, it's easier to see and read the ways in which Black living has always mattered in early America (particularly before 1830) and at present. It's in the act of mattering that Black lives find the quietude or interiority necessary to enjoy or make joy. This joy is left behind and collected in printed texts and remnants in manuscript by those women, men, and children who invite us to read for and anticipate them.

If we, as readers, take pleasure and its possibility seriously, pleasure can help us read Black persons and their living in relation to themselves and to each other and in a manner that is not necessarily tied to a white gaze. Reading can be and serves us best, at times, as an affective and bodily experience that is not entirely dependent upon book learning but instead seeks after just how much Black living matters and has always mattered—in and outside of the library and its holdings.

Notes

Introduction

1. Duke Franklin Humanities Institute, "Fred Moten & Saidiya Hartman at Duke University," YouTube, 5 October 2016, www.youtube.com/watch?v=t_tUZ6dybrc.

2. Toni Morrison, "Home," in *The House That Race Built: Original Essays by Toni Morrison, Angela Y. Davis, Cornel West, and Others on Black Americans and Politics in America Today*, ed. Wahneema Lubiano (New York: Vintage, 1998), 10.

3. Duke University Department of African and African American Studies, "Keynote Address: Professor Farah Jasmine Griffin," YouTube, 14 July 2015, www.youtube .com/watch?v=yXngPCy_YYQ.

4. Kevin Quashie, *Sovereignty of Quiet: Beyond Resistance in Black Culture* (New Brunswick, NJ: Rutgers University Press, 2012), 6.

5. Elizabeth Alexander, *Black Interior: Essays* (Saint Paul, MN: Graywolf, 2004), 5.

6. Toni Morrison, "Rediscovering Black History: It's Like Growing Up Black One More Time," *New York Times*, 11 August 1974.

7. Quashie, *Sovereignty of Quiet*, 6.

8. Ibid., 6.

9. Ralph Ellison, "'A Very Stern Discipline:' An Interview with Ralph Ellison," *Harper's Magazine*, 1 March 1967, 76.

10. For a particularly important discussion of this living—as theory and as a point of sociopolitical concern—see Stephanie M. H. Camp, "Pleasures and Resistance: Enslaved Women and Body Politics in the Plantation South, 1830–1861," *Journal of Southern History* 68.3 (August 2002): 533–72.

11. Alexander, *Black Interior*, x.

12. Glenn Hendler, *Public Sentiments: Structures of Feeling in Nineteenth-Century American Literature* (Chapel Hill: University of North Carolina Press, 2001), 3.

13. Duke University, "Keynote Address."

14. The quotation in the subhead title is by Camp, "Pleasure and Resistance," 538.

15. James Baldwin, *The Fire Next Time* (New York: Vintage International, 1962), 42–43.

16. Kevin Young, *The Grey Album: On the Blackness of Blackness* (Minneapolis, MN: Graywolf, 2012), 270.

17. Katherine McKittrick, "Rebellion/Invention/Groove," *Small Axe* 20.1 (March 2016, no. 49): 90.

18. I thank Dr. Shani Mott (and her continued work on this subject) for the many conversations that introduced me to the profitability of suffering as a scholarly pursuit.

19. For a discussion of "ultimate concern," see, of course, the following works of Paul Tillich: *Courage to Be*, 2d ed. (New Haven, CT: Yale University Press, 2000); *Dynamics of Faith* (New York: Perennial Classics, 2001); and *Love, Power, and Justice: Ontological Analyses and Ethical Applications* (New York: Oxford University Press, 1954).

20. Phillis Wheatley, *Complete Writings*, ed. Vincent Carretta (1773; New York: Penguin Books, 2001), 148.

21. David Walker, *Walker's Appeal in Four Articles Together with a Preamble, to the Coloured Citizens of the World, But in Particular, and Very Expressly to those of the United States of America, Third and Last Edition* (Boston: Revised and Published by David Walker, 183), 3.

22. Hortense Spillers, "Moving on Down the Line," *American Quarterly* 40.1 (March 1988): 84.

23. See also Derrick Spires, *The Practice of Citizenship: Black Politics and Print Culture in the Early United States* (Philadelphia: University of Pennsylvania Press, 2019).

24. Rom. 11:8; Matt. 13:15; Isa. 44:18. All biblical citations are from the King James Version.

25. John Marrant, "A Funeral Sermon," in *Face Zion Forward: First Writers of the Black Atlantic, 1785–1798*, ed. Joanna Brooks and John Saillant (Boston: Northeastern University Press, 2002), 166.

26. Heb. 11:1.

27. James Albert Ukawsaw Gronniosaw, *Narrative of the Most Remarkable Particulars of James Albert Ukawsaw Gronniosaw, Written by Himself*, 2d ed. (Newport, RI: S. Southwick, 1774), 25.

28. See Treva Lindsey at NYU Florence, "Black Portraiture(s) II—The Sweetest Taboo: Theorizing Black Female Pleasure," YouTube, 29 May 2015, www.youtube.com/watch?v=7wp8XEtdkvQ&t=844s.

29. Special thanks are due to Jim Green (of the Library Company of Philadelphia) for encouraging me to think about how pleased David Walker might have been to set type and to make demands of his community and his nation.

30. Special thanks to Dr. Alexis Pauline Gumbs for pointing out Wheatley's penmanship and the utility or pleasures of its beauty.

31. McKittrick, "Rebellion/Invention/Groove," 90.

32. See Treva Lindsey at John Hope Franklin Center at Duke University, "'I Woke Up Like This:' Desire & Respectability in Shondaland," YouTube, 9 February 2015, www.youtube.com/watch?v=EmxZsmj7N3U.

33. Barbara Christian, "Response to 'Black Women's Texts,'" *NWSA Journal* 1.1 (Autumn 1988): 34.

34. Brian K. Blount, "Reading Revelation Today: Witness as Active Resistance," *Interpretation* 54.3 (2000): 398.

35. McKittrick, "Rebellion/Invention/Groove," 88.

36. Quashie, *Sovereignty of Quiet*, 29, 3.

37. Blount, "Reading Revelation Today," 398.

38. Lindsey, "Sweetest Taboo."

39. Frances Smith Foster, "Looking Back Is Tricky Business," *Narrative* 18.1 (January 2010): 27.

40. Ellison, "'Very Stern Discipline,'" 76.

41. Phillip Troutman, "Grapevine in the Slave Market: African American Geopolitical Literacy and the 1841 Creole Revolt," in *The Chattel Principle: Internal Slave Trades in the Americas*, ed. Walter Johnson (New Haven, CT: Yale University Press, 2004), 203–33; and Toni Morrison, "Angela Davis and Toni Morrison: Literacy, Libraries and Liberation," YouTube, 27 October 2010, www.youtube.com/watch?v=zLR_TcGHzRU.

42. Troutman, "Grapevine in the Slave Market," 203, 206, 207.

43. Toni Morrison at Cornell University, "Toni Morrison on Language, Evil and the 'White Gaze,'" YouTube, 18 March 2013, www.youtube.com/watch?v=FAs3E1AgNeM.

44. Kevin Young, *The Grey Album: On the Blackness of Blackness* (Minneapolis, MN: Graywolf Press, 2012), 175, 175, 178.

45. Yolanda Pierce, *Hell without Fires: Slavery, Christianity and the Antebellum Spiritual Narrative* (Gainesville: University Press of Florida, 2005), 3; Phillip M. Richards, "Anglo-American Continuities of Civic and Religious Thought in the Institutional World of Early Black Writing," in *Beyond Douglass: New Perspectives on Early African-American Literature*, ed. Michael J. Drexler and Ed White (Lewisburg, PA: Bucknell University Press, 2008), 86.

46. Wheatley, *Complete Writings*, 156.

47. Ibid., 149.

48. Ibid., 157.

49. Katherine Clay Bassard, *Spiritual Interrogations: Culture, Gender and Community in Early African-American Women's Writing* (Princeton, NJ: Princeton University Press, 1999), 24.

50. Young, *Grey Album*, 56.

51. Joanna Brooks, "Our Phillis Ourselves," *American Literature* 82.1 (2010): 1–28; Young, *Grey Album*, 70.

52. Katherine Clay Bassard, "Daughter's Arrival: The Earliest Black Women's Writing Community," *Callaloo* 19.2 (1996): 515.

53. Young, *Grey Album*, 70.

54. Hortense Spillers, "Moving on Down the Line," *American Quarterly* 40.1 (March 1988): 89; Katherine Clay Bassard, *Spiritual Interrogations*, 24.

55. Bassard, *Spiritual Interrogations*, 24.

56. Ibid., 24–25.

57. Wheatley, *Complete Writings*, 162; Bassard, *Spiritual Interrogations*, 25.

58. Joseph Rezek, "The Print Atlantic: Phillis Wheatley, Ignatius Sancho and the Cultural Significance of the Book," *Early African American Print Culture*, ed. Lara Langer Cohen and Jordan Alexander Stein (Philadelphia: University of Pennsylvania Press, 2012), 22.

59. Joanna Brooks, "The Early American Public Sphere and the Emergence of a Black Print Counterpublic," *William and Mary Quarterly* 62.1 (January 2005): 75; Frances Smith Foster, "A Narrative of the Interesting Origins and (Somewhat) Surprising Developments of African American Print Culture," *American Literary History* 17.4 (Winter 2005): 715.

60. Rezek, "Print Atlantic," 22.

61. Robert B. Stepto, *A Home Elsewhere: Reading African American Classics In The Age of Obama* (Cambridge, MA: Harvard University Press, 2010), 144–46.

62. Foster, "Narrative," 715.

63. Brooks, "Early American Public Sphere," 73.

64. Henry Louis Gates Jr., "Introduction: Talking Book," in *Pioneers of the Black Atlantic: Five Slave Narratives from the Enlightenment, 1772–1815*, ed. Henry Louis Gates Jr. and William L. Andrews (Washington, DC: Civitas Counterpoint, 1998), 2.

65. Vincent Carretta, *Phillis Wheatley: Biography of a Genius in Bondage* (Athens: University of Georgia Press, 2011), 97.

66. Wheatley, *Complete Writings*, 145.

67. Peter Hinks, "John Marrant and the Meaning of Early Black Freemasonry," *William and Mary Quarterly* 64.1 (2007): 112.

68. Audre Lorde, "Uses of the Erotic," in *Sister Outsider: Essays and Speeches* (Berkeley: Crossing Press, 1984), 53.

69. Allen Dwight Callahan, *The Talking Book: African American and the Bible* (New Haven, CT: Yale University Press, 2006), 187; James A. Noel and Matthew V. Johnson Jr., "Psychological Trauma, Christ's Passion, and the African American Faith Tradition," *Pastoral Psychology* 53.4 (March 2005): 361–69; Molefi K. Asante and Kariamu Welsh, "Myth: the Communication Dimension to the African American Mind," *Journal of Black Studies* 11.4 (June 1981): 387–95.

70. Ralph Ellison, "The World and the Jug," in *The Collected Essays of Ralph Ellison*, ed. John F. Callahan (New York: Modern Library Edition, 1995), 23.

Chapter 1. Phillis Wheatley's Pleasures

1. Vincent Carretta, *Phillis Wheatley: Biography of a Genius in Bondage* (Athens: University of Georgia Press, 2011), 99–101.

2. Christopher Castiglia and Julia Stern, "Introduction," *Early American Literature* 37.1 (2002): 1.

3. Ibid., 2.

4. Lauren Berlant, "Intimacy: A Special Issue," *Critical Inquiry* 24.2 (Winter 1998): 282.

5. Joan Morgan, "Why We Get Off: Moving Towards a Black Feminist Politics of Pleasure," *Black Scholar* 45.4 (Winter 2015): 37.

6. Astrid Franke, "Phillis Wheatley, Melancholy Muse," *New England Quarterly* 77.2 (June 2004): 224–251.

7. Phillis Wheatley, *Complete Writings*, ed. Vincent Carretta (1773; New York: Penguin Books, 2001), 10.

8. Castiglia and Stern, "Introduction," 2–3; Treva B. Lindsey at NYU Florence, "Black Portraiture(s) II—The Sweetest Taboo: Theorizing Black Female Pleasure," YouTube, 29 May 2015, www.youtube.com/watch?v=7wp8XEtdkvQ&t=926s.

9. See Caroline Wiggington, "The Consolation of Phillis Wheatley's Elegies," in *In the Neighborhood: Women's Publication in Early America* (Amherst: University of Massachusetts Press, 2016), 84–108; and Joanna Brooks, "Our Phillis Ourselves," *American Literature* 82.1 (2010): 1–28.

10. Castiglia and Stern, "Introduction," 2–3.

11. Kevin Quashie, *Sovereignty of Quiet: Beyond Resistance in Black Culture* (New Brunswick, NJ: Rutgers University Press, 2012), 8.

12. Ibid., 6.

13. Ralph Ellison, "'A Very Stern Discipline:' An Interview with Ralph Ellison," *Harper's Magazine*, 1 March 1967, 76.

14. Kevin Young, *The Grey Album: On the Blackness of Blackness* (Minneapolis, MN: Graywolf Press, 2012), 22.

15. Katherine Clay Bassard, *Spiritual Interrogations: Culture, Gender and Community in Early African-American Women's Writing* (Princeton, NJ: Princeton University Press, 1999), 3.

16. Morgan, "Why We Get Off," 36.

17. Jennifer Christine Nash, *The Black Body in Ecstasy: Reading Race, Reading Pornography* (Durham, NC: Duke University Press, 2014), 2.

18. James Baldwin, *The Fire Next Time* (New York: Vintage International, 1993), 42–43.

19. Lindsey, "Sweetest Taboo."

20. Treva B. Lindsey and Jessica Marie Johnson, "Searching for Climax: Black Erotic Lives in Slavery and Freedom," *Meridians: Feminism, Race, Transnationalism* 12.2 (2014): 187.

21. Wheatley, *Complete Writings*, xiv.

22. *Proceedings of the Massachusetts Historical Society* (Boston: MHS, 1863–64), 268.

23. Julie Ellison, *Cato's Tears and the Makings of Anglo-American Tradition* (Chicago: University of Chicago Press, 1999), 115.

24. Lindsey, "Sweetest Taboo."

25. Ivy Schweitzer, "'My Body/Not to Either State Inclined:' Early American Women Challenge Feminist Criticism," *Early American Literature* 44.2 (2009): 406.

26. Katherine Clay Bassard, "The Race for Faith: Justice, Mercy and the Sign of the Cross in African American Literature," *Religion and Literature* 38.1 (Spring 2006): 101.

27. June Jordan offers a brief and important discussion of these lines too in "The Difficult Miracle of Black Poetry in America or Something like a Sonnet for Phillis Wheatley," *Massachusetts Review* (Summer 1986): 257.

28. Henry Louis Gates Jr., "Editor's Introduction: Writing 'Race' and the Difference It Makes," in *"Race," Writing, and Difference* (Chicago: University of Chicago Press, 1985). See Katherine Clay Bassard, "The Daughter's Arrival: The Earliest Black Women's Writing Community," *Callaloo* 19.2 (1992): 515; Barbara Christian, *Black Feminist Criticism: Perspectives on Black Women Writers* (New York: Pergamon Press, 1985), 120; June Jordan, "The Difficult Miracle of Black Poetry in America or Something Like a Sonnet for Phillis Wheatley," in *Some of Us Did Not Die: New and Selected Essays of June Jordan* (New York: Basic/Civitas Books, 2002), 174–86; Alice Walker, "In Search of Our Mothers' Gardens," in *In Search of Our Mothers' Gardens: Womanist Prose*, 1st ed. (San Francisco: Harcourt Brace Jovanovich, 1983), 237. Phillip M. Richards, "Phillis Wheatley and Literary Americanization," *American Quarterly* 44.2 (June 1992): 163–91. Robert Reid-Pharr, *Conjugal Union: The Body, the House, and the Black American* (New York: Oxford University Press, 1999), 4.

29. Wheatley, *Complete Writings*. All subsequent line numbers refer to this work.

30. Jordan Alexander Stein, "Early American #Blacklivesmatter," *Common-Place* 16.2 (Winter 2016), http://commonplace.online/article/early-american-blacklivesmatter/.

31. See Rafia Zafar, *We Wear the Mask: African Americans Write American Literature* (New York: Columbia University Press, 1997), 17; William H. Robinson, ed., *Critical Essays on Phillis Wheatley* (Boston: G. K. Hall, 1982); Phillip M. Richards, "Phillis Wheatley and Literary Americanization," *American Quarterly* 44.2 (June 1992): 163–91.

32. Ralph Ellison, "The World and the Jug," in *The Collected Essays of Ralph Ellison*, ed. John F. Callahan (New York: Modern Library Edition, 1995), 159.

33. Wheatley, *Complete Writings*, 153.

34. Reid-Pharr, *Conjugal Union*, 4.

35. Brooks, "Our Phillis Ourselves," 7.

36. For further discussion, see also Frances Smith Foster, "Introduction: By Way of an Open Letter to My Sister," in *Love and Marriage in Early African America*,

ed. Frances Smith Foster (Boston: Northeastern University Press, 2008), xiii–xxvi; Lindsey and Johnson, "Searching for Climax."

37. See also Phillip M. Richards's useful reading of this poem in "Phillis Wheatley and Literary Americanization," *American Quarterly* 44.2 (June 1992): 163–91; Dr. Isaac Watts, "Psalm XIX to the Tune of the 113 Ps: *The Book of Nature and Scripture*," in *The Psalms of David, Imitated in the Language of the New Testament and Apply'd to the Christian State and Worship* (London: J. Oswald and J. Buckland, 1748), 3:17–19; Roland E. Murphy and O. Carm, "Wisdom and Creation," *Journal of Biblical Literature* 104.1 (March 1985): 3–11; William J. Scheick, *Authority and Female Authorship in Colonial America* (Lexington: University Press of Kentucky, 1998); June Jordan, "The Difficult Miracle of Black Poetry in America or Something like a Sonnet for Phillis Wheatley," *Massachusetts Review* 27.2 (Summer 1986): 252–62.

38. Kevin Quashie, "The Other Dancer as Self: Girlfriend Selfhood in Toni Morrison's Sula and Alice Walker's *The Color Purple*," *Meridians: Feminism, Race, Transnationalism* 2.1 (2001): 196.

39. Wheatley's poetic voice refers to blooming a number of times: "To Maecenas," "To the University of Cambridge in New England," "On the Death of Rev. Dr. Sewell," "Thoughts on the Works of Providence," "A Hymn to the Evening," "To a LADY on her coming to North-America with her Son, for the Recovery of her Health," "To a LADY on her remarkable Preservation in a Hurricane in North-Carolina," "On the Death of J.C. an infant," "Niobe."

40. Paula Loscocco, *Phillis Wheatley's Miltonic Poetics* (New York: Palgrave McMillan, 2014), 79.

41. Quashie, "Other Dancer as Self," 192.

42. Wheatley, *Complete Writings*, 159.

43. Quashie, "Other Dancer as Self," 207.

44. See also Elizabeth McHenry, "Rereading Literary Legacy: Considerations of the 19th-Century African-American Reader and Writer," *Callaloo* 22.2 (1994): 477–82.

45. Frances Smith Foster, "A Narrative of the Interesting Origins and (Somewhat) Surprising Developments of African American Print Culture," *American Literary History* 17.4 (Winter 2005): 721.

46. For additional discussion of Wheatley's writing communities, see also David Waldstreicher, "The Wheatleyan Moment," *Early American Studies* 9.3 (2011); Cedrick May, *Evangelism and Resistance in the Black Atlantic, 1760–1835* (Athens: University of Georgia Press, 2008); Joanna Brooks, "The Early American Public Sphere and the Emergence of a Black Print Counterpublic," *William and Mary Quarterly* 62.1 (January 2005), and "Our Phillis Ourselves"; Bassard, *Spiritual Interrogations*, 24.

47. Hortense Spillers, "Moving on Down the Line," *American Quarterly* 40.1 (March 1988): 89.

48. Barbara Christian, *Black Feminist Criticism: Perspectives on Black Women Writers* (New York: Pergamon, 1985), 34–35.

49. Joycelyn Moody, *Sentimental Confessions: Spiritual Narratives of Nineteenth-Century African-American Women* (Athens: University of Georgia Press, 2001), 52–53.

50. Glenn Hendler, *Public Sentiments: Structures of Feeling in Nineteenth-Century American Literature* (Chapel Hill: University of North Carolina Press, 2001), 3.

51. Wheatley, *Complete Writings*, 148.

52. See also John 17:23; George Whitefield, *The Indwelling of the Spirit, the Common Privilege of All Believers* (Boston: S. K. Keeland and T. Green, 1739), 10.

53. Wheatley, *Complete Writings*, 143.

54. Whitefield, *Indwelling Spirit*, 11.

55. Wheatley, *Complete Writings*, 116.

56. Whitefield, *Indwelling Spirit*, 10.

57. Baldwin, *Fire Next Time*, 41.

58. Wheatley, *Complete Writings*, 141.

59. 1 Cor. 7:22.

60. Toni Morrison at Cornell University. "Toni Morrison on Language, Evil and the 'White Gaze,'" YouTube, 18 March 2013, www.youtube.com/watch?v=FAs3E1AgNeM&t=6s.

61. Wheatley, *Complete Writings*, 143.

62. Ibid., 141.

63. Psa. 73:25–26.

64. See Joanna Brooks, "Soul Matters," *PMLA* 128.4 (2013): 947–52.

65. Wheatley, *Complete Writings*, 142–43.

66. Phil. 3:14.

67. Wheatley, *Complete Writings*, 143.

68. Isa. 57:15. Wheatley, *Complete Writings*, 150.

69. Carretta, *Phillis Wheatley*, 42–43.

70. Ibid., 42–43.

71. Bassard, *Spiritual Interrogations*, 35.

72. Jennifer Bernhardt Steadman, Elizabeth Engelhardt, Frances Smith Foster, and Laura Micham, "Archive Survival Guide: Practical and Theoretical Approaches for the Next Century of Women's Studies Research," *Legacy* 19.2 (2002): 232.

73. Brooks, "Our Phillis Ourselves," 9.

74. For a discussion of the ordinary, see Lois Brown, "Death-Defying Testimony: Women's Private Lives and the Politics of Public Documents," *Legacy* 27.1 (2010): 129–39.

75. Phillis Wheatley, *Complete Writings*, 141, 148.

76. Frances Smith Foster, "Mammy's Daughters; Or, the DNA of a Feminist Sexual Ethics," in *Beyond Slavery: Overcoming Its Religious and Sexual Legacies*, ed. Bernadette J. Brooten (New York: Palgrave Macmillan, 2010), 281.

77. See William H. Robinson, ed., *The Proceedings of the Free African Union Society and the African Benevolent Society, Newport, Rhode Island, 1780–1824* (Providence: Urban League of Rhode Island, 1976).

78. Wheatley, *Complete Writings*, 149.

79. Ibid., 141, 143.

80. Quashie, "Other Dancer as Self," 193.

81. Jasmine Nichole Cobb, "'Forget Me Not:' Free Black Women and Sentimentality," *MELUS: Multi-Ethnic Literature of the U.S.* 40.3 (Fall 2015): 37.

82. Erica R. Armstrong, "A Mental and Moral Feast: Reading, Writing, and Sentimentality in Black Philadelphia," *Journal of Women's History* 16.1 (Spring 2004): 98.

83. Charles H. Long, "Passage and Prayer: The Origin of Religion in the Atlantic World," in *The Courage to Hope: From Black Suffering to Human Redemption*, ed. Quinton Hosford Dixie and Cornel West (Boston: Beacon, 1999), 14.

84. Rosemarie Harding and Rebecca Harding, "Hospitality, Haints, and Healing," in *Deeper Shades of Purple: Womanism in Religion and Society*, ed. Stacey M. Floyd (New York: New York University Press, 2006), 100.

85. Matt. 18:20.

86. Carretta, *Phillis Wheatley*, 42–43.

87. James Baldwin, *Notes of a Native Son* (Boston: Beacon, 1984), 23.

88. Toni Morrison and Gloria Naylor, "A Conversation," *Southern Review* 21 (Summer 1985): 578.

89. Toni Morrison, *Beloved* (New York: Plume, 1987), 247.

90. Anthony B. Pinn, *Embodiment and the New Shape of Black Theological Thought* (New York: New York University Press, 2010), 56.

91. Audre Lorde, *Sister Outsider* (Berkeley: Crossing Press, 1984), 56, 56, 54, 54, 54.

92. Ibid., 56–57.

93. Quashie, "Other Dancer as Self," 193.

94. Thanks to Christy Pottroff for her mention, during a conversation at the American Antiquarian Society, of the 1770s as a time of major transition in the development of the informal and formal postal networks. The revolutionary era marks a shift in the availability of mail networks and in the ways in which mail is carried between cities and persons.

95. Hortense J. Spillers, "The Politics of Intimacy: A Discussion," in *Sturdy Black Bridges: Visions of Black Women in Literature*, ed. Roseann P. Bell, Bettye J. Parker, and Beverly Guy-Sheftall (Garden City, NY: Anchor Press/Doubleday, 1979), 88.

96. Carla Kaplan, *Erotics of Talk: Women's Writing and Feminist Paradigms* (New York: Oxford University Press, 1996), 11.

97. Alice Walker, *We Are the Ones We Have Been Waiting For: Inner Light in a Time of Darkness* (New York: New Press, 2006), 5.

98. Toni Morrison, "Home," in *The House That Race Built: Original Essays by Toni Morrison, Angela Y. Davis, Cornel West, and Others on Black Americans and Politics in America Today*, ed. Wahneema Lubiano (New York: Vintage, 1998), 12.

99. Wheatley, *Complete Writings*, 142.

100. Maya Angelou in Joe Berlinger, dir., "Dave Chappelle and Maya Angelou," *Iconoclasts*, 46:00 min., aired 30 November 2006 on SundanceTV; Bassard, *Spiritual Interrogations*, 23.

101. Bassard, *Spiritual Interrogations*, 11.

102. Kevin Quashie, "The Other Dancer as Self," 191.

103. Wheatley, *Complete Writings*, 148, 142, 141, 142.

104. Ibid., 141.

105. Ibid., 156, 156, 156, 156, 157.

106. Ibid., 141.

107. Bassard, *Spiritual Interrogations*, 23.

108. Wheatley, *Complete Writings*, 141.

109. Bassard, *Spiritual Interrogations*, 23.

110. Albert J. Raboteau, "The Blood of Martyrs Is the Seed of Faith: Suffering in the Christianity of American Slaves," in *Courage to Hope: From Black Suffering to Human Redemption*, ed. Quinton Hosford Dixie and Cornel West (Boston: Beacon, 1999), 35.

111. Wheatley, *Complete Writings*, 142.

112. See also Num. 23:10 and Rev. 14:13. Wheatley takes the phrase with revision, "we Shall die the death of the Righteous" directly from Num. 23:10. See Bassard, *Transforming Scriptures: African American Women Writers and the Bible* (Athens: University of Georgia Press, 2010); Wheatley, *Complete Writings*, 142.

113. Wheatley, *Complete Writings*, 141.

114. Frances Smith Foster, *Written by Herself: Literary Production by African American Women, 1746–1892* (Bloomington: Indiana University Press, 1993), 19.

115. Moody, *Sentimental Confessions*, 152–53; Wheatley, *Complete Writings*, 161.

116. Wheatley, *Complete Writings*, 162.

117. Spillers, "Politics of Intimacy," 105–6.

118. Wheatley, *Complete Writings*, 162.

119. Carretta, *Phillis Wheatley*, 190.

120. Ibid., 43; Robinson, *Proceedings*, 166.

121. *Proceedings of the Massachusetts Historical Society* (Boston: Massachusetts Historical Society, 1863–64), 267–74. See also Marco Tomaschett, "Sale 2058, Lot 322," New York: Swann Auction Galleries, November 2005, https://catalogue.swanngalleries.com/Lots/auction-lot/WHEATLEY-PHILLIS-Autograph-Letter-Signed?saleno=2058&lotNo=322&refNo=563170.

122. *Proceedings of the Massachusetts Historical Society*, 267–69.

123. Ibid., 267–69.

124. Spillers, "Politics of Intimacy," 105.

125. Morrison, *Beloved*, 247.

126. Ryan Hanley, "Calvinism, Proslavery, and James Albert Ukawsaw Gronniosaw," *Slavery and Abolition* 36.2 (2015): 360.

Chapter 2. James Albert Ukawsaw Gronniosaw's Joyful Conversion

1. Ryan Hanley, "Calvinism, Proslavery, and James Albert Ukawsaw Gronniosaw," *Slavery and Abolition* 36.2 (2015): 368.

2. For a discussion of the first edition's date of publication, see Leon Jackson, "The Talking Book and the Talking Book Historian: African American Cultures of Print—the State of the Discipline," *Book History* 13 (2010), and Vincent Carretta, ed., *Unchained Voices: An Anthology of Black Authors in the English-Speaking World of the Eighteenth-Century* (Lexington: University Press of Kentucky, 2004), 53n1.

3. Hanley, "Calvinism, Proslavery," 374.

4. It is thought to be the first Black-authored text published in Britain. For additional discussion of this point, see Hanley, "Calvinism, Proslavery"; Paul Edwards, "An African Literary Source for Blake's 'Little Black Boy'?," *Research in African Literatures* 21.4 (Winter 1990): 180.

5. Yolanda Pierce, *Hell without Fires: Slavery, Christianity and the Antebellum Spiritual Narrative* (Gainesville: University Press of Florida, 2005), 3.

6. See Carretta, *Unchained Voices*, 55n36.

7. Kevin Young, *The Grey Album: On the Blackness of Blackness* (Minneapolis, MN: Graywolf Press, 2012), 18, 35.

8. Ibid., 35, 54.

9. Srivinas Aravamudan, *Tropocopolitans: Colonialism and Agency, 1688–1804*, 236. See also Helen Thomas, *Romanticism and Slave Narratives: Transatlantic Testimonies* (New York: Oxford University Press, 2000), 168.

10. Pierce, *Hell without Fires*, 5.

11. George Whitefield, *A Sermon on Regeneration*, 2d ed. (Boston: T. Fleet for Charles Harrison, 1739), 7.

12. 2 Cor. 5:17.

13. George Whitefield, *The Marks of the New Birth* (Boston: Rogers and Fowle, 1740), 6.

14. Pierce, *Hell without Fires*, 9.

15. James Albert Ukawsaw Gronniosaw, *Narrative of the Most Remarkable Particulars of James Albert Ukawsaw Gronniosaw, Written by Himself*, 2d ed. (Newport, RI: S. Southwick, 1774), 25.

16. Ibid., 3.

17. Ryan Hanley, *Beyond Slavery and Abolition: Black British Writing, c. 1770–1830* (New York: Cambridge University Press, 2019), 101.

18. For a discussion of W. Shirley as the countess's cousin, see Laura Barrio-Vilar, "Narrating the African Self in the Late Eighteenth Century: Issues of Voice, Authority and Identity in Gronniosaw's 1770 Narrative," *Journal of Kentucky Studies* 20 (2003): 117–22.

19. Gronniosaw, *Narrative*, 4.

20. Ibid., 3, 3–4, 4.

21. Ibid., 3.

22. Ibid., 7.

23. Jennifer Harris, "Seeing the Light: Re-Reading James Albert Ukawsaw Gronniosaw," *English Language Notes* (June 2005): 43–57.

24. Gronniosaw, *Narrative*, 10.

25. Ibid., 7, 7, 7, 8, 7.

26. Harris, "Seeing the Light," 46.

27. John Bunyan, *Pilgrim's Progress* (1678; New York: Signet Classic, 2002), 11.

28. Jer. 31:35.

29. Gronniosaw, *Narrative*, 7.

30. Ibid., 10, 10, 11, 11.

31. Ibid., 13, 13, 14, 14.

32. Ibid., 14, 15, 15, 15.

33. Joanna Brooks, *American Lazarus: Religion and the Rise of African American and Native American Literatures* (New York: Oxford University Press, 2003), 100.

34. Gronniosaw, *Narrative*, 16.

35. Similar language appears throughout the Psalms and in Matt. 14:30.

36. John 12:20–23.

37. Gronniosaw, *Narrative*, 16.

38. Ibid., 16.

39. This incident also occurs in the writings of James Albert Ukawsaw Gronniosaw, Ottobah Cugoano, Olaudah Equiano, and John Jea. For a discussion of these versions, see Henry Louis Gates Jr., *The Signifying Monkey: A Theory of Afro-American Literary Criticism* (New York: Oxford University Press, 1988); see also Henry Louis Gates and Nellie Y. Mckay, "From Phillis Wheatley to Toni Morrison: The Flowering of African-American Literature," *Journal of Blacks in Higher Education* 14 (Winter 1996–97): 96.

40. Leon Jackson, "The Talking Book and the Talking Book Historian African American Cultures of Print—The State of the Discipline," *Book History* 13 (2010): 265.

41. Gates, *Signifying Monkey*, 131.

42. Henry Louis Gates Jr., "The Trope of the Talking Book," in *Signifying Monkey*, 131; Henry Louis Gates Jr., "Introduction: The Talking Book," in *Pioneers of the Black Atlantic: Five Slave Narratives from the Enlightenment*, ed. Henry Louis Gates Jr. and William L. Andrews (Washington, DC: Civitas Counterpoint, 1998), 3.

43. Gronniosaw, *Narrative*, 22.

44. Gates, *Signifying Monkey*, 137; Nellie Y. McKay and Henry Louis Gates Jr., "From Phillis Wheatley to Toni Morrison: The Flowering of African-American Literature," *Journal of Blacks in Higher Education* 14 (Winter 1996–97): 95–100.

45. Gates, "Introduction," 1–2.

46. Gates, "Trope of the Talking Book," 131; Gates, "Introduction," 3.

47. Katherine Clay Bassard, *Spiritual Interrogations: Culture, Gender and Community in Early African-American Women's Writing* (Princeton, NJ: Princeton University

Press, 1999), 20. See also Harryette Mullen, "African Signs and Spirit Writing," *Callaloo* 19.3 (Summer 1996): 671. See also Brooks, *American Lazarus*, 14, and Sandra M. Gustafson's discussion of Marrant in *Eloquence is Power: Oratory and Performance in Early America* (Chapel Hill: University of North Carolina Press, 2000), 108.

48. Toni Morrison, "The Site of Memory," in *Inventing the Truth: the Art and Craft of Memoir*, ed. William Zinsser (New York: Houghton Mifflin, 1995), 83–102.

49. George Whitefield, *The Indwelling of the Spirit, the common Privilege of All Believers* (Boston: S. K. Keeland and T. Green, 1739), 10–11.

50. Young, *Grey Album*, 19.

51. John Marrant, "A Funeral Sermon," in *Face Zion Forward: First Writers of the Black Atlantic, 1785–1798*, ed. Joanna Brooks and John Saillant (Boston: Northeastern University Press, 2002), 169.

52. Hanley, "Calvinism, Proslavery," 367.

53. Gronniosaw, *Narrative*, 17, 17, 17, 18.

54. Ibid., 18–19.

55. Ibid., 19.

56. Ibid., 19–20, 20.

57. Rev. 1:7.

58. Gronniosaw, *Narrative*, 20.

59. Ibid., 20.

60. Ibid., 22, 22, 23.

61. Ibid., 23.

62. Ibid., 21.

63. Ibid., 23, 23, 24.

64. Ibid., 24, 24, 25.

65. Ibid., 25, 26.

66. Ibid., 48, 46.

67. Hanley, "Calvinism, Proslavery," 372.

68. Hanley, *Beyond Slavery*, 113.

69. Hanley, "Calvinism, Proslavery," 372.

70. Cedrick May, *Evangelism and Resistance in the Black Atlantic, 1760–1835* (Athens: University of Georgia Press, 2008).

Chapter 3. Desiring John Marrant

1. For a greater bibliographic discussion of John Marrant's publication dates (and there are several), see Joseph Rezek, "Author," in *Early American Studies* 16.4 (Fall 2018): 599–606; see also Tiya Miles, "'His Kingdom for a Kiss': Indians and Intimacy in the Narrative of John Marrant," in *Haunted by Empire: Geographies of Intimacy in North American History*, ed. Ann Laura Stoler (Durham, NC: Duke University Press, 2006).

2. Cedrick May, "John Marrant and the Narrative Construction of an Early Black Methodist Evangelical," *African American Review* 38.4 (Winter 2004): 558.

3. John Marrant, *A Narrative of the Lord's Wonderful Dealings with John Marrant, a Black* (London: R. Hawes), 38.

4. John Marrant, "A Journal of the Rev. John Marrant, from August the 18th, 1785, to the 16th of March, 1790," in *Face Zion Forward: First Writers of the Black Atlantic, 1785–1798*, ed. Joanna Brooks and John Saillant (Boston: Northeastern University Press, 2002), 97.

5. Marrant, *Narrative*, 7.

6. Jane Landers, "Black Frontier Settlements in Spanish Colonial Florida," *OAH Magazine of History* 3.2 (Spring 1988): 28.

7. Marrant, *Narrative*, 7.

8. For a greater discussion of Marrant's move from New York to St. Augustine and finally to Charleston, see Alphonso F. Saville IV, "The Gospel According to John Marrant: Religious Consciousness in the Black Atlantic, 1755–1791," PhD diss., Emory University, 2017, ProQuest, 10628001.

9. Marrant, *Narrative*, 7.

10. Ibid., 7.

11. Charles H. Long, *Significations: Signs, Symbols, and Images in the Interpretation of Religion* (Philadelphia: Fortress, 1986), 7.

12. John Marrant, "A Funeral Sermon," in *Face Zion Forward: First Writers of the Black Atlantic, 1785–1798*, ed. Joanna Brooks and John Saillant (Boston: Northeastern University Press, 2002), 165.

13. George Whitefield, *The Indwelling of the Spirit, the common Privilege of All Believers* (Boston: S. K. Keeland and T. Green, 1739), 11.

14. Marrant, *Narrative*, 15.

15. James H. Cone, *God of the Oppressed* (New York: Seabury, 1975), 18.

16. Psa. 68:31; Rev. 7:14.

17. See Rev. 5, Acts 16, Matt. 4, John 1.

18. See Adam Potkay, "Olaudah Equiano and the Art of Spiritual Autobiography," *Eighteenth-Century Studies* 27.4 (Summer 1994): 680; Benilde Montgomery, "Recapturing John Marrant," *A Mixed Race: Ethnicity in Early America*, ed. Frank Shuffleton (New York: Oxford University Press, 1993), 107; Sandra M. Gustafson, *Eloquence Is Power: Oratory and Performance in Early America* (Chapel Hill: University of North Carolina Press, 2000), 102.

19. Kevin Young, *The Grey Album: On the Blackness of Blackness* (Minneapolis, MN: Graywolf Press, 2012), 24.

20. Marrant, *Narrative*, iii.

21. Nancy Ruttenberg, *Democratic Personality: Popular Voice and the Trial of American Authorship* (Stanford, CA: Stanford University Press, 1998), 84.

22. Hortense Spillers, "Moving on Down the Line," *American Quarterly* 40.1 (March 1988): 89.

23. Marrant, *Narrative*, 8–9, 9.

24. Ibid., 10.

25. Amos 4:13.

26. Marrant, *Narrative*, 10.

27. Ibid., 12.

28. Joanna Brooks, *American Lazarus: Religion and the Rise of African American and Native American Literatures* (New York: Oxford University Press, 2003), 46.

29. Yolanda Pierce, *Hell without Fires: Slavery, Christianity and the Antebellum Spiritual Narrative* (Gainesville: University Press of Florida, 2005), 4.

30. Marrant, *Narrative*, 8.

31. George Whitefield, *The Marks of the New Birth* (Boston: Rogers and Fowle, 1740), 6.

32. Christopher Castiglia and Julia Stern, "Introduction," *Early American Literature* 37.1 (2002): 1.

33. Marrant, *Narrative*, 14–15.

34. See Jordan Alexander Stein, "Mary Rowlandson's Hunger and the Historiography of Sexuality," *American Literature* 81.3 (September 2009): 469–95.

35. John 6:35.

36. Marrant, *Narrative*, 15.

37. Ibid., 16.

38. Ibid., 17.

39. Ibid., 17.

40. Ibid., 18.

41. Katherine Clay Bassard, *Spiritual Interrogations: Culture, Gender and Community in Early African-American Women's Writing* (Princeton, NJ: Princeton University Press, 1999), 23.

42. Ibid., 258.

43. Joanna Brooks, "The Early American Public Sphere and the Emergence of a Black Print Counterpublic," *William and Mary Quarterly* 62.1 (January 2005): 89.

44. Rev. 5:4.

45. Rev. 5:2.

46. Rev. 5:6.

47. Rev. 5:6–7.

48. Rev. 5:12.

49. Marrant uses the language of "king" to describe this Cherokee leader. He seems to have no interest using the words that this community leader might have used to describe his own role among the Cherokee. Marrant's disinterest speaks to his commitment to a particular kind of Christian story. He isn't in the business of truth-telling. Rather, he needs his imagined readership to understand that he knows God, and he can and does bring salvation to those who don't know his god.

50. Marrant, *Narrative*, 22.

51. Ibid., 23.

52. See Rom. 10:17–18.

53. See also Rom. 16:16, 1 Cor. 16:20, 2 Cor. 13:12, 1 Thess. 5:26, 1 Pet. 5:14, which speak of the kiss as a salutary greeting of charity.

54. Brooks, *American Lazarus*, 111.

55. Stein, "Mary Rowlandson's Hunger," 486.

56. Ibid., 486.

57. Marrant, *Narrative*, 8, 13, 14.

58. Miles, "His Kingdom for a Kiss," 177.

59. Rafia Zafar, *We Wear the Mask: African Americans Write American Literature, 1760–1870* (New York: Columbia University Press, 1997), 59.

60. Whitefield, *Indwelling of the Spirit*, 10.

61. Isa. 53:7.

62. Matt. 26:1–2.

63. Spillers, "Moving on Down the Line," 258.

64. Isa. 53:5.

65. Isa. 53:7.

66. Matt. 26:16, 26:46, 26:48–49. Marrant, *Narrative*, 29.

67. Marrant, *Narrative*, 23.

68. Gustafson, *Eloquence Is Power*, 104.

69. Marrant, *Narrative*, 23.

70. Ibid., 23.

71. Luke 22:69.

72. Miles, "His Kingdom for a Kiss," 181.

73. Marrant, *Narrative*, 24.

74. Ibid., 24–25.

75. Ibid., 25.

76. Miles, "His Kingdom for a Kiss," 183.

77. Marrant, *Narrative*, 29.

78. Ibid., 29.

79. Acts 12:14–15.

80. Marrant, *Narrative*, 29.

81. Ibid., 29, 30.

82. 2 Cor. 5:17.

83. Marrant, *Narrative*, 32, 32, 32, 33.

84. Ibid., 36.

85. Ibid., 36, 36, 36, 37, 37, 37.

86. Marrant, "Journal," 94.

87. Brooks, *American Lazarus*, 112.

88. May, "John Marrant," 553.

89. Prince Hall, *A Charge Delivered to the Brethren of the African Lodge on the 25th of June 1792* (Boston: Bible and Heart, 1792), 10.

90. Elizabeth Alexander, *Black Interior: Essays* (Saint Paul, MN: Graywolf, 2004), x.

Chapter 4. David Walker's Good News

1. David Walker, *Walker's Appeal, in Four Articles; Together with A Preamble to the Coloured Citizens of the World, But in Particular, and Very Expressly, to Those of the United States of America* (Boston: Published by David Walker, 1830), verso. All citations of *Walker's Appeal* are from this third and final edition unless otherwise noted.

2. Ibid., verso.

3. Christopher Apap, "'Let No Man of Us Budge One Step': David Walker and the Rhetoric of African American Emplacement," *Early American Literature* 46.2 (2011): 319–350; Dolan Hubbard, "David Walker's 'Appeal' and the American Puritan Jeremiadic Tradition," *Centennial Review* 30.3 (Summer 1986): 342.

4. Walker, *Appeal*, 62.

5. Gordon Fraser, "Distributed Agency: David Walker's Appeal, Black Readership and the Politics of Self-Deportation," *ESQ* 65 (Second Quarter 2019): 229.

6. Lori Leavell, "'Not Intended Exclusively for the Slave States': Antebellum Recirculation of David Walker's Appeal," *Callaloo* 38.3 (Summer 2015): 679–95; and also Lori Leavell, "Poe's Steadfast Servant in the Aftermath of Walker's Appeal," *Mississippi Quarterly* 66.4 (Fall 2013): 539–63. Fraser, "Distributed Agency."

7. Marcy J. Dinius, "'Look!! Look!! At This!!': The Radical Typography of David Walker's Appeal," *PMLA* 126.1 (January 2011): 55.

8. Ibid., 56.

9. Walker, *Appeal*, verso, 7.

10. Apap, "Let No Man," 322.

11. Walker, *Appeal*, verso, 80.

12. Ibid., 3.

13. Peter Thompson, "David Walker's Nationalism—and Thomas Jefferson's," *Journal of the Early Republic* 37.1 (Spring 2017): 63.

14. Walker, *Appeal*, 3.

15. Rom. 7:24.

16. Rev. 3:17.

17. Phillip M. Richards, "Anglo-American Continuities of Civic and Religious Thought in the Institutional World of Early Black Writing," in *Beyond Douglass: New Perspectives on Early African-American Literature*, ed. Michael J. Drexler and Ed White (Lewisburg, PA: Bucknell University Press, 2008), 84.

18. Walker, *Appeal*, 81.

19. Bao Nguyen—Grad, Admin Comparative Literature, "Fred Moten's Lecture: (Audio Only) "Manic Depression: A Poetics of Hesitant Sociology," YouTube, University of Toronto, 7 April 2017, www.youtube.com/watch?v=gQ2k0dsmIJE.

20. Walker, *Appeal*, 33, 4.

21. Ibid., 79.

22. Derrick R. Spires, *The Practice of Citizenship: Black Politics and Print Culture in the Early United States* (Philadelphia: University of Pennsylvania Press, 2019), 3.

23. Walker, *Appeal*, 7, 73.

24. Ibid., 79.

25. Thompson, "David Walker's Nationalism," 75.

26. Apap, "Let No Man," 330.

27. John Marrant, *A Sermon Preached on the 24th day of June 1789, Being the Festival of St. John the Baptist, at the Request of the Right Worshipful The Grand Master Prince Hall* (Boston: Bible and Heart, 1789), 4.

28. Walker, *Appeal*, 81, verso.

29. Ibid., 4–5, verso.

30. Ibid., 37.

31. Gene Andrew Jarrett, "To Refute Mr. Jefferson's Arguments Respecting Us: Thomas Jefferson, David Walker, and the Politics of Early African American Literature," *Early American Literature*, 46.2 (2011): 297.

32. Prince Hall, *A Charge delivered to the African Lodge, June 24, 1797* (Boston: Published by the desire of the Members of said Lodge, 1797), 12.

33. Hortense Spillers, "Moving on Down the Line," *American Quarterly* 40.1 (March 1988): 85.

34. Joanna Brooks, *American Lazarus: Religion and the Rise of African American and Native American Literatures* (New York: Oxford University Press, 2003), 145.

35. Hall, *Charge*, 12–13.

36. Walker, *Appeal*, 19, 11.

37. Peter Coviello, "Agonizing Affection: Affect and Nation in Early America," *Early American Literature* 37.3 (2002): 441.

38. Kevin Quashie, *Sovereignty of Quiet: Beyond Resistance in Black Culture* (New Brunswick, NJ: Rutgers University Press, 2012), 8.

39. Walker, *Appeal*, 5, 8.

40. Ibid., 20, 25.

41. Ibid., verso, 4.

42. Ibid., 21, 18.

43. Ibid., 15.

44. Spires, *Practice of Citizenship*, 3–4.

45. Walker, *Appeal*, 80, 86.

46. Nguyen, "Fred Moten's Lecture."

47. Walker, *Appeal*, 34–35, 79.

48. Frances Smith Foster at Emory School of Law, "Making Happiness in Early African America—Frances Smith Foster," YouTube, 30 September 2010, www.youtube.com/watch?v=8ByQMERWjnc.

49. Walker, *Appeal*, 84.

50. Ibid., 84.

51. Gene Andrew Jarrett, "To Refute Mr. Jefferson's Arguments," 293.

52. Ibid., 299.

53. Dinius, "Look!!," 66.

54. Walker, *Appeal*, 85.

55. Dinius, ""Look!!," 67.

56. Walker, *Appeal*, 85.

57. Dinius, "Look!!," 67.

58. Walker, *Appeal*, 85.

59. Apap, "Let No Man," 322.

60. Charles H. Long, *Significations: Signs, Symbols, and Images in the Interpretation of Religion* (Philadelphia: Fortress, 1986), 153; and Charles H. Long, "Passage and Prayer: The Origin of Religion in the Atlantic World," in *The Courage to Hope: From Black Suffering to Human Redemption*, ed. Quinton Hosford Dixie and Cornel West (Boston: Beacon, 1999), 11–21.

61. Walker, *Appeal*, 54.

62. Ibid., 60, 88.

63. Ibid., verso.

64. Ralph Ellison, "The World and the Jug," in *The Collected Essays of Ralph Ellison*, ed. John F. Callahan (New York: Modern Library Edition, 1995), 159.

65. James Baldwin, *Notes of a Native Son* (Boston: Beacon, 1984), 23.

66. Coviello, "Agonizing Affection," 441.

67. Walker, *Appeal*, 34–35.

68. John Marrant, *Sermon*, 78.

Coda

1. William H. Robinson, ed., *The Proceedings of the Free African Union Society and the African Benevolent Society, Newport, Rhode Island, 1780–1824* (Providence: Urban League of Rhode Island, 1976), 166. The question mark in the date is as in the original letter.

2. For a discussion of Wheatley's life during the Revolutionary War, see Cornelia Dayton, "Citizenship Denied: John Peters and Phillis Wheatley Peters in Middleton, Massachusetts," *New England Quarterly* 94.3 (September 2021): 309–51.

3. Vincent Carretta, *Phillis Wheatley: Biography of a Genius in Bondage* (Athens: University of Georgia Press, 2011), 43.

4. Christy Clark-Pujara, *Dark Work: the Business of Slavery in Rhode Island* (New York: New York University Press, 2016), 122.

5. Robinson, *Proceedings*, 153, 162.

6. Ibid., 162.

7. Clark-Pujara, *Dark Work*, 122.

8. Robinson, *Proceedings*, 165.

9. Ibid., 166.

10. Robinson, *Proceedings* 166.

11. Clark-Pujara, *Dark Work*, 124.

12. Phillis Wheatley, *Complete Writings*, ed. Vincent Carretta (1773; New York: Penguin Books, 2001), 162.

13. Robinson, *Proceedings*, 166.

14. Jennifer L. Morgan, "Archives and Histories of Racial Capitalism: An Af-

terword," *Social Text* 33.4 (December 2015): 154, https://doi.org/10.1215/01642472-3315862.

15. Saidiya Hartman, "Venus in Two Acts," *Small Axe* 26 (June 2008): 2.

16. Laura E. Helton, Justin Leroy, Max A. Mishler, Samantha Seeley, and Shauna Sweeney, "The Question of Recovery: An Introduction," *Social Text* 33.4 (December 2015): 2, https://doi.org/10.1215/01642472-3315766.

17. Lois Brown, "Death-Defying Testimony: Women's Private Lives and the Politics of Public Documents," *Legacy* 27.1 (2010): 130.

18. Brian Connolly and Marisa Fuentes, "Introduction: From Archives of Slavery to Liberated Futures?," *History of the Present* 6.2 (Fall 2016): 107.

19. Hartman, "Venus," 5.

20. Kevin Quashie, *Sovereignty of Quiet: Beyond Resistance in Black Culture* (New Brunswick, NJ: Rutgers University Press, 2012); Brown, "Death-Defying Testimony," 132.

21. Kevin Young, *The Grey Album: On the Blackness of Blackness* (Minneapolis, MN: Graywolf, 2012), 41.

Index

Beecher, Mrs. William, 49
Beecher, William, 129
Bible: 1 John 4:8, 33; 2 Corinthians 4:16,
  39; 2 Corinthians 12:9, 39; Acts, 81; Acts
  9:9, 84; Acts 12, 98; Acts 16, 90; Amos
  4:12, 84; Corinthians, 37, 56, 90, 98–99;
  and Gronniosaw, 20, 54–58, 60, 63–64,
  69, 71–73; Hebrews, 55; Hebrews 7:14,
  73; Hebrews 11:1, 57; Hebrews 13:14,
  79; Isaiah, 55; Isaiah 42:16, 58; Isaiah
  53, 93–94; James 1:23, 69; Job 38, 60;
  Job 42:2–3, 60; John, 55, 81; John 1:29,
  73; John 12:27, 64; Mark 6:27, 63; and
  Marrant, 21, 66, 77, 79, 81–86, 88–99;
  Matthew, 81; Matthew 26, 93–94; New
  Testament, 77, 91; Numbers, 109; Old
  Testament, 38, 77, 81, 84, 91, 93; Psalms,
  55; Revelation, 55, 81; Revelation 1:7, 71;
  Revelation 3:17–18, 109; Revelation 5,
  21, 89, 95; Revelation 5:7, 95; Romans,
  90, 98, 109; Romans 7:24, 107; Thessalo-
  nians, 90, 98; and Walker, 109–10; and
  Wheatley, 38–40, 46
biblical revisionism, 21, 38, 81
Black death, 130
#BlackLivesMatter, 8–13
Blackness, 17, 66–67
book learning, 12, 26, 35, 65, 67–68, 92,
  112–13, 133
Boone, Daniel, 97
Bornu, 53, 60, 75
Brooks, Joanna, 17, 32, 64, 84, 91
brotherhood, 21, 58, 61, 63, 98, 101–2, 111;
  brothers-in-Christ, 18. See also community; fellowship
Brown, Lois, 130
Bunyan, John, 20, 55, 73; Pilgrim's Progress,
  61

Cain (biblical), 29–30
Calvinism, 51, 55–57, 59, 68, 77, 82, 101
Campbell, William, 100
captivity and conversion narratives, 5, 55, 92
Caribbean, 125
Carretta, Vincent, 18, 39, 70
Castiglia, Christopher, 23–25
Chappelle, Dave: "When Keeping It Real
  Goes Wrong," 55
Cherokee People, 79, 82–83, 85, 88–98,
  100, 149n49
Christian, Barbara, 10, 35
Christianity, 3, 125–26; brothers-in-Christ,

18; and Gronniosaw, 18–20, 51, 54–61,
  64–65, 68–75; and Marrant, 19, 20–21,
  69, 75, 77–102; and reading, 6–8, 20, 92,
  94–95; sisters-in-Christ, 14; and Walker,
  21, 106, 110, 113–18; and Wheatley, 14,
  25–26, 28–31, 36, 37–38, 42, 46–47, 51.
  See also Calvinism; Congregationalism;
  Dutch Reformed Church; Jesus Christ;
  Methodists; Protestantism; Quakers;
  Word of God
close reading, 4, 131
Coggeshall, Cato, 14, 19, 35, 40
collaboration, 4, 6, 9, 11
Collins, Barry, 49, 124
Collins, Orbour. See Tanner (Collins),
  Obour
colonialism (European), 15, 18, 29, 56, 58,
  78, 92, 100, 125, 130
colonization, 19, 92, 105–6, 111, 118. See also
  American Colonization Society (ACS)
Combahee River, 99
community, 1, 4–5, 7; Christian, 3, 6, 13,
  36, 49, 51, 55, 59, 61, 75, 92, 125–27, 132;
  community building, 10, 44, 126; and
  Gronniosaw, 55, 59, 61, 75; and Hall,
  113; Indigenous, 83, 96–97, 149n49; and
  Marrant, 19, 78–79, 85, 86, 88, 92, 96–99,
  101–2, 149n49; and Walker, 107, 109–12,
  116–17, 132, 136n29; and Wheatley, 19,
  25, 35–36, 40, 44; writing community, 15,
  17–18, 35, 51, 55, 75, 86, 88, 102. See also
  brotherhood; fellowship; sisterhood
Cone, James, 81
Congregationalism, 35, 42, 49
Connolly, Brian, 130
conversion, 3, 5; and Gronniosaw, 8, 20, 51,
  53–76; and Marrant, 7–8, 78–102; and
  Tanner, 46–47; and Wheatley, 35–36
Cornish, Samuel, 108, 111
Countess of Huntingdon. See Hastings,
  Selina (Countess of Huntingdon)
Coviello, Peter, 122
creativity, 2, 11–14, 32, 34, 44, 51, 80, 81, 88,
  103, 119, 132; creative activism, 107, 110,
  121–22
critical generosity, 8, 11
Crucifixion, 46–47, 94
Cuba, 79; Havana, 53
Cugoano, Ottobah, 88, 146n39; Narrative
  of the Enslavement of Ottobah Cugoano,
  66
Cumberland, 48–49

51, 54–61, 63–65, 68–75; and community, 55, 59, 61, 75; and conversion, 8, 20, 51, 53–76; and desire, 20, 56–57, 62, 65–70, 73; and faith, 8, 18–20, 22, 51, 53–59, 67–69, 74–75, 89; and joy, 56–58, 60, 62–63, 74–75; *A Narrative of the Most Remarkable Particulars in the Life of James Albert Ukawsaw Gronniosaw, an African Prince,* 18, 20, 51, 53–76, 81–82, 88–92
Gumbs, Alexis Pauline, 137n30
Guy, William, 54

Hagar trope, 41
Hale, Edward, 49
Hall, Prince, 19, 21, 101–2, 112, 132; "Charge," 113
Hammon, Briton, 20; *Narrative of the Uncommon Sufferings, and Surprizing Deliverance of Briton Hammon, a Negro Man,* 55
Hammon, Jupiter, 15, 30
Hammond, Thomas, 126
Hammond, Turnbridge, 123
Harris, Jennifer, 60
Hartman, Saidiya, 129–30
hashtags, 9–11, 13, 22. *See also* #BlackLivesMatter
Hastings, Selina (Countess of Huntingdon), 15, 18–19, 23–25, 35, 41, 51, 58–59, 75, 77, 82, 101
Hazard, Samuel, 54
Hendler, Glenn, 36
Herod, King (biblical), 63, 98
historiography, 10, 92, 106
Holland, 53, 64–65, 69–70, 100
Holy Spirit/Ghost, 8, 36, 56, 72, 78, 80, 87, 93, 95–96, 111
Hopkins, Samuel, 14, 18, 24, 35, 40, 42; *The System of Doctrines,* 129
Howe, Irvin, 31

inner space, 2
interiority: and desire, 2, 15, 23, 25–26, 114; and Marrant, 85–86, 91; and pleasure, 1–5, 8, 18–19, 22, 26–28, 43; and reading, 5–6, 131–33; and slavery, 25–27; and Walker, 114, 122; and Wheatley, 23–28, 32, 34–40, 43, 45, 50
interpretative community, 16
intersectionality, 50
intertextuality, 6, 17, 20, 67, 88–89
intimacy, 10, 24, 91–92, 94–95, 98, 122;

with God, 20, 55–57, 74–75, 80, 82, 88; and pleasure, 26, 43–44, 132; and reading, 17, 34, 68–69, 88–89, 133; rhetorical, 11; Wheatley and Tanner's, 16, 20, 40–50
Isaiah (biblical), 93
Islam, 60
Israel, 84

Jacobs, Harriet, 29
James (biblical), 69
Jarrett, Gene, 119
Jea, John, 88, 146n39; *The Life, History, and Unparalleled Sufferings of John Jea, the African Preacher,* 66–67
Jefferson, Thomas, 30, 119–20
Jerusalem, 64
Jesus Christ: and Gronniosaw, 20, 54–56, 59, 61, 63–64, 68–74; and Marrant, 7, 77–94, 96, 98–102; and Wheatley, 6, 36–39
Jewry Street Church, 82
Jezebel trope, 41
Job (biblical), 60
John, St. (apostle), 89, 95, 109
Johnson, Jessica Marie, 27
John the Baptist (biblical), 63
jokes, 22, 27, 97
Jonah (biblical), 100
Jordan, June, 140n27
joy, 4, 11, 127, 132–33; and #BlackLivesMatter, 9–10; and Gronniosaw, 56–58, 60, 62–63, 74–75; and interiority, 1–3, 5, 8; and Marrant, 21, 78, 80–81, 84, 86, 88, 101; and Walker, 21, 103, 117–22; and Wheatley, 14, 17, 25–28, 37, 44–47, 51. *See also* desire; eroticism
Judaism, Levitical, 79
Judas (biblical), 94–95

keeping it real, 5

lamb of God, 73, 81, 89, 95–96
Laodicea, 109
Legge, William (Earl of Dartmouth), 30–31
Liberia, 105, 111, 118
libraries, 14–15, 124, 128, 130–33. *See also* archives
Library Company of Philadelphia, 136n29
Library of Congress, 128
Lindsey, Treva B., 11, 27
literacy, 3, 5, 22, 113, 133; affective, 7, 12, 93, 102, 108; aliteracy, 12; desire for, 30,

66–69; folk-faith, 131; geopolitical, 12; religious, 36, 63, 65, 82–84, 88–89, 91–96; visual, 12. *See also* talking books
London Evening Post, 75
Long, Charles H., 80, 120
Lorde, Audre, 19–20, 43–44, 46
Louisiana, 106
Loyalists, 79, 100–101
Lyma, Sarah D., 123–27, 130
Lyndon, Phylis, 15

Madison, James, 109
Maecenas, 24
Malbone, Sarah, 123, 127
Mammy trope, 41
Marrant, John, 3–6, 11, 58, 67, 76, 111, 122, 132; and anticipation, 79, 83, 86, 91, 93, 101; and Christianity, 7, 19, 20–21, 66, 69, 75, 77–102; and community, 19, 78–79, 85, 86, 88, 92, 96–99, 101–2, 149n49; and conversion, 7–8, 78–102; and desire, 21, 78, 81–99; and faith, 8, 19–22, 75, 77–81, 84–97, 102; "A Funeral Sermon," 69, 80; *Journal,* 101; *A Narrative of the Lord's Wonderful Dealings with John Marrant, a Black,* 18, 66, 75, 77–103; Sermon (1789), 19
Marvatt, John, 123, 126
Marvatt, Patience, 123, 127
Mary (biblical), 98
Massachusetts: Boston, 14, 18–19, 23–24, 29–30, 32, 40, 42, 45, 48, 77–79, 101, 105, 108, 112, 120, 124–25; Menotomy, 113; Worcester, 48, 124
Massachusetts General Coloured Association, 108, 110
Massachusetts Historical Society, 49
materiality: politics of, 16
Matthew (biblical), 93
May, Cedrick, 75, 77
McKittrick, Katherine, 4, 9
Methodists, 6, 35, 51, 58, 75, 77, 92, 101, 113, 125
methodology of book, 3–4. *See also* close reading; critical generosity
Middle Passage, 20, 29, 30, 53, 76
Mills, Thomas, 54
misreading, 9, 30, 66–69, 124, 129–31
Mohegan People, 31
Moorhead, Mr., 46
Morrison, Toni, 1–2, 12, 15, 29, 43, 45
Moten, Fred, 110, 117

Mott, Shani, 136n18
mutual aid, 19, 125

Native Americans, 21, 31, 66, 79, 82–83, 85, 88–98, 100, 149n49
Naylor, Gloria, 43
New England, 15, 35, 39–40
Newport, Rhode Island, 13, 39–40, 45, 123–24, 126, 129; mutual aid communities in, 19, 125; publishing in, 14, 18, 51, 54, 58; religious communities in, 24, 27, 42, 49, 132; writing community in, 18
New South Congregational Church, 42
Newton, John: "Amazing Grace," 107
New York City, 53, 54–55, 108
New York State, 65, 70, 75–76, 78–79; Long Island, 30
North Carolina, 105–6, 121; Wilmington, 108
North Sea, 100
Nova Scotia, Canada, 19, 77–79, 85, 101, 125, 132

Occom, Samson, 31
Old Independent Meeting House, 75
Old South Church, 42

passion, 10, 28–29
Passover, 94
Paul (apostle), 20, 37–39, 54, 55–57, 77, 80–81, 84, 90, 98, 101, 109–10
Pemberton, Mr., 35
Peter (biblical), 98
Peters, John, 15, 28, 48, 129
Philippi, 80
Pierce, Yolanda, 54–55, 85
plantations, 5, 70, 79, 93, 99
play, 10–11, 17, 29, 34, 61, 63, 94
pleasure, definition, 4
Pocock, Admiral, 53
Pottroff, Christy, 143n94
predestination, 59, 62, 77, 82, 101
print Atlantic, 16
protest, 1, 9, 12
Protestantism, 3, 6, 14, 54–55, 57, 92. *See also* Calvinism; Christianity; Congregationalism; Dutch Reformed Church; Methodists; Quakers; Word of God
Providence, Rhode Island, 125, 132

Quakers, 74
Quamine, John, 14–15, 19, 27, 40

103, 105–11, 114, 116–20; *Walker's Appeal in Four Articles Together with a Preamble to the Colored Citizens of the World,* 21, 102–3, 105–22

Washington, George, 30

Wesley, John and Charles, 58, 101

West Indies, 100

Wheatley, John, 23, 26, 29

Wheatley, Phillis, 5, 11, 22; and anticipation, 28, 32–34, 39, 50, 124; in archives, 14–15, 17, 27, 41, 48, 124, 127–31; and Christianity, 14, 25–26, 28–31, 36, 37–38, 42, 46–47, 51; and community, 19, 25, 35–36, 40, 44; *Complete Writings,* 13; and desire, 15, 19, 25–26, 28, 30–32, 37–38, 44–50, 124; and faith, 6, 8, 14, 18–20, 26, 28, 31, 33–51; friendship with Tanner, 3, 6, 8, 13–16, 19–20, 24–25, 29, 33–36, 39–51, 123–29, 132; frontispieces, 15, 23, 25, 30, 50; "On Being Brought from Africa to America," 28–30; "On Imagination," 24; "On the Death of Rev. Sewell," 24; and pleasure, 4; *Poems of Various Subjects, Religious and Moral,* 3, 13, 15, 23, 32, 40,

42, 54, 58; "Thoughts on the WORKS of PROVIDENCE," 29, 32–34; "To the Earl of Dartmouth," 30–31

Wheatley, Susanna, 25, 31, 37, 42, 46

Whitefield, George, 6, 15, 18, 35–37, 55–56, 68–69, 70, 79–80, 84–85, 93, 96

white gaze, 1–3, 133

white supremacy, 2, 9, 29

Whitwell, Mr., 25

Wooldridge, Mr., 25

Wooster, Madame, 41

Word of God, 8, 37, 109; and Gronniosaw, 20, 55, 57, 68–69, 71–73; and Marrant, 7, 19–21, 75, 80–97, 99, 102; and reading, 6–7, 20, 82–83, 88–97, 102; and Walker, 6, 114; and Wheatley, 36, 42, 45

writing community, 15, 17–18, 35, 51, 55, 75, 86, 88, 102

Yamma, Bristol, 14, 19, 27, 40

Young, Kevin, 4, 12–13, 26, 54, 81, 131

Zafar, Rafia, 92

Zion, 101

Tara A. Bynum is an assistant professor of
English and African American Studies at the
University of Iowa.

The New Black Studies Series

The University of Illinois Press
is a founding member of the
Association of University Presses.

———————————————

University of Illinois Press
1325 South Oak Street
Champaign, IL 61820-6903
www.press.uillinois.edu